Human Capital and Global Business Strategy

Human capital – the performance and the potential of people in an organisation – has become an increasingly urgent issue for business leaders. Dramatic demographic shifts, the globalisation of organisations, increasing business complexity, and generational differences are causing many organisations to place a more deliberate focus on human capital as a key element in strategic planning and execution.

This book helps business leaders determine how to address human capital as part of their business strategy, to drive value and realise the potential of the organisation. Topics are presented clearly, allowing readers to quickly grasp and apply key concepts and ideas. The authors share both their academic research and practical experience from around the world, providing first-hand case studies and examples to help bring theoretical topics to life. With a strong practitioner focus, this book will provide business leaders and HR professionals with new insights into how to improve business performance through a unique, strategic approach to human capital.

Howard Thomas is Dean of the Lee Kong Chian School of Business at Singapore Management University. Professor Thomas is internationally recognised as a leading expert in the field of strategic management. He is the author, co-author or editor of many acclaimed management books, including *Handbook of Strategy and Management* (2001), *Strategy: Analysis and Practice* (2005), and *Strategic Leadership in the Business School* (Cambridge University Press, 2011).

Richard R. Smith is a Senior Lecturer at Singapore Management University in the areas of global business and human capital. He is also a retired partner from Accenture where he led the global Leadership Effectiveness practice. Smith has more than 25 years of experience in organisation strategy, change management, and human capital leadership.

Fermin Diez is an Adjunct Professor at Singapore Management University and is also a Senior Partner and Head of Talent Consulting for Mercer in AsiaPacific, the Middle East and Africa. He has over 30 years' experience in HR and consulting as well as corporate roles in Asia, Australia, Latin America, and the USA.

HUMAN CAPITAL AND GLOBAL BUSINESS STRATEGY

Howard Thomas
Richard R. Smith
Fermin Diez

CAMBRIDGE
UNIVERSITY PRESS

University Printing House, Cambridge CB2 8BS, United Kingdom

Cambridge University Press is part of the University of Cambridge.

It furthers the University's mission by disseminating knowledge in the pursuit of education, learning and research at the highest international levels of excellence.

www.cambridge.org
Information on this title: www.cambridge.org/9781107613287

© Howard Thomas, Richard R. Smith and Fermin Diez 2013

First published 2013

A catalogue record for this publication is available from the British Library

Library of Congress Cataloguing in Publication data
Thomas, Howard, 1943–
Human capital and global business strategy / Howard Thomas,
Richard R. Smith, and Fermin Diez.
    pages   cm
Includes bibliographical references and index.
ISBN 978-1-107-03315-3 (hardback) – ISBN 978-1-107-61328-7 (paperback)
1. Human capital.   2. Strategic planning.   I. Smith, Richard R., 1962–
II. Diez, Fermin, 1960–   III. Title.
HD4904.7. T4964 2013
658.3′01–dc23
2013023922

ISBN 978-1-107-03315-3 Hardback
ISBN 978-1-107-61328-7 Paperback

DEDICATIONS

To Su-Yen and my children who are the source of Fermin's strength and inspiration.

To Teresa and my 3Ms, who are Rick's team and partners in life's journey.

To Lynne and the Thomas family, who are Howard's foundation and who light up Howard's life.

To our students past and present at Singapore Management University who have shaped our thinking through numerous discussions, explorations, and trials on the topics of human capital and strategy.

CONTENTS

FIGURES

TABLES

FOREWORD by Pradeep Pant

For some years now, Howard Thomas has enjoyed making fun of the silk handkerchief that always resides in the top pocket of my blazer. So I considered it a step up in our relationship when he approached me with the serious request that I write the foreword to this book. I quickly said yes.

It also helped that Howard and his coauthors Rick Smith and Fermin Diez are taking on an issue that I deal with every day in my job – the issue of human capital as a strategic imperative. When you're growing your revenues year-over-year by orders of magnitude ... When you're methodically expanding your geographic footprint ... When you're constantly adding to the categories in which you compete ... When you're regularly entering new trade agreements and encountering new competitors – and new *kinds* of competitors ... When you're managing ever-greater scale and complexity ... When your employee profile is becoming more multicultural and multigenerational ... When your multinational corporation increasingly depends on your financial contribution to meet investor expectations ... And when all those things are happening at once ... you don't need anyone to tell you that human capital is a strategic imperative. You need someone to help you put the right people in the right jobs on a large scale and with the greatest urgency. Who better to provide that help than the three authors of this book? In Fermin, you get the leader of Mercer's Human Capital consulting business throughout Asia Pacific and Africa and a former Head of HR at Freescale Semiconductor and VP at Pepsi. In Rick, you get the retired head of Accenture's global Leadership Effectiveness practice, with expertise in the areas of organization strategy, change management and human capital leadership. And in Howard, you get the Dean of Lee Kong Chian School of Business and Chair of Strategic Management at Singapore Management University (SMU), whose chief academic interests are in strategic management and risk & decision analysis. Howard had the vision to write a book on strategic human capital, while Rick and Fermin had the pressing need for a textbook suitable for the MBA courses they were teaching at SMU. This is where it gets exciting for everyone working in the great growth markets of the early 21st century. Rampant growth creates needs. Needs attract people who know things. People who know things collect around centres of learning that focus on solving new problems rather than rehashing old ones. And that's when you start to realise that none of you are just doing a job; you're all part of a business renaissance. If you're ready to play a role in the human capital corner of that renaissance, you may want to consider your answers to these questions:

- *Are your organisation's people investments aligned with your most important business goals?*
- *Will your company buy, build, or borrow the workforce capabilities you need?*
- *Do you know who your critical employees are, and are you investing in them accordingly?*
- *Does your organisation have the right leaders in place to drive transformational new strategies?*
- *Will your company have the leaders in place for the future success of the enterprise?*
- *Are you measuring performance appropriately and rewarding it in the right way?*
- *Do you use workforce data and rigorous analytics to drive people decisions?*
- *Can you confidently tell your Board that you are managing human capital risks in the strategy process?*

If you break into a cold sweat at the mere consideration of these questions, then get this book. Read it. Get more copies and give it to people you rely on to make the right decisions in your company. And together you can move forward with a common understanding that culture, leadership, structure, talent management, human capital metrics, and change management are critically important to business success in the growth markets of the early 21st century. However, it takes an overarching human capital strategy to make a global business plan work. I am thrilled that they're going to be teaching these concepts at SMU, and I can't wait for the first graduating class to have benefitted from that teaching. I mean that literally – I am not able to wait. Our needs are banging at the door. We are going to read this book ourselves at Mondelēz International. We are going to operationalise its renaissance wisdom. And the next time I see Howard, I will tell him that the silk handkerchief in my blazer pocket was a semaphore, signalling the need for help with my human capital strategy, and what a relief it is that he finally deciphered it.

Pradeep Pant

Executive Vice President and President, Asia Pacific

and Eastern Europe, Middle East & Africa (EEMEA), Mondelēz

International; formerly with Kraft Foods Inc.

ACKNOWLEDGEMENTS

This book began as a lunch meeting between the three authors about the need for more awareness of human capital in strategy execution as a critical competency for our students as well as practitioners. It was Howard who encouraged us by saying: 'Let's write a book!' So as to not disappoint the Dean ... here it is.

The authors would like to thank Paula Parish, our tireless editor, and Claire Poole at Cambridge University Press for all their help and advice in making our writing into a cohesive book. We would also like to thank Gillian Goh for her excellent work with the manuscript preparation. Dorasen Khoo at SMU helped keep this author team connected and coordinated through the project.

Special thanks to Ruchika Salotra for her help in preparing the case studies and the team at the Singapore Human Capital Institute for ongoing support. Also to Haig Nalbantian, Jason Jeffay, Jay Doherty and their teams at Mercer for their contributions. Pat Milligan, Don Ferrin, Thomas Menkhoff, and Orlando Ashford were instrumental in their support for this project. Thank you to Martin Ibanez-Frocham, Yinn Ewe, Jochen Reb, Devasheesh Bhave, Jonathan Doh, Stephanie Gault, Yaarit Silverstone, Grace Yip, Yulia Yasmina, Low Choy Huat, Bob Thomas, David Smith, Peter Cheese, and Ting Wang, all of whom provided valuable feedback and insight along the way.

1 Introduction

> No institution can possibly survive if it needs geniuses or super-men to manage it. It must be organised in such a way as to be able to get along under a leadership composed of average human beings.
>
> Peter Drucker

Introduction

The purpose of this book is to emphasise the role of strategic human capital in the development of stronger global business strategies. This book is specifically aimed at helping business leaders understand the essential elements of human capital in their organisations. Human capital, the performance and the potential of the people in an organisation, is a critical issue for leaders to address. We will examine how the critical elements of human capital such as culture, leadership, talent, structure, change, and performance metrics are essential to strategic learning and the continued evolution of the firm's strategic positioning.

Strategy is the expression in practice of the strategic intent or aspiration that stretches the organisation to innovate, change, leverage resources, and develop new skills. Intent is an architecture or framework used to develop the distinctive competencies of an organisation, which can be leveraged for competitive advantage. Strategy encompasses the formulation and articulation of a strategy through a planning process or strategic analysis, a set of goals, and the associated processes of strategic implementation and execution enacted by policies to achieve the goals. It follows that a good strategy is achieved through an understanding of not only how to achieve strong competitive advantage, but also how to execute that position and the competitive vision over time.[1]

The strategy implementation process must be closely aligned with the strategy formulation process to create results. Alfred Chandler, a renowned business historian at the Harvard Business School, defined strategy as: 'The determination of the basic long-term goals and appropriate objective of an enterprise coupled with the adoption of courses of action and the allocation of resources necessary for carrying out these goals.'[2]

In strategy execution there is clear attention on the role of strategic leadership to set the direction, develop solid plans, and carry out the necessary strategic change processes. Critical to the execution is the identification of resources that will comprise the distinctive core competencies, dynamic capabilities, and strategic assets that support the firm's sustainable competitive advantage.[3]

The resource-based view suggests that the firm can be considered as a collection of resources or assets that are unique drivers of strategy and growth of the firm.[4] With this orientation, it is the resources of the firm that are of primary importance, rather than the external factors. A resource is an asset with an important relationship to the execution of a strategy: for example, geographic location, patents, innovation, strong brand, established distribution network, or skilled human resources. In the case of human capital, the strategic value is infrequently stressed in many of the strategy textbooks as it can be more challenging to quantify.

It is one thing to make note of resources available to the firm, but another to use them to actively create value. Strategic capability is the ability to perform an activity that involves complex patterns of coordination between people and other resources. Capabilities are non-imitable, intangible, rare, and non-tradable.[5] Examples include expertise in research and development (R&D), high-quality manufacturing, and superior customer reputation and service.

For example, in the airline industry there are low-cost carriers that sell air travel at the lowest possible price as a means of gaining customers. Ryanair and Southwest are good examples of this approach, offering a no-frills flight experience at a low price. Their target customers tend to be travellers looking for an economical way of getting from point A to point B. At the other extreme we find the 'five-star' airlines such as British Airways, Singapore Airlines, and Qatar Airways, which provide full service on the ground and in the air, aimed at the business traveller. Both types of air carrier are in the business of moving passengers but their strategies are very different. Ryanair and Southwest do it by being low-cost carriers while full-service carriers provide extra services and capabilities with either a national or international orientation. They constitute different strategic groups.[6] The services provided are different, as is the price charged. But, importantly for the purposes of this book, the type and nature of the human capital will also be different. Whereas a low-cost carrier would tend to address management processes designed to take costs out of the overall system, a full-service carrier concentrates on how to improve the overall travel experience for its passengers, resulting in the ability to charge a price premium. As a result, the organisational culture, leadership, structures, and talent must be aligned to enable employees to fulfil the strategy and change the organisation's direction.

The use of terms such as strategic assets, core competencies, and dynamic capabilities are used interchangeably in the literature and in practice. Here we will use the notion of core competence, widely accepted in practice and based on the work of Prahalad and Hamel.[7] They propose that organisations can create distinctive resources that can bring significant value through collective learning in the firm. This notion of building organisational competence is difficult to put into practice as it defines the way that things get done inside the firm. A key element of achieving distinctive core competence is the capabilities of the people in the organisation, or *human capital.*

Just as the literature defines dynamic capabilities, we can also reflect on these in light of the human capital of the organisation. Since the time that Chandler introduced the notion of structure and strategy in his 1962 book, *Strategy and Structure: Chapters in the History of the American Industrial Enterprise*, thinking about the nature of firms and strategy has continued to evolve and there is a much needed link between human capital and strategy in the literature and in practice.[2] Globalisation and new operating models have been driving changes in talent, human capital, and human capital strategy. For our purposes, we will use the following definition: 'Human capital is the people, their performance, and their potential in the organisation.'

The key emphasis of human capital is therefore not only the bundle of skills, but also the integration of a diverse set of skills. Human capital is generally considered of value when it makes a disproportionate contribution to customer-perceived value. To be considered unique, the human capital of the organisation should be considered distinctive relative to that of its competitors or at a superior level with respect to others. The notion of human capital for competitive advantage (the ability to open new markets and find new sources of value) is seeded in the basis of dynamic capabilities. Human capital is an important part of the ability to execute strategy.

The office products giant 3M has long been credited with having not only the right ideas but the right people to execute them. A main staple of 3M's strategy continues to be that a certain percentage of their revenue must come from products introduced by the company in the last five years. This strategic emphasis on innovation forces the company not only to hire the most creative talent possible, but also to accept failures when a potential new idea does not work so that these creative people can continue searching for more ideas.

As a consequence, there is a real and commonly shared concern about more clearly identifying and understanding human capital in an organisation from a strategic standpoint. Leaders want to determine gaps and significant areas that can be better leveraged to sustain competitive advantage, and untapped potential. Finding ways to leverage the strategic human capital of the firm has the potential to create new core competencies as firms look to find new ways to improve the speed at which they respond to the marketplace, foster more innovation, adapt to the competitive landscape, enable consistency of performance, develop the right future talent, and create a global mindset.

Thinking differently about business strategy

Sometimes strategists look too closely at the external factors affecting the firm and pay too little attention to internal capabilities. This imbalance can lead to inadequate framing of the strategic problems, leading to unrealistic strategic decisions, false sets of assumptions, or simply failed strategies, as the internal capabilities may not allow the plans to be implemented. While popular frameworks such as Porter's five forces model and environmental scanning provide models to address elements of the strategic context, they can direct too much attention to the external and economic factors that are affecting the firm.

A strengths, weaknesses, opportunities, and threats (SWOT) analysis can help to provide a balanced view on both internal and external factors. While this framework has been criticised for being too broad or lacking sufficient rigour in addressing competition, most would argue it is of value in determining an organisation's relative strengths and matching them with available opportunities.

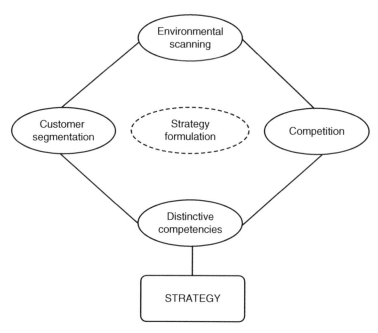

Figure 1.1 Strategy formulation
Source: adapted from McGee, Thomas, and Wilson, *Strategy Analysis and Practice* (McGraw Hill, 2010)

Strategy formulation typically involves some level of environmental scanning, a review of competitive positioning, an analysis of customer segments, and the key distinctive competencies of the firm. Many organisations develop a strategy based on these factors, yet often do not consider the factors associated with the availability and the value of human capital. Based on the work of McGee, Thomas, and Wilson, we note the strategy formulation process as illustrated in Figure 1.1.

The output of strategy formulation is usually a business strategy that defines the performance goals the organisation seeks to achieve and sets parameters for the decisions and investments it will make to support those goals.

It has been noted that strategic organisation change is often difficult to implement. In fact, some estimates indicate that 50 to 70 per cent of all new change efforts fail to reach their objectives.[8] One of the many reasons for this startling statistic is the lack of alignment of 'fit' between the organisational context of strategy and the strategy implementation process. A successful strategy requires appropriate linkage between strategy analysis and the processes of implementing that strategy effectively in the practical context.

Strategy implementation must consider the culture of the organisation, leadership capability, structures and organising mechanisms, and the management

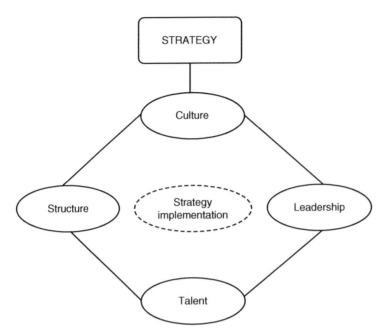

Figure 1.2 Strategy implementation or human capital strategy
Source: adapted from McGee, Thomas, and Wilson, *Strategy Analysis and Practice* (McGraw Hill, 2010)

of talent, as shown in Figure 1.2. These elements each play, individually and collectively, a critical role not only in shaping the strategy, but also in determining the success of implementation.

Another way to think about strategy implementation is to view this essentially as a 'human capital strategy'; as a way we can largely address the people side of the business (along with the organisational configuration) to implement strategy successfully. Therefore, human capital strategy is defined as a unique set of prioritised choices about people investments that enables the organisation to achieve its business strategy and performance goals. This may be called a 'people strategy' or 'talent strategy' in some organisations.

Human capital strategy should not be confused with a human resources (HR) strategy. An HR strategy typically reviews the human capital strategy to determine the appropriate actions for the human resources function (HRF). Typical areas that are addressed in an HR strategy include: compensation programmes, development initiatives, incentive programmes, hiring plans, HR data management, and HR effectiveness planning. At the same time, some are taking a broad view of HR strategy, such as Cascio and Boudreau in their recent book on strategic human resource management.[9] They argue that HR strategy must incorporate and consider environmental factors as well as organisational factors since HR influences and is influenced by organisational context. For example, an organisation may determine that a new strategy requires the company to upgrade talent quality in critical roles, build workforce pride and commitment, clarify expectations to drive performance, and build strong front-line management. The HR function strategy would then deliver on those imperatives and in turn deliver programmes to support these areas. While the HR strategy is a critical component, we suggest that the human capital strategy can be more closely aligned with strategy execution.

When business strategy evolves, so must the human capital strategy, to ensure that the significant people investments being made reinforce each other and collectively drive new, desired business outcomes, and effect strategic change. Keeping strategic decision-making in step with the human capital strategies is a key element in driving successful strategy implementation efforts. As illustrated in Figure 1.3, the human capital strategy is an essential part of the strategy process and drives the implementation efforts.[10]

Throughout this book we will address each of the key aspects of human capital strategy as it relates to business direction and strategy. Human capital is often an essential element of the strategic change and execution processes.

Recognition of human capital as a source of value

For decades, economists have considered human capital as a source of competitive advantage for nations, following Gary Becker who popularised the concept.[11] As they examine education levels, workforce demographics, and general availability of skills, the idea of human capital has become one of the most important factors in the production and growth of economic wealth. Increasingly, the idea of national human capital also points to important linkages between human capital and long-term economic growth, as the strength of a nation can only be sustained by the strength of the next educational generation. Several nations have launched human capital initiatives as they recognise the importance of human capital as a part of the national agenda.

One such example can be found in Malaysia. In 2011 the Prime Minister created a new initiative to address the human capital of the nation. The primary purpose is to develop initiatives and direction to address the availability of talent in line with the country's economic growth and transformation plans. For a country like Malaysia, the availability of human capital can be either a driver

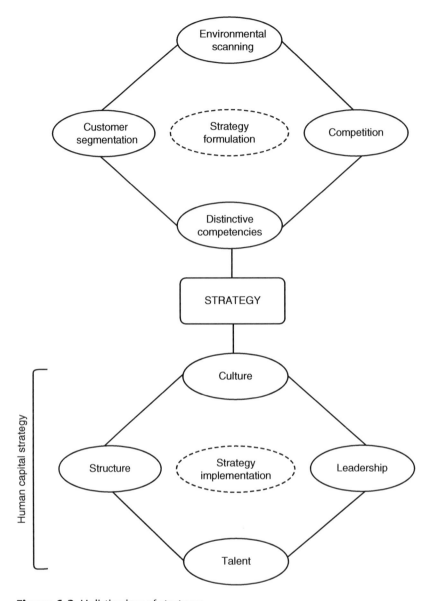

Figure 1.3 Holistic view of strategy
Source: adapted from McGee, Thomas, and Wilson, *Strategy Analysis and Practice* (McGraw Hill, 2010)

for success or a barrier to growth. To drive this initiative, Malaysia created TalentCorp, a new organisation with the mission of building effective partnerships and making a difference in addressing Malaysia's talent needs. The aim is to enable the country to reach its aspiration of being a high-income nation. For many countries similar national human capital initiatives are coming to the forefront of political-economic agendas.

A recent report by the World Economic Forum highlights that collaboration in talent mobility among stakeholders on all sides of the employment equation is most effective in addressing labour market shortages.[12] The report points out that talent markets are impeded by four key problems: widespread unemployment, skills gaps, information gaps, and private and public constraints. The report includes many examples of collaboration among companies, governments, academic institutions, and non-profits to address talent challenges.

In Canada, the Toronto Financial Services Alliance was established by the City of Toronto as a public–private partnership between government, academia, and financial services organisations to attract talent and thereby strengthen the Toronto financial services sector. The partnership aims to close information gaps by identifying specific skills and talent needs of the industry at college and university levels. The creation of the Centre of Excellence in Financial Services Education in 2009 was a result of this ongoing partnership.

Saudi Aramco, the world's largest oil and gas company, relies on rigorous workforce planning methods, substantial targeted investments in education and training, and expansive talent mobility programmes that give its employees exposure to the management practices and tools used by other major firms around the world. These programmes contribute to internal mobility at all career levels. Saudi Aramco also works closely with the government of Saudi Arabia and key academic institutions to secure a steady flow of talent to the company and throughout the country.

Strategic human capital is generally classified as an 'intangible asset', as it is often team-embedded in an organisation and built up as a strategic capability over time. Other intangible assets include brands, trademarks, and customer goodwill. While these assets are not physical or listed on a balance sheet, they are organisationally determined and growing in importance in economic and business activity.[13] This can be commonly seen in the valuation of assets in cases involving acquisitions or asset sales that include intangibles.

The relationship between human capital and the resource-based view (RBV) of the firm has been explored in recent years.[14] Some of the RBV strategists have linked various aspects of human capital to business strategy, for example, Barney's work on organisational culture as a potential source of sustained competitive advantage.[15] From the human resource management discipline, researchers and practitioners have long viewed the nature of human capital from different vantage points. While some address the link to strategy and the resource-based view, others take a performance-based view of human resource management (HRM) practices.[16] Boxall and Purcell summarised the interplay of strategy and human resource management to help bridge the disciplines in their book, *Strategy and Human Resource Management*.[17] While more research is needed in this area, it seems clear that the attention to human capital as a part of global business strategy has come of age.

Human capital as a part of business strategy

Regardless of the type of business strategy, the need to successfully implement strategy is important. Business leaders are increasingly recognising that whether the strategy is based on acquisition, differentiation, cost leadership, or a niche area, human capital is critical to success of that strategy.

One good example of implementing change by addressing the core elements of human capital is provided by Carlos Ghosn, then COO of Nissan, as he led the successful turnaround of the company against the backdrop of crisis for the Nissan–Renault alliance in the early 2000s.[18] Ghosn took stock of the situation when he arrived and reviewed the business practices, culture, talent management practices, leadership and structures. In addition to fundamental financial challenges due to re-engineering product development and the costs of production and the supply chain, the human capital assumptions on how work was organised and performed had to be rethought. He made major changes to the organisation structure by establishing cross-cultural teams across Nissan and Renault to identify common potential synergies in R&D, engineering, marketing, manufacturing, etc. and nine cross-functional teams in each company including most business areas that would then drive the major changes that had to be made. These teams became the catalyst for the turnaround as they broke traditional paradigms and began to change the culture of the organisation. Leadership through these teams coupled with the open and authentic leadership of Ghosn made a powerful difference in helping managers see beyond former functional boundaries. Ghosn notes that the success of this organisation change was built on establishing trust through transparency, with strong attention to nurturing a new corporate culture that remained sensitive to the history of Nissan and the best elements of Japan's national culture.[19] At the same time, he challenged current assumptions in the Nissan system such as lifetime employment (a luxury that Nissan could not afford), the orientation towards seniority versus meritocracy in rewards, and the use of *keiretsu* suppliers versus open bidding. He challenged these assumptions to effect appropriate strategic change while also empowering his leadership team to take the right actions for execution. By devoting the right attention to the areas of leadership, structure, talent management, and organisational culture, Ghosn helped drive sustainable strategic change.

Popular literature and the press are filled with success stories featuring strong, effective leadership that make a big impact. While many of these stories draw attention to the individual leader, the more important story is how they managed the human capital of the firm to create the results. Just as the Ghosn example shows, having a leader who is sensitive to structure and culture while making the right changes to the human capital strategy of the organisation can make a considerable difference.

Another organisation that has embarked on a human capital strategy is the professional services firm Accenture.[20] After experiencing tremendous growth and success in the core businesses of consulting, outsourcing, and technology services, the firm recognised the risk of losing their competitive edge. Growing from 60,000 employees to more than 250,000 employees over a nine-year period created a number of challenges in developing the breadth of leadership at the same pace. In addition, the organisation culture, structure, and talent management systems needed to be reviewed in light of the future direction. This became an action item as a part of the board of directors and was led by the CEO, Bill Green. Accenture developed a multi-year human capital strategy to paint a picture of how the talent, leadership, culture, and operating model would look in the future. This has become an ongoing and important part of the strategy process for the firm that is now led by the chief leadership officer who reports to the CEO. Accenture believes that its human capital strategy will help create a global talent advantage for the firm.[21]

Regardless of the business strategy, the attention to human capital becomes critical in the planning and execution of the process of strategy. As more businesses recognise the critical nature of addressing human capital as a part of strategy formulation and implementation, we expect to see more orientation towards human capital strategy around the world.

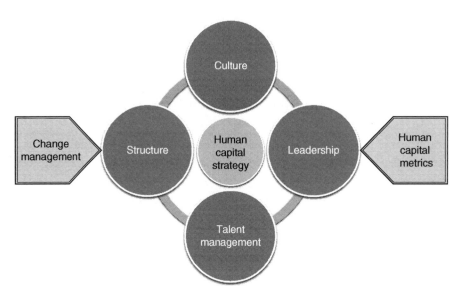

Figure 1.4 Human capital strategy

Overview of this book

The purpose of this book is to help drive the importance of human capital in the strategy process. We propose a simple conceptual model of human capital, as shown in Figure 1.4, and address the importance of each element in the succeeding chapters.

Chapter 2: Culture

We first define the firm culture and then review the impact of organisational culture on strategy and business performance. We then address the challenges in managing a desired culture. The internal and external influences of culture are discussed along with ways of determining and perpetuating a desired culture for the organisation.

Chapter 3: Leadership

We discuss the importance of leadership development and examine concepts of, and approaches to, strategic leadership. There is specific attention to the tools and techniques for developing future leaders.

Chapter 4: Structure

We address the interrelated nature of strategy and structure and examine the forms that may fit with particular business strategies. The design of teams, jobs, and other elements are reviewed in light of creating an effective structure.

Chapter 5: Talent management

The issue of creating the right workforce with the skills needed to carry out the strategy is discussed here. Key elements of recruitment, development, performance management, and forecasting are reviewed.

Chapter 6: Human capital metrics

We review ways of measuring the areas of human capital and, specifically, workforce capabilities, behaviours, and competencies. The growth in the use of many data sources with new analytic approaches is creating new mechanisms for linking human capital to business strategy and plans.

Chapter 7: Change management

Each of the elements of human capital are an important part of managing change in business strategy. We review the elements of managing and directing change consistent with the execution of business plans.

Chapter 8: Conclusion

While each of the components in Chapters 2 to 7 is important, the power of an overarching human capital strategy is a necessity to bring them all together as a part of business plans. We therefore discuss how business leaders can integrate these elements into their global business plans and develop overarching human capital strategies.

We hope you will benefit from this book and recognise that the attention to human capital is essential in framing strategy, planning, and developing dynamic human capital capabilities.

Key questions for consideration

- *Are your organisation's people investments aligned with the most important business goals?*
- *Will your company buy, build, or borrow the workforce capabilities needed?*

- *Do you know who are your critical employees and are you investing in them accordingly?*
- *Does your organisation have the right leaders in place to drive transformational new strategies?*
- *Will your company have the leaders in place for the future success of the enterprise?*
- *Are you measuring the performance appropriately and rewarding it the right way?*
- *Do you use workforce data and rigorous analytics to drive people decisions?*
- *Can you confidently tell your Board that you are managing human capital risks in the strategy process?*

REFERENCES

[1] McGee, J., Thomas, H., and Wilson, D. (2010) *Strategy Analysis and Practice*. London: McGraw-Hill.

[2] Chandler, A. (1962) *Strategy and Structure: Chapters in the History of the American Industrial Enterprise*. Cambridge, MA: MIT Press.

[3] Teece, D. J. (2009) *Dynamic Capabilities and Strategic Management*. Oxford: Oxford University Press.

[4] Penrose, E. (1959) *The Theory of the Growth of the Firm*. Oxford: Basil Blackwell.

[5] Barney, J. (1991) 'Firm Resources and Sustained Competitive Advantage', *Journal of Management* 17(1): 99–120.

[6] McGee, J., and Thomas, H. (1986) 'Strategic Groups: Theory, Research and Taxonomy', *Strategic Management Journal* 7(2): 141–160.

[7] Prahalad, C. K., and Hamel, G. (1990) 'The Core Competence of the Corporation', *Harvard Business Review* 68(3): 79–91.

[8] Beer, M., and Nohria, N. (2000) 'Cracking the Code of Change', *Harvard Business Review* 78(3): 133–141.

[9] Cascio, W., and Boudreau, J. (2012) *Introduction to Strategic Human Resource Management*. Cambridge University Press.

[10] Thomas, H. (2010) *Strategic Management Lecture Materials*. Singapore Management University.

[11] Becker, G. (1964) *Human Capital: A Theoretical and Empirical Analysis, with Special Reference to Education*. New York: National Bureau of Economic Research.

[12] World Economic Forum (2012) *Talent Mobility Good Practices – Collaboration at the Core of Driving Economic Growth*.

[13] Hand, J. R. M., and Lev, B. (2003) *Intangible Assets: Values, Measures, and Risks*. New York: Oxford University Press.

[14] Hitt, M. A., Bierman, L., Shimizu, K., and Kochhar, R. (2001) 'Direct and Moderating Effects of Human Capital on Strategy and Performance in Professional Service Firms: A Resource-Based Perspective', *Academy of Management Journal* 44(1): 13–28.

[15] Barney, J. B. (1986) 'Organizational Culture: Can it be a Source of Sustained Competitive Advantage?', *Academy of Management Review* 11(3): 656–665.

[16] Lepak, D. P., and Snell, S. A. (1999) 'The Human Resource Architecture: Toward a Theory of Human Capital Allocation and Development', *Academy of Management Review* 24(1): 31–48.

[17] Boxall, P., and Purcell, J. (2003) *Strategy and Human Resource Management.* New York: Palgrave Macmillian.

[18] Yoshino, M., and Egawa, M. (2002) Nissan Motor Co., Ltd., *Harvard Business School Case* (9): 303–042.

[19] Millikin, J. P., and Fu, D. (2005) 'The Global Leadership of Carlos Ghosn at Nissan', *Thunderbird International Business Review* 47(1): 121–137.

[20] Smith, D., Silverstone, Y., and Lajtha, A. (2011) *A New Lens on Business Advantage: Human Capital Strategy and the Drive for High Performance.* Accenture Business and Leadership Publication.

[21] Accenture (2012) 2010–2011 Corporate Citizenship Report.

2   Culture

> A lot of knowledge in any kind of organisation is what we call task knowledge. These are things that people who have been there a long time understand are important, but they may not know how to talk about them. It is often called the culture of the organisation.
>
> Howard Gardner

Introduction

Managers are facing increasing demands in looking for strategic advantage and ideally a sustainable competitive advantage in the marketplace. As shown in Chapter 1, each of the elements of human capital strategy is critical for strategy execution. Of these elements, organisation culture has a tremendous impact on the ability to sustain competitive advantage.

Culture is a critical element in business success, as noted by Kotter and Heskett in their research on corporate culture and performance.[1] Companies with adaptive, high-achieving cultures will positively influence the bottom line. For those firms with culture aligned to their business strategy, the performance is quite remarkable as they achieved: more than 4 times revenue growth, over 700 times the net income growth, and a 9 times stock price increase relative to other companies in the same period. While there are many factors that contribute to business performance, culture plays a key role in supporting the business plans and is a key lever in the human capital strategy of the organisation.[2] Research has also shown that distinct culture types have an impact on employee attitudes which impact performance.[3]

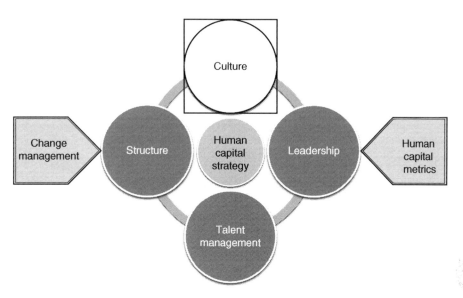

Figure 2.1 Culture
Source: adapted from Schein, Organizational Culture and Leadership (Jossey-Bass, 1992).
Reproduced with permission of John Wiley & Sons, Inc.

Of course, each of the elements in our human capital strategy model does not stand in isolation. The culture of the firm has a high linkage with leadership effectiveness, as the way that leaders interact with the people, provide direction, and manage expectations will have an immediate effect on the culture. At the same time, a new leader who does not understand the nuances of the company culture may quickly find that she or he is not effective or may even be ostracised. We will explore the interaction between leadership and culture further in this chapter.

The linkage between talent and culture is also a critical one as the efforts associated with talent management such as recruiting, performance management, and career development should all reflect and support the desired culture in the organisation. For example, if the business focus is on efficient operations, the desired culture can be reinforced through performance appraisals that emphasise efficiency in both content as well as process. The same can be done with recruiting and other talent management processes as effective tools for providing signals on the desired behaviours in the organisation.

In this chapter, we will examine the role of culture in achieving business results:

- *What is organisation culture?*
- *How does culture support strategy and execution?*
- *What should a business leader consider about culture?*

- *What are ways of measuring and understanding a company's culture?*
- *How do we change or shape the organisation culture?*

About organisation culture

The culture defines *how* things get done inside a firm. While processes and procedures may be defined and even embedded into workflows and IT systems, the general ways of working are driven from the accepted behaviours and norms in the firm. In many ways, culture can be seen as the personality or way of working within an organisation that is generally ingrained into common work practices and styles for managing.

Attributes of culture for an internet services company such as Google might include innovative, participative, team orientation, and nimbleness. These attributes have been a key part of the success of the company as it adapts to a quickly changing online marketplace. If we were to consider a global financial services business like Citigroup, the cultural attributes might include accountability, process orientation, meritocracy, professionalism, and dependability.[4] Characteristics such as these have allowed many large financial services organisations to maintain stability, customer trust, and scalable results.

While we can think of many characteristics of companies with which we have experience, research by Edgar Schein has shown that there are several levels of culture,[5] as shown in Figure 2.2. At the surface we might find 'artifacts' which are attributes that can be observed, felt, and heard in a firm. Such things as the physical workplace architecture, dress code, office jokes, trophies, verbal sayings, and common greetings are all artifacts of culture.

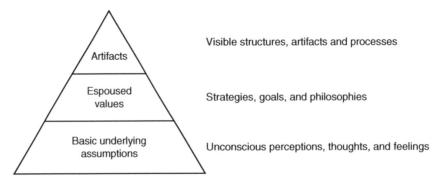

Figure 2.2 Three levels of culture
Source: based on research findings of Heskett and Kotter, Corporate Culture and Performance (The Free Press, 1992)

Table 2.1 The Coca-Cola Company values

Live our values
Our values serve as a compass for our actions and describe how we behave in the world.
Leadership: The courage to shape a better future
Collaboration: Leverage collective genius
Integrity: Be real
Accountability: If it is to be, it's up to me
Passion: Committed in heart and mind
Diversity: As inclusive as our brands
Quality: What we do, we do well

Source: Coca-Cola Company, *Mission, Vision & Value* [Online] Available from: www.coca-colacompany.com/our-company/mission-vision-values

At the next level we might uncover values. The values of a firm are generally stated and documented as a part of the human capital strategy. Many companies spend time to consider the type of standards, moral principles, and norms desired throughout the organisation. These may be summarised in a set of values or principles that are published for employees and are often measured through surveys or as part of the performance review processes. The Coca-Cola Company defines a set of values as set out in Table 2.1.

At the foundation of culture are underlying assumptions about what things are actually valued in the organisation. Generally these assumptions are typically well integrated into the office dynamic so that they are hard to recognise from within the enterprise. Information at this level can be perceived by outsiders only through careful observation since it is often taken for granted and not recognised. An example of an underlying assumption may include the protocol in hierarchy or the degree of acceptable confrontation when differences arise. People in the organisation do not think about how to act in these situations, they just 'know how things are done' since it is embedded as part of the cultural foundation.

Aligning the underlying assumptions with the values and artifacts is important in creating a consistent and clear culture in the organisation. In addition, the culture must be aligned with the business strategy to support the desired behaviours needed to drive plans and activities. Culture can be both a critical enabler of business strategy as well as a potential barrier in making changes.

Culture in support of strategy and execution

Considering that the culture is the character or personality of the organisation, we should then consider what type of behaviours support the direction and plans for the business. Of course, each company culture is unique as it is typically shaped over years by the people, environment, and situation of the enterprise. While some might consider culture to be an uncontrollable result of activities over time, many insightful leaders now see the need for aligning and shaping the culture in a way that supports long-term plans.

For example, for a business with a customer-centric strategy, an associated culture that creates 'default' behaviour and orientation around the needs and values of the customer becomes critical. A stated strategy of strong customer orientation where the differentiation hinges on customer service and loyalty can create conflict and confusion if the culture is focused on low-cost operation. In this case, decisions on customer wait times, call response times, policy exceptions, customer record keeping, and the like could be in debate between operational cost and customer value.

It is important for the culture to be aligned with the strategy to help facilitate the execution. If we consider basic business strategies, as outlined by Treacy and Wiersema, we can envision potential cultural elements that become critical for each, as shown in Table 2.2.

The alignment of firm culture to the strategy is an important effort that management must address as part of the human capital strategy. While many business leaders can describe the culture of their firm, few have worked to actually define and document the desired culture of the organisation in a way that fits with the business strategy. This alignment is necessary for the execution of strategy and the consistency of activities during strategic change.

Wal-Mart has a tremendous story of growth with a clear strategy of being a low-cost retailer. The relentless focus on finding ways to save money for customers has driven Wal-Mart's success in global sourcing, supply chain innovation, and store management. The corporate culture can be described as customer-focused with a high respect for people (see Table 2.3). The founder, Sam Walton's concern and respect for staff from the foundation of the company creates an environment of trust that persists to this day. Walton met staff, calling them by their first name and encouraged change to maintain the competitive edge. To this day, staff members think about '*how Sam would have done it*'.

Table 2.2 Potential cultural elements

Basic business strategy	Potential cultural implications
Low-cost provider	Economic orientation, focus on efficiency, economic innovation, process orientation, time-based models, and operational focus
Product-centric differentiation	Focus on product quality, product innovation, technical orientation, open to change, continuous learning, risk-taking and nimbleness
Customer intimacy	Customer orientation, service focus, innovation of customer experience, employee growth, flexibility, external focus, and market responsive

Source: adapted from Treacy and Wiersema, *The Discipline of Market Leaders: Choose Your Customers, Narrow Your Focus, Dominate Your Market* (Perseus Books, 1997)

The Wal-Mart Corporation employs more than 2,000,000 employees and operates more than 10,000 stores. Operating at this scale with success cannot be done without having a defined culture that helps guide behaviour 'the Wal-Mart way'. The rapid expansion and consistency of Wal-Mart's performance is enabled by the defined culture of the organisation.

As businesses and governments work to improve performance, it seems that efforts are given to areas other than culture. We often see corporate initiatives on restructuring, new processes, automation, expansion or strategic alliances in an effort to improve performance. More recently, we start to see leaders who understand the importance of determining the desired culture and driving this behaviour model throughout the enterprise. As we consider that culture provides a set of 'default' behaviours, it seems that culture becomes a key priority for management teams.

Taking stock of organisation culture

When an outsider walks into the office, what do they notice? Often they may take note of things that employees may take for granted and do not question since it is just the way that things are in this organisation. Every company has a certain 'way' of doing business that has shaped the bounds of acceptable

Table 2.3 The Wal-Mart culture

Open door
Our management believes open communication is critical to understanding and meeting our associates' and our customers' needs. Associates can trust and rely on the open door; it's one of the most important parts of our culture.
Sundown rule
Observing the sundown rule means we do our best to answer requests by the close of business on the day we receive them. Whether it's a request from a store across the country or a call from down the hall, we do our very best to give each other and our customers same-day service. We do this by combining our efforts and depending upon each other to get things done.
Grassroots process
Sam's philosophy lives on today in Wal-Mart's grassroots process, our formal way of capturing associates' ideas, suggestions and concerns.
Three basic beliefs and values
Our unique culture has helped make Wal-Mart one of the world's most admired companies. Since Sam Walton opened Wal-Mart in 1962, our culture has rested on three basic beliefs. We live out these beliefs each day in our interactions with our customers and each other.
Ten-foot rule
The 10-foot rule is one of our secrets to customer service. During his many store visits, Sam Walton encouraged associates (employees) to take this pledge with him: 'I promise that whenever I come within 10 feet of a customer, I will look him in the eye, greet him, and ask if I can help him.'
Servant leadership
Sam Walton believed that effective leaders do not lead from behind their desks. 'It's more important than ever that we develop leaders who are servants, who listen to their partners – their associates – in a way that creates wonderful morale to help the whole team accomplish an overall goal,' Sam said.
Teamwork
Sam Walton, our founder, believed in the power of teamwork. As our stores grow and the pace of modern life quickens, that philosophy of teamwork has only become more important over the years.
Wal-Mart cheer
Don't be surprised if you hear our associates shouting this enthusiastically at your local Wal-Mart store. It's our cheer, and while it might not sound serious, we take it seriously. It's one way we show pride in our company.

Source: courtesy of Walmart: http://careers.walmart.com/company-beliefs-and-values/

and expected behaviour by those who are associated with the organisation. Sometimes this culture is very pronounced and recognisable and at other times it may be more subtle with variations based on location or division. After all, the culture is shaped by a number of factors, some of which are in the control of the enterprise as well as others that come from external sources.

Culture is shaped by internal business influencers such as control systems, structures, leadership roles, rituals and routines, symbols, physical work environment, and stories. External factors that influence culture can include the nature of the industry, customers, suppliers, public perception, marketplace conditions, and even natural disasters. With so many potential variables, it can seem difficult to somehow manage and actually shape an organisation's culture. Let us start by first considering many of these potential influences on culture.

Internal culture influences

The signals of culture are all around us from the moment we walk through the front door of a company. *Are we greeted with sincere interest to help or are we greeted with guarded suspicion? Are the décor and location of the office focused on low-cost or high-comfort surroundings? Are formal processes and documentation used or are interactions more casual and open?* While many of these can be situational, they make up the landscape of culture signals. Such signals become invisible to those who are immersed in the organisation every day, while being potentially startling to those who join from the outside. The degree of person–organisation fit is commonly considered as the alignment of the personality and values of the individual with that of the organisation. Research illustrates the importance of this person–organisation fit to achieving job satisfaction and trust in the business.[6]

One of the immediate signals to employees about what is important to the organisation relates to control systems, or how an organisation monitors progress.[7] Control systems can refer to the rather sophisticated manufacturing systems that keep production lines moving, but here we consider a more general view of systems and measures that management uses to understand how the enterprise is performing. As the old adage goes: 'What gets measured gets done.' Such is also the case when considering the impact on culture. What gets measured can be an important behaviour signal about values and expectations. Consider a customer contact centre that posts a large electronic display showing call volumes handled by individuals. The measure reinforces a focus on efficiency in call handling and speedy resolution of issues; a different result might be obtained if we measured call waiting times, customer satisfaction, and query resolution. Depending on the measure chosen, it creates an expectation and understanding of what is important and potentially what is not important.

Company structure also sends an important cultural signal based on reporting lines, spans of control, hierarchy, and authority levels. While structure does not dictate how things get done, it sends important messages to the organisation. Companies that have rather rigid structures with very well-defined and detailed role descriptions along with rulebooks may well reinforce the clear expectations but may have difficulty when flexibility is required. Consider a firm with authority set to a minimum for each level in the organisation. In this case, managers must ask for approval from the boss for every potential exception, which can help control costs, but may unintentionally signal a lack of trust or confidence in subordinates. In addition to hierarchy, organisational silos, a side-effect of structural designs, can create cultural impacts by isolating groups and fostering a focus on one dimension of the business. While there are always many considerations in organisation design, we must pay particular attention to the potential cultural impact of the structures and management lines. We will explore the topic of organisation structure more fully in Chapter 4.

Leadership behaviour and style can be one of the most important influences on culture. However, we should not falsely believe that leadership is the primary driver of culture or that leaders can actually control the culture directly. Leaders often set the tone in the organisation and guide a number of critical factors that affect culture such as the measurements, structures, and work environment. On a day-to-day basis, leaders make an impact by the way they interact with others, the manner in which they take decisions, and the nature and tone of their communications. Consider a leader who seeks input from others in a collaborative style before making a decision. In this mode he/she may not only be improving the quality and context of the decision, but also signalling an important value for collaboration and teamwork. We will explore the topic of leadership more fully in Chapter 3.

Talent management practices can be one of the important personal signals for behaviour consistent with the culture and expectations. The selection of potential employees, the way promotions are determined, the recognition of performance, and the design of performance incentives are all ways of influencing culture. These can be powerful human resource (HR) tools for shaping organisational behaviour in a way that is consistent with the desired culture. When these processes are not in line with the stated values or desires of the firm, confusion can develop. For example, many companies espouse the importance of teamwork and team orientation. Consider a manager who organizes his department in working teams and encourages people to focus on team results. Imagine the incongruity when they each receive an individual performance appraisal and individual performance award that does not reflect the team accomplishments or goals. The area of talent management plays a key role related to culture and will be explored more fully in Chapter 5.

Rituals and routines in an organisation are often embedded without much consideration, yet they have an impact on the way work gets done. The nature of management meetings, communication methods, and management reports are general aspects that make a subtle impact on the view of the organisation. For example, a weekly staff meeting conducted by a manager may set the tone for interactions. Suppose the manager runs the meeting with the same agenda each week where he/she provides the staff with updates and direction without pausing to invite questions or comments. While the intent is to share information, the inadvertent message might also be delivered that input or discussion is not welcomed. Consider as well the team leader who takes everyone out for happy hour every Friday to say thank you and wrap up the week. Even years after he has left the firm, the tradition remains with the department. These routines and rituals as an individual occurrence may seem insignificant, but multiplied by hundreds and thousands of times over the years will shape expectations and the cultural foundations. Over time, meetings like these can become more habitual than necessary for business results. Habitual patterns in an organisation form rituals that are sometimes explained as '*That is just the way we do things around here*' when questioned by outsiders.

In a similar way, power structures or the way power is distributed in the organisation can make an impact as these demonstrate important distinctions in roles and areas. In a culture where power is used to influence decisions and gain preference, we will likely find more emphasis on individualism versus teamwork. In many businesses the CFO holds significant position power even though there may not be direct authority over business operations. In a manufacturing environment, significant power is often given to plant managers as they are accountable not only for the results of the plant, but also as the company representative for that location. The power in the firm provides clear signals on where to air new ideas or where to go for help in influencing decisions or for seeking favour. While often unsaid, the power maps can provide important clues on how the organisation works and on the resulting culture.

Another internal influence of culture is the symbols that exist in the enterprise. Every firm has symbols that include logos and designs, but also symbolic items that provide important clues to the company culture. Logos and brands can make impressions and statements about how the organisation works internally as well as how it wants to be known externally. When Standard Chartered Bank launched the brand identity 'Here for good' they immediately used this to help reinforce their core values and culture of the organisation. Symbols not only include logos, brands, and designs, but also extend to symbols of power such as parking spaces and executive washrooms. Casual space in the office with lounge chairs and sofas can also serve as a symbol that might reinforce creative or innovating thinking. Executive leaders with private lunch rooms, exclusive elevators, and private planes should understand the impact that these symbols have on the culture of the organisation.

Like symbols, stories and myths have a long-lasting impact on the foundation of a culture. In every organisation stories often build up about people and events, and convey a message about what is valued. When terrorists attacked in Mumbai in 2008, the employees of the Taj Mumbai behaved in a way that exemplified the culture and values of the organisation. Certainly a life-threatening situation such as this can create chaos, but the evidence shows that the employees acted in a way that placed the safety of the guests over their own wellbeing – in some cases, sacrificing their own lives. The Taj Hotel group takes pride in the customer-centric culture and it showed through in this ultimate test.[8] The story of this experience and the memories of the employees who died in this unfortunate crisis remain a powerful part of the Taj Group. Like the other internal influences, symbols and stories may also create inconsistent messages about what is important in the firm since legends of bad behaviour can also be passed around the organisation for a long time.

External culture influences

Internal factors play a primary role in shaping a culture while external conditions can set the context and considerations that may influence it as well. One of the primary external considerations is the industry within which the company operates. Companies in the same industry share some common attributes from the markets they serve, occasional strategic alliances, movement of employees between organisations, and basic business model. Consider the similarities between the cultures of multinational oil companies, in contrast to, say, large investment banks. The adventurous nature of upstream oil exploration and production in remote parts of the earth coupled with the industrial orientation of downstream refining, production and distribution create some common traits across the super majors. At the same time, a look into the global investment banks that are dealing with analytical portfolio management, executive relationships, valuations, and complex financial deals creates a few common traits across the firms. Of course, each company still has a unique culture based on its special circumstances and its internal culture shaping, described above.

Market conditions can have an impact on the organisation in an indirect way by setting the context within which the management operates. When the global semiconductor industry faced dire circumstances following the internet boom, each company faced common challenges of overcapacity, extreme price competition, and innovation demands. These challenges created similar responses across several companies as production units were consolidated to low-cost locations, staff numbers were reduced to a minimum, and austerity programmes were introduced. This 'lean and mean' orientation across the industry has created common cultural traits in the sector due to the needs of the industry driven by the marketplace.

Customers can also have an impact on the organisational culture. For retail organisations, it is important for customer service staff to be able to relate to and understand the needs of their clientele. Upscale hotel chains such as the Shangri-La and Ritz Carlton target affluent customers and consequently work to create a comprehensive guest experience. These firms are known for their customer-centric orientation and must have a culture that fits with the target customers. In the same way, the customers also have an impact on the culture due to their expectations and interactions with the organisation. These customer expectations and experiences help to perpetuate the culture as employees work to meet the needs of the customers whether in a consumer or business-to-business situation.

Organisational cultures are sometimes tested by external factors such as natural disasters or unplanned events that impact the enterprise. In these cases, the normal rules of behaviour may not apply due to prevailing circumstances. During the earthquake and resulting tsunami in Japan on 11 March 2011, many leaders and businesses had to quickly take action in ways that did not fit traditional cultural norms. Unfortunately, in some cases the strong culture prevented others from taking action immediately. The response to such disasters can have an impact and potentially shape the culture of the organisation in some way.

External factors of industry, market conditions, customers, suppliers and even disasters can have a strong impact on the organisational culture. It is important to recognise these influences to determine how to best shape the right culture in light of these factors.

Perpetuating a culture

What keeps a particular culture sustained in an organisation? While the internal and external factors continuously influence the culture, many firms unintentionally perpetuate their culture through processes and routines that help reinforce behaviours, beliefs, and assumptions. In fact, even before we consider perpetuation within the company, it is important to recognise that the recruiting processes and screening criteria for new potential employees typically include a culture screen. This screening for cultural fit may be intentional or unintentional, and has a large impact on perpetuating the culture by only hiring 'like-me' profiles into the business. Of course, there is a potential danger of discriminating against certain profiles, which can adversely impact certain groups, so leaders must be sure that proper HR processes are being followed. Another potential risk from cultural fit screening is the missed opportunity for increasing the diversity of the organisation. Consider a firm that only hires people with engineering degrees based on the roots of the company and the desire for everyone to relate to the discipline of engineering regardless of their role in the organisation. Imagine the missed opportunity for this company to bring in people with a different mindset who might challenge some of the conventional thinking and potentially lead to new improvements or breakthrough ideas. While the idea of screening for cultural fit may be a tempting, and sometimes unintentional, way to perpetuate the current way of working, managers should take care to encourage the new thinking that comes with diversity.

It is said that first impressions can be lasting ones and this is the case with the first day in a new job. Once people are hired into the organisation, we may send them to orientation or some type of induction training to learn more about the company. While this induction training and general orientation may follow a simple programme that is outlined by HR, it can leave a lasting impression. Consider the insurance company that had just hired a group of bright, energetic MBA graduates for a new product area. The traditional orientation was conducted by a clerk in HR with an orientation on compliance to the rules, completion of forms, along with a clear demonstration that she was not satisfied with the organisation. The excited graduates were surprised to meet someone like this after talking with others in the firm during the interview process. Several began to wonder if this was what it was really like as an employee and began to question their assumptions about the firm. When they finished the three-day orientation process, they arrived in the new area with mixed emotions. The excitement about starting was a bit diminished and, instead of looking at the opportunities around them to build the new product area, they began to question the feasibility and focus on the problems around them. While there are many factors that influence situations like this, it seemed clear that the orientation process did not help create the right cultural orientation that the company desired.

The culture is also perpetuated by the way that leadership engages and communicates with the organisation.[5] When the company leadership announce changes, do they issue a memo to the entire firm or leave this to each manager to address? When changes are introduced do leaders discuss these with their people or are the changes kept at the management level? Of course, there are many circumstances that may dictate how communication is handled in each situation; however, the employees will quickly understand and interpret the patterns of communication from leadership. The communication and direct engagement patterns serve as a signal about what is acceptable, expected, and appreciated in the way of working together. As leadership changes take place, many times the communication patterns and methods remain the same, thus perpetuating the cultural assumptions.

In addition to official company communication, informal communication networks also help perpetuate the culture through stories and legends. New employees often learn about the company from their co-workers who describe how things work in the organisation. The stories of prior events of heroic feats such as the stranded FedEx delivery employee who was concerned about his ability to meet the company promise of 'absolutely, positively delivered overnight'.

A blizzard in the California Sierras prevented communication and delivery of packages for customers from a local FedEx office. Unable to deliver as promised for customers due to communication lines being down, a junior FedEx staffer decided to rent a helicopter. Without asking for permission from his managers, he put the helicopter expense on his personal American Express card and instructed the pilot to fly to the top of the mountain where the failed equipment was located. There, the employee jumped onto the snow-covered mountain top, trudged three-quarters of a mile in deep snow and fixed the line to get FedEx back in business.

His decision to charter a helicopter to meet the objective of delivering parcels was rewarded by management and the story has been spread throughout the company as well as among customers. The FedEx employee who took it upon himself to charter a helicopter is now a legend in the industry. Positive stories like this help reinforce the understanding of the values and the culture of the business. In fact, FedEx quickly learned the positive power of this story in conveying a message about their organisation, such that they have since launched a website that contains this and other positive stories demonstrating their commitment to excellence.[9]

Nordstrom Department Stores are known for their strong customer service and a culture that is relentlessly customer-driven. To perpetuate this culture, Nordstrom uses stories to help reinforce the desired behaviours and outcomes. In daily pre-shift meetings at Nordstrom stores, employees share detailed stories about their recent interactions with customers. In the hallways of Nordstrom's executive offices, letters from customers are mounted on the walls, enlarged and framed so they cannot possibly be ignored by the people who run the company. On the desk of Pete Nordstrom, the company's President of Merchandising, sit albums full of letters from customers and employees, each telling a story about a memorable experience they had with Nordstrom. These actions encourage employees to look for opportunities to create their own stories. They know that most customer interactions will be fairly routine but that from time to time exceptional circumstances will arise. Those circumstances can lead to memorable tales, and those tales are more powerful than any advertising the company could buy.

Of course, not all stories are positive: actions such as controversial decisions for terminating employees, managers who may have publicly embarrassed people, or prior union conflicts all have an impact on how people see the boundaries of acceptable or expected behaviour in the organisation. From the reports of Enron's collapse, Jeff Skilling never told employees to act unethically. He simply demanded extreme results and made it clear that any behaviour was acceptable to produce them. These leadership messages and the corresponding stories sent clear signals to the people on what was expected and what was acceptable.

Not only can culture define the ways of working, it also can have a significant impact on the overall performance of the organisation. It is therefore critical to consider what type of culture is appropriate for the business that fits with the business strategy and plans.

Determining the desired culture

While it seems logical to have a culture that fits with the business strategy, how do we determine what type of culture works best? Many have remarked on the culture and work environment of Google. As a high-tech company oriented toward innovation, Google has a track record of success and a culture that promotes innovation and creativity. At Google we might find employees lounging on the sofas or relaxing in one of the many themed rooms designed to help people reflect and think differently. This is also reinforced with the performance management processes that encourage innovation and teamwork.

The culture of Google can be considered fun, but it has a serious business side as innovation and ideas are critical to continued business success. This is a culture that works for Google, but should we adopt a similar culture for other organisations? Imagine one of the largest banking institutions in the world today, adopting the Google culture. Instead of showcasing the security and reliability of the bank, they now focus more on innovation and creativity. How creative do you want your bank to be with your deposits? Certainly each culture should be crafted in a way that fits with the organisation's purpose and strategy.

Cultures vary in styles as well as strength and influence on behaviours. Some enterprises have a deeply embedded culture that has been shaped over many years, while other company cultures may not be noticeable and may seem to have little impact on day-to-day business operations. In general, strong cultures have been shaped by management, often the founder or strong leader who puts a number of practices and principles in place to drive the organisation in a certain direction. In addition to having a strong leader, a long-term commitment to reinforce these practices and principles must exist and be demonstrated over several years. These practices and ways of working become reinforced in the organisation at all levels. Those who have a difficult time adhering to the behaviours are typically reminded by co-workers and others to encourage them to keep within the norms and may have an impact on performance.[10] Often people will leave the company if they have trouble fitting into the strong culture, as shown by research through meta-analysis of person–organisation fit.[11] Typically, companies with a strong culture are anchored to a genuine interest in the wellbeing of employees, customers, and shareholders. Companies with strong cultures will endure changes in the marketplace, different leadership styles, and even strategy changes. Of course, this inflexibility can be a problem for a business with a strong culture. Changing a strong culture is extremely difficult and can only be done with significant effort over time.[12]

Weak cultures on the other hand can be changed and moulded since they lack the consistency of a strong culture. Typically a weak culture is in place due to inconsistent messages on values, principles, and direction. Frequent leadership changes or leaders who do not actively share a business philosophy can leave the firm to determine its own ways of doing things. This can lead to internal differences and conflicts when it comes to decisions or a clear view on what is important to the company. In addition it can be difficult for employees to feel a sense of identification with the company since it lacks the 'personality' of a strong culture company. Making changes within a weak culture is considerably easier than in a strong culture, but can create confusion if the organisation is not accustomed to strong direction or principles.

For many years, it was believed that strong cultures are always best for organisation performance since there is an identifiable conformity to the norms and accepted practices to guide behaviour. Research has shown however that those firms with adaptive characteristics are better able to respond to the changing needs of the business. In other words, those firms that are able to adapt to the changes needed for the improvement of the business will more easily adjust with a higher level of business results.[1]

An adaptive culture consists of a few important characteristics. First, employees in adaptive cultures have a strong willingness to try new things and accept change as a relative constant. Many will see change as a new and exciting challenge and engage in the effort to execute new strategies or ways of working. There is generally a sense of pride and confidence in the firm. Second, people in adaptive cultures will demonstrate a sense of teamwork and genuine support for each other. Competitive and political agendas are not acceptable as members of the organisation openly demonstrate supportive behaviours for others in making changes or trying new things. Third, management encourages employees to remain flexible and adaptive by seeking out individuals who take initiative and act with a sense of ownership for the business or area. Managers also foster prudent risk-taking and innovative ideas through recognition and acknowledgement of employees who take on new things or identify new opportunities. Fourth, the employer demonstrates concern for the well-being of the employees through both formal programmes as well as informal actions by leadership.

While an adaptive culture embraces change, it does have elements that provide consistency and identity for the people in the organisation. Generally, the values in the organisation remain solid and at the forefront as key anchors for decision-making and direction. The stated values are not just put away on a shelf; they are used and known by the people in the business. The other important reason that allows a culture to stay consistently adaptive is the emphasis on the legitimate interests of the stakeholders such as customers, employees,

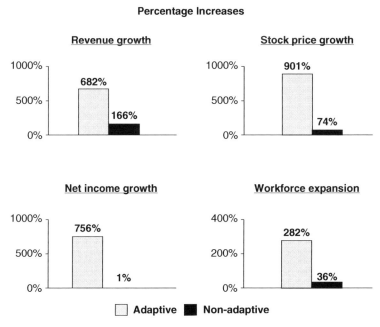

Figure 2.3 Impact of adaptive cultures on business performance
Source: adapted from Kotter and Heskett, *Corporate Culture and Performance* (The Free Press, 1992)

shareholders, and local communities. By focusing on core values and stakeholder interests, the employees clearly understand and trust that management is only implementing changes for improvement.

In their research on culture and the impact on business performance, Kotter and Heskett found striking results for those companies with adaptive cultures. Those firms that exhibited adaptive characteristics were much more successful as measured by revenue growth, net income growth, and workforce expansion, as shown in Figure 2.3.

An adaptive culture can help provide competitive advantage since it allows the business to adjust to changing markets, new business plans, and dynamic customer needs.[13] Adaptive organisations can more easily embrace new strategies and move quickly to execution of plans to change the business. As shown here, adaptive organisations are more likely to create strong results for shareholders in most situations.

Mergers and acquisitions

While working to shape one culture is a challenge, imagine the complexity when we combine two organisations. It turns out that culture is a key factor in determining success in strategic alliances.[14] In fact, not recognising the challenges inherent in culture can create major challenges in merger and acquisition (M&A) situations. Susan Cartwright and Cary Cooper summarised this phenomenon and recognised that many 'organisational marriages' continue to prove disappointing due to cultural differences.[15] Understanding cultural differences becomes critical when considering the costs and integration challenges between companies. In fact, the M&A landscape is littered with difficult business situations and mixed results due to poor planning or execution of culture integration. Buono and Bowditch outline the impact of culture during a merger in their work with a major bank merger to demonstrate how cultures can collide.[16]

When faced with an acquisition or merger, four options for addressing culture seem to emerge (see Figure 2.4). The first and simple option might be to keep separate cultures for each of the entities. This could be appropriate for group structures that operate more like a holding company or potentially a diversified conglomerate. By keeping the separate cultures, each organisation can continue to build on historical strengths and potentially minimise disruption to the business. This can also help keep the market image clear and avoid confusing the end customers. Even with separate cultures, there is still an opportunity to share learning and practices across the organisations to find areas for potential improvement. Even with a strategy to keep separate cultures, it is important to address this area as a part of the M&A activities to ensure alignment with the new strategy.

The second option is to operate a culture within a culture. In other words, allow the acquired company to keep and build the current culture within the

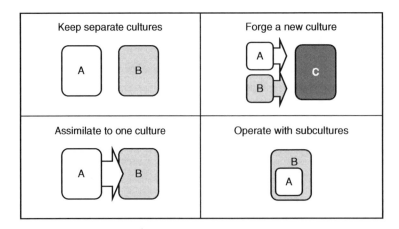

Figure 2.4 Culture integration options during a merger

context of the overall acquiring company culture. We call this operating with a subculture when there is a distinct culture for one part or division of an organisation. This can often help with integration as a way to defer some of the complex issues associated with how work gets done. Allowing the subculture can minimise the disruption for both customers and employees. Some companies may even take this as a strategy if the acquiring company can serve as a 'skunk work' or innovation lab for new ideas and as a potential model for study by the rest of the firm. Even with a subculture plan, it is still important to determine how to manage the interface points on integration to ensure alignment with strategy.[17]

The third culture integration option is to complete a cultural assimilation where the acquiring company imposes their culture on the other firm. This can be a quick and efficient way of defining the desired culture and moving rapidly with integration activities. Assimilation of a culture in this way only requires compliance from the employees in the short term, not necessarily commitment. This can be a good way of easing into the new ways of doing things in an organisation. In some situations, direct assimilation using the acquiring company culture can be a way of putting a healthy culture in place while replacing an unhealthy culture. As research shows, the challenge arises as this may introduce a great deal of change in the acquired firm and may impose unrealistic expectations in the short term. The risks associated with this approach should be carefully considered.[18] The culture assimilation approach can work well when the business strategy calls for integration of operations in situations where the acquisition provides market share without necessarily unique market differentiators.

The fourth approach for integration of cultures is to create a new culture using elements of both parties in the merger. This is particularly helpful when a 'merger of equals' takes place and neither party is clearly dominant. Forging a new culture can build a foundation for long-term synergy and potential new positioning. This can be an exciting opportunity to create a new identity, encourage innovation, and build commitment for the future. This approach avoids the sometimes difficult situation of creating the perception of winners and losers. The creation of the new culture must be done in a way that is in concert with the business strategy and fits with the vision and values for the new entity.

Regardless of what type of business and culture integration, mergers and acquisition situations require special attention to culture. A classic example is the creation of New United Motor Manufacturing, Inc. (NUMMI), a joint venture between Toyota Motors of Japan and General Motors of the USA, established in the 1980s. In this case, both companies contributed to the new venture and agreed to follow the Toyota way for manufacturing in a factory based in California. The introduction of the Toyota processes included different ways of working that empowered the factory line workers. While the focus of the venture was on learning technology and process from the other party, careful attention was paid to the culture to make the venture successful. As a result of NUMMI, Toyota was successful in its objective of entering the US market for manufacturing, sales, and service of their vehicles while GM was successful in learning new processes and ways of working to improve quality and efficiency. Both organisations benefited from the learning on cultural differences and the opportunity to create a special culture at NUMMI.

CASE STUDY

Culture change following acquisitions

Recent acquisitions made this Asian steel producer one of the world's most geographically diversified producers, with operations in twenty-six countries and commercial presence in over fifty countries. To further their position in the steel industry as an integrated supplier in one of the most diverse regions in the world, they realised a need to lower costs and create differentiated products by consolidation. Through M&A activity the company acquired not only diversified businesses, but also a set of divided cultural beliefs. The management team recognised that the variations in culture and lack of unified ways of working would create potential barriers to success. In addition, the planned synergies of the mergers could be in jeopardy.

The leadership launched a culture programme that would closely link to the business strategy. Over the course of a few months, the management team, along with an outside consultant, conducted over fifty one-to-one interviews with senior management across both organisations to better understand the current situation and identify the desired culture based on the business strategy. From these interviews, the team was able to more clearly define a desired culture for the organisation. The project team then worked in joint organisational teams from each entity to create a shared vision of the desired culture with clear examples to help bring it to life.

They launched a culture assessment tool that sampled employee input on aspects of the current culture. From the measurement of the current culture, they could more clearly understand some of the differences and issues. The team identified the gaps between the current and desired cultures for both entities and developed an overall view of areas that needed to change. After prioritising and agreeing with management on the top areas for culture change, the team launched a comprehensive initiative to address the creation of a new culture shared by everyone.

To help drive this change at all levels, the project team detailed the cultural implications at an organisational and departmental level to help make it real for people. The team also helped break down the desired leadership attributes for ongoing reinforcement by the HR team. The company continues the strong business performance and has made great strides in achieving its business strategy by addressing the culture of the organisation.

Defining the desired culture

Whether it is an M&A situation, a new start-up organisation, or a strategic transformation, it is important to determine the desired culture that fits with the business strategy. As stated above, the culture can have a significant impact on strategy execution and business performance, which makes the process for defining the desired culture quite important. There are three important steps to defining a desired culture:

1. Understand the business mission, values and vision;
2. Identify the critical behavioural elements or anchors of the strategy; and
3. Determine the culture shaping mechanisms in the organisation.

The definition and redefinition of culture should be done with each change in business strategy to make sure there is a strong linkage between the plans for the business and actions of the people. When business leaders neglect the planning and consider culture, they miss an opportunity to align the vision with the behaviours in the organisation.

Understanding the mission or the purpose of the organisation provides the context to guide the vision and business strategy. The mission generally defines what business we are in and why it exists. The vision provides a desired future state that summarises the business strategy. Organisation values describe what is important to the organisation in guiding behaviours and conduct. As we noted at the beginning of this chapter, the company values play an important part in helping people understand expectations.

From the mission, values, and vision we can begin to identify critical behavioural elements. To define the desired culture, it is often best to more closely examine the specific elements of the business strategy and ask what behaviours we are expecting from people in the firm. For example, if our business strategy is to aggressively grow and capture market share in emerging markets, we might identify supporting behaviours such as entrepreneurship, creativity, and innovation related to our need for growth.

We might also identify needs for valuing global diversity, cultural sensitivity, openness to others, and demonstrating corporate social responsibility. While there may be many behaviours identified for success as there are many competencies needed to make the business successful, we must consider the key elements that we want to reinforce as 'anchors' that guide management actions and processes. Our company with plans for rapid expansion in emerging markets might settle on anchors such as market-sensitive and rapid innovation. If these are desired aspects of the culture, the management team will need to determine how to bring these to life as a part of the culture. It is one thing to state the desired behaviours; it is quite another to make them part of the culture.

With the desired culture attributes or anchors defined, we must then determine how these can be brought to life and continually reinforced. In other words, what mechanisms do we have that can shape the culture to support these anchors? As we know from psychology, any level of inconsistency or mixed message in reinforcement of behaviours will create uncertainty about expectations.[19] If we want to shape the culture towards rapid innovation, we will want to look for ways that encourage people to try new things that make a difference for customers. Management will need to be tolerant of risk-taking and be able to accept failure. Management systems and decision-making will need to allow quick decisions for people to move forward with ideas with speed. Meetings and communications should help facilitate successful innovations and new ideas being launched as management works to reinforce the behaviours and desire to continuously innovate for emerging market success. If leaders were to create conflicting messages by stopping innovation projects to do cost-cutting, it may create uncertainty about what is important. For this reason, it is critical to relentlessly reinforce the desired cultural attributes until these become ingrained in the enterprise. This takes time as the culture is developed over years of operation during which it collects an organisational memory and understanding from all the daily experiences and stories shared among members of the firm. Defining the desired culture can be done in a few short weeks; developing that culture is a continuous process.

Measuring the organisation culture

When considering the current culture of the organisation, we may have some general ideas about the common characteristics, but we may not fully understand how the culture is translated into different locations or divisions. After all, each sub-organisation may have slightly or sometimes vastly different ways of working. It can therefore be helpful to measure the culture to gain an understanding of the attributes and to provide management feedback on how the desired culture is being reinforced throughout the enterprise.

The most common way of measuring culture is through the use of surveys that are designed to check for characteristics and the intensity of such characteristics. Some of these assessment tools also provide the ability for benchmarking. When considering a culture assessment tool, it is important to understand what dimensions of culture are assessed. Since the survey will show the results across multiple characteristics, it is good to develop a desired result based on the desired culture. This will allow management to determine the areas where the desired culture is not being realised along with an improved understanding of the current culture.

Several service firms and universities offer culture assessment services that provide a proven survey instrument and process for helping a firm gauge the current culture. While there are many instruments and potential variables to measure, each organisation should determine what instrument meets their needs. Table 2.4 contains examples of culture variables as measured in a culture survey.

Another method of assessing culture is the use of targeted groups. During a focus group, people from the organisation are brought together to discuss various aspects of culture with a trained facilitator. The facilitator may pose a number of broad questions or topics and ask the group to discuss their thoughts and share their experiences in the firm. The facilitator is generally a neutral party from the human resources area or from outside the organisation. While the facilitated sessions do not yield quantifiable data, the summarisation

Table 2.4 Sample culture measurement dimensions

Adaptability	Mission	Consistency	Involvement
Creating change	Vision	Core values	Empowerment
Customer focus	Goals and objectives	Agreement	Team orientation
Organisational learning	Strategic direction and intent	Coordination and integration	Capability development

Source: adapted from Denison, *Corporate Culture and Organisational Effectiveness* (Wiley, 1990). Reproduced with permission of John Wiley & Sons, Inc.

can include powerful examples and stories shared by the participants that can help bring the nature of the culture to life.

In many cases, companies find that a survey followed by focus groups create the most powerful results since the quantitative results can be brought to life with the qualitative aspects of the focus group. Like other assessments, the data can provide leaders with good insights on their organisations and highlight potential areas for improvement. Implicit in the assessment process is the commitment by management to take actions to address current challenges that have been highlighted in the measurement process. While the measurement of culture can be completed in a few weeks, the challenge lies in determining how to shape and change the culture.

CASE STUDY

Culture measurement

A financial services firm in the USA used culture measurement to successfully drive a new culture programme. As a leading provider of financial services to selected customers worldwide, the firm was quite successful with its services through strategic partnerships, technological innovations and multiple service channels. Yet, the management was concerned about shaping the right culture for the future of the enterprise.

The management team created a three-year roadmap with strategic objectives and recognised the importance of addressing the culture in the organisation. Fortunately, the firm had conducted a culture analysis a few years prior and had some experience in reviewing culture. This time the team completed a culture assessment to understand the current state and changes over the past few years. The differences between the surveys done three years apart showed progress in some areas, while some level of inconsistency was found in newer areas of the organisation.

The team then conducted a desired culture survey with the top 400 leaders to understand what behaviour was expected to support the strategy. After reviewing the gaps between the current and desired culture, the project team prioritised the areas and drafted a plan to help align the management to the desired culture. They identified misalignment among the different levels of the management in regard to the desired culture.

As a result of this effort, the firm identified key themes, top ten culture priorities, and areas of alignment/misalignment to be addressed. A leadership scorecard was developed to help track culture initiatives and area results on a more regular basis. The office of the CEO developed an overall plan that linked the culture initiatives with the strategic plans and a journey map. The buy-in and emphasis on culture was spread throughout the company.

Shaping and changing organisation culture

Once a company has determined the desired culture and understands what areas need to be addressed from a culture assessment, management has the opportunity to determine a plan to shape and improve the culture. The identification of improvement areas from the assessment can appear to be straightforward, but can often provide perplexing questions for leaders of the firm. Questions such as: '*How do we create more trust in our regional offices?*' or '*What can we do to reduce the perception of bureaucracy in our operations?*' The answers to these questions are not always clear and the processes for addressing them are not tackled easily. As noted earlier, even if leaders do not make any decisions about culture or take any actions, the culture will continue to emerge and grow. The risk in not deliberately shaping the culture is that it may not be in line with the values and strategy.

When determining the need to change a culture, managers should be mindful of the difference between incremental and transformational culture change. Reshaping culture can be a difficult challenge as it requires the changing of assumptions, processes, and general beliefs held by individuals in the organisation. Leaders must be fully committed to making the changes necessary to bring about culture change since even the subtle messages and ways of doing things carry messages to others about what is expected and rewarded.

Consider a manufacturing company that has launched new initiatives in line with execution excellence. The strategy is to outperform the competition by improving the efficiency in processes and meeting expectations (on time and on budget – every time). Management has committed to change the culture of the operations with an emphasis on execution and driving excellence into everything that they do. After the initial training on the discipline of execution excellence, the employees were ready to give it a try but looked closely to others and to management for signs of what was expected. While each manager was espousing the value of the new philosophy, the signals to the organisation were still the same. Meetings still started late as people took their time getting assembled, measurement systems were focused on the former priorities of individual output, and quality inspectors still ruled the shop floor with their ability to disrupt production based on their findings. While the management communications espoused execution excellence, there were very few signs of this new culture in the day-to-day operations. After several months of communication on execution excellence, the messages faded and the manufacturing continued on without much change from the months prior to the declaration of this new culture change. As with many culture initiatives, it is difficult to drive such a change without dealing with it holistically.

CASE STUDY

Addressing culture change

To support their market success as a leading wireless provider in Europe, this telecommunications company developed and rolled out new services at a pace which made it reconsider how best to manage such a scale of change and complexity. Management decided that the company needed a redesign of its strategy, structure, processes, and culture to become an intensely customer-focused unit.

As a starting point, management appointed a project team to take action. This team along with an outside consultant surveyed and interviewed employees in order to understand the current state. They then redesigned the structure and appointed personnel to key positions within the line organisation.

To understand the current culture challenges, the team used a culture inventory survey to assess culture and behavioural styles. By comparing the 'current' and 'ideal' cultural profiles, a number of key cultural gaps were identified in the company. One gap area was in the technical section of the organisation. A specific technical behaviour change programme introduced a range of initiatives to close the gaps. Across the entire firm a comprehensive matrix of accountabilities and responsibilities helped to provide organisational clarity along with the new behavioural clarifications.

As a result of this emphasis on culture and organisational alignment, a new level of clarity and understanding was spread throughout the company. Redesigned and improved processes aligned accountability with responsibility and authority. An overall communication plan and mapping helped improve and clarify information flows and general communications. New leadership development programmes helped build a shared vision among the teams. In under a year, the transformation led to a reduction of unplanned systems downtime by more than 50 per cent while on-time delivery and reliability of new systems improved dramatically. Efficiency gains of 20 to 30 per cent have been measured and output is up by more than 20 per cent. The organisation has recognised an improvement and created a culture that will sustain the success.

When undertaking such a transformational culture change, management must employ a blend of direct and indirect tactics. Direct activities such as communications, training, and measures can help introduce the changes planned but cannot sustain them in the organisation. Indirect activities such as messages through informal networks, actions of leaders, recognition, and day-to-day decision-making are critical for 'proving' to the people in the company that there is strong commitment to making this change in the way things get done. Direct attempts to change values and assumptions underlying culture are rarely successful alone. To transform culture we must drive changes in manifested behaviours, working to impact underlying values, norms, and assumptions, by allowing individuals to bring those values, norms, and assumptions into line with how their behaviour has changed.

In their research on corporate cultures, Goffee and Jones contend that managers must understand the competitive situation and then determine how to transform the culture.[20] Cultural change should be considered as part of any organisational transformation (including strategy, structure, performance management, talent system, and leadership). In fact, transformational efforts can be accelerated by aligning the cultural context with the other technical and social elements of the organisation, taking the constraints of existing culture into account. Often we may find new business plans and strategies that consider the market opportunity or income improvement, yet lack the analysis of the cultural impact and culture change plan required.

Building a successful enterprise change requires more than a clever strategy and providing direction, it is critical to create and shape the culture to bring about the changes required for success. As we have seen from the research on adaptive cultures, leaders who consider building a culture that is nimble and can respond quickly to market developments are able to create a more responsive enterprise. Firms that create a culture that continuously learns, adjusts its plan, and improves its efficiency without creating bureaucracy will discover that they have developed a valuable intangible asset. An adaptive culture can help make a competitive differentiation in more quickly capturing market advantage.

As explored at the start of this chapter, there are several levels of culture to be addressed. Culture transformation is primarily about changing the cultural context and secondarily about changing the cultural foundations. An organisation's processes and policies (e.g. performance measurement and rewards system, leadership practices, training, communications, etc.) are the strongest levers that can be pulled to change the cultural context and instil culture transformation.

As shown in Figure 2.5, culture can easily be addressed at the surface level by changing processes and organisation structures. However, these actions may not make significant changes in the underlying beliefs and assumptions in the organisation. The management systems and measures provide a more meaningful impact on behaviour as signals that create a clear expectation to people and provide a consistent way for management to guide the way things get done. Making more substantive culture change is typically more difficult as it will require a more indirect effort of managing through informal leaders, social network channels, and group discussions.[21] With concentrated effort over time, the organisation will develop new attitudes, norms, and ways of working. This is a deep change process that can only be accomplished over months and years of persistent effort.

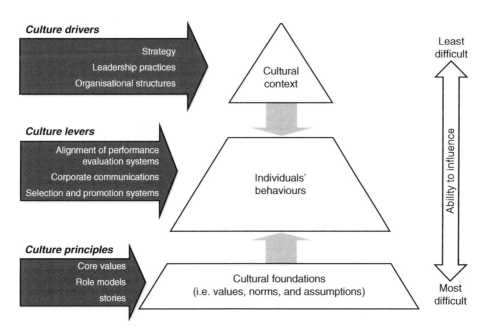

Figure 2.5 Degrees of culture change

It is worth mentioning the impact of symbols and stories in the creation and transformation of culture. As we explored earlier, the use of stories and symbols can provide a powerful organisation clue on what is important and expected from people. During times of culture change, stories can provide a great reference and examples for change catalysts. As we know from research, the environment can have an impact on customer orientation and outcomes.[22] Consider, for example, the case of a company working to shift to a more customer-centric culture. To help make this shift, management sent many of the operations line managers out to meet with customers even if they had no role directly with customers. After a few months, each of the managers had experienced how their products were used by the customers and gained an improved understanding of customer needs. While this was helpful insight, it was the stories that the line managers shared with others that began to spread around the other departments and caught the attention of most employees. The stories about the customers, their business situations, perceptions of the products, and questions were the talk around break tables and hallways. The stories shifted the attention to a much stronger customer orientation across the organisation. The use of stories can play an important part in making a culture shift, but can also create unintended negative consequences if the stories shared are about poor behaviour or unfavourable feedback in the new strategy. After all, the stories cannot be controlled in the organisation but they can be created with good intent. Since stories provide a fundamental way of building collective thinking in the organisation, these help signal a shift in the culture if managers can use them in the right way.

Another consideration when transforming culture is the direction of the shift related to business strategy. For example, when developing a culture change plan in promoting a high growth plan, managers will want to consider how the new culture supports the entrepreneurial aspects of working to create positive growth momentum. At the same time, for organisations that may be working to optimise company assets we would need to consider the aspects of culture that can help drive the focus on effectiveness and efficiency. In other cases we may find companies that need to be more agile and flexible in working in an uncertain environment and therefore emphasise change capability to build adaptability. For those organisations looking to improve with innovation, we might see an orientation towards learning, risk-taking, knowledge-sharing and external market orientation. Collaboration and knowledge management can become critical components to culture and success.[23] Knowledge management consists of processes within a firm to identify, create, and distribute the adoption of insights and experiences so that individual learning becomes organisational learning.[24] Regardless of the direction, each firm should chart a unique course with the desired changes in culture closely coupled with the plans for the business.[25]

For a manager leading an organisation there are several areas to keep in mind when working to manage and change the culture:

- **Align leaders** – identify the desired culture to guide the path of change and ask for leader commitment.[26] Ensure adequate time is provided for leaders to debate, confirm, and clearly articulate the behavioural patterns required to achieve the desired culture.[27]
- **Launch with clarity** – take an early stand on what the organisation is. A proactive approach promotes understanding and acceptance and embeds the new behaviours more consistently.
- **Emphasise value creation** – identify a finite number of initiatives that will drive value and focus effort and resources accordingly.
- **Deliberately drive behaviour** – to reinforce or discourage particular behaviours, select the drivers (factors that influence behaviour) that will have the greatest impact on the culture that is needed.
- **Choose words carefully** – time and again, the language used is key to ensuring alignment of effort. Be deliberate about choosing and reinforcing the 'right' language and terminology. The same words can have very different meanings across organisations, so take the time needed to understand what is being referenced.

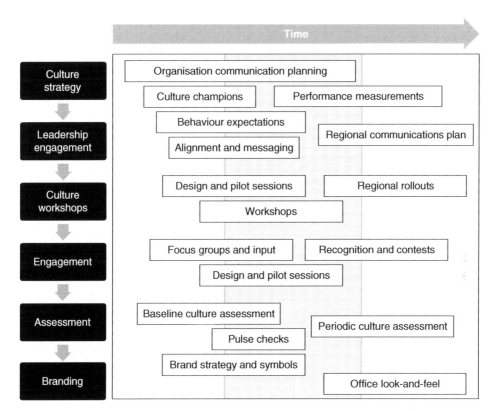

Figure 2.6 Sample culture roadmap
Source: based on data provided by GlobeSmart® an Aperian Global culture profile tool

- **Track and celebrate progress** – measurement is the best-understood (and least-leveraged) integration lever. Track signs that your organisation is headed in the direction intended. Identify metrics and measure and reinforce them with vigilance.

Managing a culture change effort requires diligence and persistence by the management team. Typically a general roadmap such as Figure 2.6 is used that identifies specific themes and activities over time to help management keep on the track of change. Of course, this is a dynamic journey that will require regular monitoring and feedback to make adjustments along the way.

While a clear roadmap can be helpful in providing the direction during culture change, it is important to differentiate between activities and behavioural results. The feedback loop is particularly important here as we better understand the dynamics of the organisation. It is critical to have top stakeholder buy-in for culture change as we need to be able to adjust course and develop new action plans as changes and unexpected occurrences take place in the business.

CASE STUDY

Culture change planning

One of the top utilities in Africa was facing critical challenges with operations. Operations were complex and included a number of notable power stations, including the largest coal-fired power station in the world, and a nuclear power station.

The company was facing supply/demand challenges, a diverse workforce, and increasing regulation. At the same time the management decided to embark upon the culture transformation required to support the objectives of the business. At first, the project team launched a number of programme initiatives, but insufficient progress was made as people became confused by the volume and complexity of the messages from each initiative. The team then made some adjustments after realising that operating model, culture, leadership and behaviours were misaligned.

To understand the desired culture more clearly, the team launched a culture analysis to determine both the desired culture and the current state of culture. From surveys, focus groups, and selected interviews, the team defined the desired culture and determined the major gaps from the current state. From this analysis, management had a clear understanding of primary areas of misalignment.

As a result, the management addressed the priority issues by putting clear metrics in place along with documented accountability for performance. The expected behaviours associated with the core values were documented for each department in a way that could be understood in the context of the work. The authority levels for decision-making were clarified to improve the speed and nimbleness of the organisation. Leadership sessions were held to share expectations, followed by tailored development sessions for the top leaders. An overall HR talent management initiative was launched to address the need to improve the consistency of people-management processes. While comprehensive in nature, the overall programme moved quickly and began realising results in the first year of implementation.

As we manage the plan for addressing key culture gaps, it is important for managers to determine magnitude and impact of each gap between the desired and current culture. Managing these gaps between the desired and current culture becomes a critical and frequent activity for leaders as they constantly assess progress while assessing the magnitude of the gaps and the potential impact. In addition, they must also differentiate between the critical needs and the requests for convenience in the firm. Like any company going through change, people are likely to come up with ideas that may improve their role or working conditions, without consideration for the rest of the operations or unit. Managers must be prudent to consider the holistic culture priorities and not be sidetracked by individual organisational unit objectives.

Understanding the influence of national cultures

Up to this point we have discussed the culture of the firm without consideration of the context of the country. Obviously, the organisational culture is influenced by the culture of the country where we are operating. It is important to note the national culture when considering operations across borders. While some country culture differences may be slight, others can be quite strikingly different. For global or regional efforts, it is important that we consider country cultures in the context of culture change. Over the past twenty years, academic researchers have been examining the differences in key dimensions across country boundaries. Robert House and others have led the cooperative effort with project GLOBE. These findings have helped us better understand the differences between country cultures and how we might consider these within the organisational context.[28]

While the scope of this book is the culture of the enterprise, it is important to note that there are many considerations in global business today in working across borders.[29] As discussed, there are likely to be subcultures that may exist from unique circumstances or from the national influences of the country. As Geert Hofstede notes in his research in this area over several decades, country or location cultures are shaped by values and practices.[30]

Several tools exist to help measure the macro-level behavioural expectations by country. Figure 2.7 illustrates one dimension across multiple country cultures.

In this example, the dimensions of task versus relationship show a stark contrast between different general default positions of various people from different countries of origin. Based on this scale, people who are task-oriented define others based on what they do, not just on whom they know. Conversely,

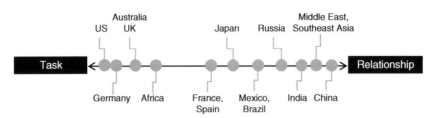

Figure 2.7 Contrast of task versus relationship orientation across cultures
Source: adapted from GlobeSmart [Online] Available from: www.globesmart.com

they evaluate others on the basis of their accomplishments, not just on connections or affiliations. People who are relationship-oriented define others based on *whom* they know and *how* they are connected, not just on *what* they know or *what* they can do. These individuals will spend a greater amount of time establishing commonality before getting down to business. Task orientation emphasises tangible time events and segmentation of time, and promptness and relationship orientation emphasises the importance of people over time. Promptness is not a priority and appointments can be broken. This can potentially impact meeting times and deliverable deadlines.

The dimensions by country culture can be quite complex; it is important to determine how to address this in the context of the organisational culture. The country cultures add an additional dimension and managers must also consider the country of origin of the enterprise. For example, Japanese companies may have a different orientation when expanding into Europe than do Brazilian companies. It is important to consider the organisational context as well as the country context.

Summary

As we have reviewed, culture is a key element in human capital strategy as it guides the individual behaviours and expectations in the firm. Research has shown that culture makes a difference to results as companies with adaptive, high-achieving cultures will positively influence an organisation's bottom line. The organisation culture can potentially provide sustained competitive advantage as a key resource for the firm.[31] The culture defines how things get done in a business. In many ways, culture can be seen as the personality or way of working within an organisation that is generally ingrained into common work practices and styles for managing.

Culture is shaped by internal business influencers such as control systems, structures, leadership roles, rituals and routines, symbols, physical work environment, and stories. External factors that influence culture can include the nature of the industry, customers, suppliers, public perception, marketplace conditions, and even natural disasters. The desired culture can be defined by understanding the business strategy, identifying the critical behavioural elements, and determining the culture shaping mechanisms. Special care should be taken in M&A situations to clearly identify the plan for culture as organisations come together. When working across borders, it may also be necessary to consider the country-based cultures and customs.

Measuring culture can be done with a variety of instruments and methods depending on the context and needs of the enterprise. Once a clear current baseline is understood and the desired culture clarified, specific gaps or areas of change can be identified for emphasis. Developing a roadmap for culture change requires diligence by management. Culture is a critical element for success in business strategy with clear links to the other areas of human capital strategy. Successful organisations typically centre on a unique culture that helps drive the business strategy to realisation.

Key questions for consideration

- *How would you describe the culture of organisations that you have been a part of?*
- *What are the aspects of organisation culture that stand out for you?*
- *If you were starting a new company, what type of culture would you want to create?*
- *Think about a successful business; how has the culture helped define the success?*
- *How have you influenced the culture of your organisations?*

FURTHER READING

Flamholtz, E., and Randle, Y. (2011) *Corporate Culture: the Ultimate Strategic Asset*. California, Stanford Business Books.

Hofstede, G. H., Hofstede, G. J., and Minkov, M. (2010) *Cultures and Organisations: Software of the Mind: Intercultural Co-operation and its Importance for Survival*. New York, McGraw-Hill.

Kotter, J. P., and Heskett, J. L. (1992) *Corporate Culture and Performance*. New York, Free Press.

Schein, Edgar H. (2009) *The Corporate Culture Survival Guide.* San Francisco, John Wiley & Sons Inc.

REFERENCES

[1] Kotter, J. P., and Heskett, J. L. (1992) *Corporate Culture and Performance.* New York, Free Press.

[2] Tushman, M. L., Tushman, M., and O'Reilly III, C. A. (2006) Winning Through Innovation. Harvard Business Press.

[3] Hartnell, C. A., Ou, A. Y., and Kinicki, A. (2011) 'Organizational Culture and Organizational Effectiveness: A Meta-analytic Investigation of the Competing Values Framework's Theoretical Suppositions', *Journal of Applied Psychology* 96(4): 677.

[4] Citigroup (2011) *Code of Conduct* [Online] Available from: www.citigroup.com [Accessed: June 2012].

[5] Schein, E. H. (1990) 'Organisation Culture', *American Psychologist* 45(2): 109–119.

[6] Arthur Jr, W., Bell, S. T., Villado, A. J., and Doverspike, D. (2006) 'The Use of Person-organization Fit in Employment Decision Making: An Assessment of its Criterion-related Validity', *Journal of Applied Psychology* 91(4): 786.

[7] Johnson, G. (1988) 'Rethinking Incrementalism', *Strategic Management Journal* 9: 75–91.

[8] Deshpande, R., and Raina, A. (2011) 'The Ordinary Heroes of the Taj', *Harvard Business Review* 89(12).

[9] Fedex (2012) *FEDEX Stories* [Online] Available from: www.fedexstories.com [Accessed: June 2012].

[10] Greguras, G. J., and Diefendorff, J. M. (2009) 'Different Fits Satisfy Different Needs: Linking Person-environment Fit to Employee Commitment and Performance Using Self-determination Theory', *Journal of Applied Psychology* 94(2): 465.

[11] Kristof-Brown, A. L., Zimmerman, R. D., and Johnson, E. C. (2005) 'Consequences of Individuals' Fit at Work: A Meta-analysis of Person-job, Person-organization, Person-group, and Person-supervisor Fit', *Personnel Psychology* 58: 281–342.

[12] Schein, E. H. (1996) 'Three Cultures of Management', *Sloan Management Review* 38(1): 9–20.

[13] Sorensen, J. B. (2002) 'The Strength of Corporate Culture and the Reliability of Firm Performance', *Administrative Science Quarterly* 47(1): 70–91.

[14] Stahl, G., and Mendenhall, M. (Eds.) (2005) *Mergers and Acquisitions: Managing Culture and Human Resources.* Stanford Business Books.

[15] Cartwright, S., and Cooper, C. L. (1993) 'The Role of Culture Compatibility in Successful Organizational Marriage', *Academy of Management Executive* 7(2): 57–70.

[16] Buono, A. F., Bowditch, J. L., and Lewis, J. W. (1985) 'When Cultures Collide: the Anatomy of a Merger', *Human Relations* 38(5): 477–500.

[17] Harvard Business School Press (2001) *Harvard Business Review on Mergers and Acquisitions.* Boston, Harvard Business School Press.

[18] Brahy, S. (2006) 'Six Solution Pillars for Successful Cultural Integration of International M&As', *Journal of Organizational Excellence* 25(4): 53–63.

[19] Ilies, R., Nahrgang, J. D., and Morgeson, F. P. (2007) 'Leader-member Exchange and Citizenship Behaviors: A Meta-analysis', *Journal of Applied Psychology* 92(1): 269.

[20] Goffee, R., and Jones, G. (1996) 'What Holds the Modern Company Together?', *Harvard Business Review* 74(6): 133–148.

[21] Higgins, J. M., and McAllaster, C. (2004) 'If You Want Strategic Change, Don't Forget to Change Your Cultural Artifacts', *Journal of Change Management* 4(1): 63–73.

[22] Grizzle, J. W., Zablah, A. R., Brown, T. J., Mowen, J. C., and Lee, J. M. (2009) 'Employee Customer Orientation in Context: How the Environment Moderates the Influence of Customer Orientation on Performance Outcomes', *Journal of Applied Psychology* 94(5): 1227.

[23] Yue Wah, C., Menkhoff, T., Loh, B., and Evers, H. D. (2007) 'Social Capital and Knowledge Sharing in Knowledge-based Organizations: An Empirical Study', *International Journal of Knowledge Management* 3(1): 29–48.

[24] Nonaka, I. (1991) 'The Knowledge Creating Company', *Harvard Business Review* 69 (6): 96–104.

[25] Flamholtz, E., and Randle, Y. (2011) *Corporate Culture: the Ultimate Strategic Asset.* California, Stanford Business Books.

[26] Wang, H., and Wong, K. F. E. (2012) 'The Effect of Managerial Bias on Employees' Specific Human Capital Investments', *Journal of Management Studies* 49: 1435–1458.

[27] Hofmann, D. A., Morgeson, F. P., and Gerras, S. J. (2003) 'Climate as A Moderator of the Relationship Between Leader-member Exchange and Content Specific Citizenship: Safety Climate as an Exemplar', *Journal of Applied Psychology* 88(1): 170.

[28] House, R. J., Hanges, P. J., Javidan, M., Dorfman, P. W., and Gupta, V. (2004) *Culture, Leadership, and Organizations: The GLOBE Study of 62 Societies.* Sage Publications.

[29] Dorfman, P., Javidan, M., Hanges, P., Dastmalchian, A. and House, R. (2012) 'GLOBE: A Twenty Year Journey Into the Intriguing World of Culture and Leadership', *Journal of World Business* 47(4).

[30] Hofstede, G. H., Hofstede, G. J., and Minkov, M. (2010) *Cultures and Organizations: Software of the Mind: Intercultural Cooperation and its Importance for Survival.* New York, McGraw-Hill.

[31] Barney, J. B. (1986) 'Organizational Culture: Can it Be A Source of Sustained Competitive Advantage?', *Academy of Management Review* 11(3): 656–665.

3 Leadership

When asked about the cost of executive development, Jack Welch replied (paraphrased): '*What is the cost of ignorance?*'

Introduction

In Chapter 2 we examined the dimensions of organisation culture which are often intertwined with the focus on leadership effectiveness. Many researchers have found that there is a strong positive correlation between leadership effectiveness and performance. David Maister, for instance, states that for each point of increase an organisation achieves in leadership effectiveness, there can be up to a forty-two point improvement in financial performance.[1] Others have found similar results all over the world. In Asia, for example, Bennett and Bell make the point that effective leadership engages employees, and engaged employees produce results. In their research they found that organisations in the top 20 per cent in employee engagement scores achieved 20.2 per cent shareholder returns, whereas average engagement companies achieved 5.6 per cent average shareholder returns and low-engagement companies actually had negative 9.6 per cent shareholder returns.[2]

In addition, the increasing global shortage of leadership talent is now recognised as a key source of risk to successful business strategy execution, business continuity and growth. In fact, boards of directors are paying more attention to their accountability for executive succession and are asking tough questions about business continuity. In a recent study by the Conference Board, people risks were determined to be 4th out of 15 risks for growing businesses but only 11th in how well they are currently managed.[3]

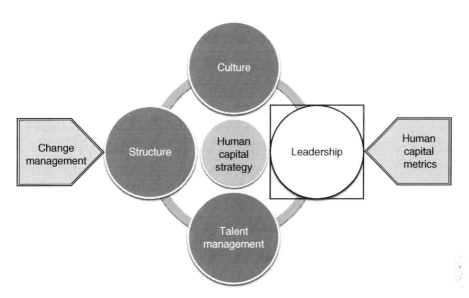

Figure 3.1 Leadership

Source: Charan, Drotter and Noel, The Leadership Pipeline: How to Build the Leadership Powered Company (Jossey-Bass, 2001). Reproduced with permission of John Wiley & Sons, Inc.

As a result, getting the next generation of talent in place to deliver results is high on the personal agenda of many CEOs. In spite of economic uncertainty in parts of the world, organisations increasingly focus on retaining and building leadership talent from within to avoid exposure to the competitive pressures and supply shortfalls of the external market. On one hand, the pace of growth and the emerging economies are fuelling demand while, on the other hand, future leaders will need to thrive in a world of change, ambiguity, paradox, and cultural diversity. Across the world, different countries suffer from different issues: aging workforce, lack of qualified candidates, brain drain, etc., which constricts the supply of future leadership talent. To make matters worse, emerging leaders are inclined to shorter job and company tenure and have less experience in strategy, people management, and execution.

Leadership is certainly critical to business success and yet the statistics show that it is tough being the boss. Consider these facts:[4]

- The average tenure of outgoing CEOs was 6.6 years in 2010 compared with 8.1 years in 2000.
- The length of CEO tenure planned by companies' boards has dropped by 30 per cent over the past 11 years, down from 10 years to 7 years.
- Externally hired CEOs stayed in office for less time than their internally hired counterparts.

When considering developing leaders, companies are faced with tough choices. In order to continue to grow profitably, they need more leaders; yet there are precious few available for hire. If they do find them, these future leaders must be developed from within, but they can be difficult to retain. Many business leaders are often perplexed by the question of whether to build their own leadership talent or recruit it externally ('build' or 'buy'). The answer for most organisations today is likely to do both, given the ongoing needs for top talent.

In this chapter, we will review how managers, with support from the human resources function (HRF), can help address these challenges, mostly from the perspective of building talent from within. At the end of the chapter we will tackle the question of how some of these tools can be used to help recruit leaders into the organisation.

CASE STUDY

Building a leadership pipeline

After filing for bankruptcy protection in one key business unit, a global energy services company brought in a number of key executives to engineer a turn-around. The new leadership successfully restored profitability through new discipline in financial and risk management. Now back on track, the company was ready to shift its strategic focus from survival to profitable growth.

To ensure that it would have the leadership talent – not just today, but in the future – to drive the new business strategy, the board wanted to shift its leadership talent strategy from 'buy' to 'build'. It sought to develop a strong pipeline of leaders with the business knowledge, strategy and implementation skills, and management and communication know-how necessary for business success. Yet defining the specific capabilities required across the business as a whole was a major challenge. In the past, the company's diverse set of businesses had been run as a portfolio, without capitalising on whatever synergies might exist among them.

The first step in building the leadership pipeline was to clarify what the company's business strategy required of its enterprise leaders, both today and tomorrow. The company worked to translate business requirements into specific leadership needs to drive growth. The result of this work was the development of an enterprise leadership model and talent management strategy aligned with the board and CEO agendas and the overall business strategy.

The second step was to develop and implement multifaceted assessment and talent review processes that would allow the company to differentiate its leadership talent pools across the enterprise and within the businesses, identify strengths and gaps, and drive development moves. Inputs to the process included performance ratings and critical success factors, 360-degree leadership feedback, self-reported career information, and feedback from a select panel of leaders about each individual's readiness, potential and development needs. From this input, the company developed role profiles for mission-critical roles, an assessment of performance potential across talent pools, and a view of leadership readiness within the organisation. Finally, having identified the leadership capabilities critical to the success of its growth strategy and the gaps in skills among its top 200 leaders, the company launched a custom-designed leadership development programme to build these targeted capabilities.

This programme combined team and individual work on selected growth challenges, workshops by executive leaders on the growth strategy and financial acumen, and workshops by external thought leaders on topics such as innovative profitable growth, flawless execution, and performance enhancement.

As a result of these efforts, the company went from empty boxes on an emergency replacement plan just a few years ago to a strong leadership bench. Because the board's executive operating committee has in-depth knowledge about the strengths and readiness of its leadership talent, it was able to fill every major role over the past year from inside the company.

The executive team also reports that its leaders are beginning to think and lead with an enterprise mindset. For example, rather than simply accepting any business that will keep assets utilised, leaders are rigorously testing the assumptions and conditions of new business to ensure *profitable* growth. Rather than pursuing growth with traditional, incremental business models, leaders are identifying bold, game-changing opportunities that will put the company at a strategic advantage. This success is attributable to the clear line of sight maintained throughout the pipeline development process from the CEO agenda and business model to the assessment process and leadership development programme.

About leadership

There is a wide variety of opinions and viewpoints on what makes an effective leader. Early theories from Fiedler and Chemers elaborated the contingency for success based on the leader's style, the needs of the situation, the leader's superior, and the nature of the group.[5] Research from Burke and Litwin focuses on individual and organisational performance in a way which clarifies what we mean by leadership effectiveness.[6] They explain that leadership influences management practices. These in turn affect the work climate of the organisation. In other words, the day-to-day behaviours exhibited by leaders, their ability to influence their teams, and their efficacy at working together with other leaders will impact on business results.

There are many leadership theories, ideas, and frameworks that comprise the leadership landscape. To help put these in context, we have summarised many of the approaches and theories here.

Trait approach – this was one of the first attempts to study leadership with the idea that certain traits made some people great leaders. While researchers have defined and discovered different types of traits over the last decades, there is some level of convergence on five factors (the big five) that make up what we call personality.[7] The big five include neuroticism, extraversion, openness, agreeableness, and conscientiousness.[8] Researchers have found a strong relationship between these factors and leadership.[9]

Skills approach – this approach assumes that leaders are able to learn and develop competencies over time (unlike trait approach which is rather fixed).[10] Most organisations today understand that developing leadership skills is important and that some combination of attributes and skills are needed to achieve outcomes.[11]

Style approach – this approach emphasises the behaviour of the leader and was popularised by studies at Ohio State University in the 1940s followed by the University of Michigan. The style approach describes the major components of a leader's behaviour and is often the mechanism by which we provide feedback to leaders.[12]

Psychodynamic leadership approach – this consists of many ways of looking at traits and understanding the tendencies or qualities that a person might exhibit. Typically this involves the use of psychometric instruments with a suggestion that various personality types are better suited to certain leadership situations or positions.[13]

Situational approach – this was developed by Hersey and Blanchard and has been used extensively in organisation leadership training around the world.[14] The idea behind this theory is that different situations require different kinds of leadership, which requires leaders to be flexible and adaptable.[15]

Transformational leadership approach – this is a currently popular focus in practice and research as it gives more attention to the charismatic elements of leadership and places emphasis on intrinsic motivation.[16] The idea of transformational leadership is that certain leaders can change people based on the ability of a leader to satisfy followers' needs.[17] This is often contrasted with transactional leadership, which is aligned to contingent rewards. Current research promises to further our understanding in this area.[18]

Servant leadership approach – this can be an approach that seems contradictory to the idea of leading others. Servant leadership emphasised that leaders be focused on the concerns of the followers and put their needs first.[19] Robert Greenleaf developed some of the ideas and the term and has established the Greenleaf Centre for Servant Leadership.[20]

Authentic leadership approach – this relatively recent area of development in leadership theory centres on the idea that leadership is genuine. Bill George developed a commonly used framework.[21] The recent uncertainty in political and economic stability has created societal interest in authentic leadership and we expect to see more in this area from both research and practice.

While exploring these and other leadership theories is beyond the focus of this book, it is important to keep them in mind as we consider the types of leadership development, tools for addressing competencies, and techniques to improve leadership capability. There are many tools and methodologies available, and in the rest of this chapter we will highlight several well-known and effective approaches in pursuit of the goal of building effective leadership.

Leadership development

As organisations plan to develop current and future leaders, there are a number of considerations such as return on investment, appropriate targets, ensuring diversity, cross-cultural differences, global perspectives, and high-potential talent retention. As research has identified, the return on investment from leadership development programmes can be challenging to estimate and capture.[22] For most large organisations the question is not *whether* we should develop leaders, but *how* we develop leaders.

In general, there are four steps companies can follow to build leadership talent internally. The first is to develop a 'talent strategy' to ensure they are aligning leadership talent with dynamic business needs. The second is to assess leadership performance, potential, readiness, and job fit against current and future needs. The third step is to design and deliver impactful leadership development experiences. The fourth and final step is to implement effective leadership performance and succession plans. Of course, none of this can exist in a vacuum; as we have mentioned elsewhere, policy solutions must be implemented systemically. In this case, compensation, workforce forecasting, mobility, performance appraisals, and career planning also play a role. Let us focus on each of the four steps in turn.

Step I: Developing a talent strategy to ensure alignment between leadership talent and business needs

A leadership strategy includes the organisation's philosophy and tactics around the definition of required leadership competencies, the process for identifying future leaders, assessment methods, and development strategies. Business needs to answer the following fundamental questions, among many others, in the process of building a leadership development strategy:

- *What capabilities, behaviours, and attitudes does the business need from its leaders to be successful in the future?*
- *What is the appropriate balance between 'building' leadership capability internally versus 'buying' it from the market? If buying is preferred, what is the availability in the market? Can the company attract and retain leaders from the market?*
- *Is the business strategy of the organisation such that 'homegrown' leaders will provide a competitive advantage?*
- *What are the key activities and positions which provide the type of experiences future leaders will need to acquire the desired skills and knowledge?*
- *What processes and systems need to be implemented to support the development of leaders?*
- *What are the key measures of success and what is the time horizon?*

In its essence, the profile of a successful leader is a blend of behaviours which align corporate values and organisational cultural norms, with the skills and

Table 3.1 Mercer's Global Leadership Competencies

Personal/ Foundational	Strategic focus	Operational focus	People focus
Learning agility	Creates strategy	Drives results	Inspires and motivates
Shows resilience	Drives innovation	Focuses on customer	Coaches and develops others
Self awareness	Develops market and business acumen	Collaborates with others	Drives performance
Cultural sensitivity	Thinks with agility	Influences and networks	Optimizes talent

Source: Mercer and Jay A. Conger, Professor of Leadership at Claremont McKenna College in California; *Insights on Global Leadership Development* (Mercer, 2011).

competencies required to fulfil the business strategy. In parallel, each individual brings their own personality traits, preferred learning style, and stage of evolution of their careers. Any strategy aimed at leadership development must take all of these into account.

Several models of leadership competencies are available and many companies have created their own in-house model. Recent research by Professor Jay Conger shows that about two-thirds of leadership requirements are universal (apply to all companies) and one-third are specific to a company's model, industry, and culture.[23] Conger's model, as illustrated by Figure 3.2, identifies sixteen essential leadership competencies for global leadership. These are grouped into four categories: strategic, operational, people, and personal. Table 3.1 also includes sample organisation-specific competencies.

Step II: Assessing the pipeline of leaders

Conducting multi-source leadership assessments is the next step in executing the leadership strategy. Any approach should include assessment solutions that target three different levels: the CEO and senior team, extended leadership, and prospective leaders showing high potential. These solutions should aim to assess performance, potential readiness, succession pathways, and possible changes to help grow performance and maximise future impact for the organisation.

After the organisation has defined its leadership and organisation-specific capabilities in the first step, the focus shifts to conducting an evaluation of leaders or leadership candidates via a consistent set of tools in order to objectively assess their competencies and capabilities. These tools can have a wide basis and can be used to gather a large amount of data about each individual. The ultimate goal is to gain an informed and accurate picture of each individual who goes through the process so as to accurately select the best people to lead the organisation, both now and in the future. Some of the most commonly used tools include:

- Behavioural event interview guides and probes;
- Assessment centres (including business simulations exercises);
- Standard interviewing and reporting templates for selection and development;
- 360-degree feedback;
- Personality testing tools (e.g., Hogan, Birkman, 16PF, DISC, etc.).

Assessment data from the use of these tools, plus individual preferences and supervisor input, can be synthesised, integrated, and consolidated into reports on a wide range of issues that affect the organisation's leadership capability. The outcome should be twofold: one is an individual report per person that allows them to understand where they are in their development and what they need to work on to get to the next level in the organisation. The other is an organisation-wide report that points at where the organisation needs to invest to improve its leadership development. In summary, this report should include information on whether the organisation needs more or fewer people in the different key roles going forward, based on various revenue and growth assumptions. It should also include an examination of whether the people in the key roles are performing at a high enough level. Ideally, it should also shed light on the engagement/retention of these individuals. But most importantly, it should provide details on the organisation's current capability gap which investigates whether the people in the role need more, deeper or different capabilities to meet future business needs. These gaps are not always distinct and they overlap. For instance, a performance gap could be related to not having the right capabilities.

It is important to note that care should be taken to avoid bias in the identification of future leaders. As research has shown, the styles of women and men may differ and organisations should help promote the development of both women and men.[22] Too often, future leaders are identified in a casual way by current leaders with unintended biases that perpetuate the lack of diversity in leadership ranks. Leading organisations are working not only to celebrate the diversity of leadership, but also to promote and encourage women leaders.

CASE STUDY

Assessing and building leadership capabilities

Recognising the rapid changes in the region, an Asia-focused development finance institution realised it needed to revise its strategy to better align with these regional developments. In response to the key drivers of external change, the institution articulated its long-term strategic plan, 'Strategy 2020', which emphasised focus on five core specialisations, including sectors such as infrastructure and education. The strategy targeted a change in lending mix, so that, over the next three years, 80 per cent of all lending would be to the newly defined specialisations.

Achievement of their desired positioning as the development partner of choice in these specialisations implied a renewed focus on in-depth sectoral knowledge. Further, a mindset of partnership and sharing was required to ensure capabilities were built and retained at an institutional level. The institution also realised that there was an increasing need to work collaboratively with external parties, as the number of potential development partners was rapidly increasing in Asia.

The institution realised that in order to achieve the enhanced technical and partnership capabilities, better management and leadership were key to success. Specifically, it needed to develop leaders of the future who could build staff capabilities, drive sharing of institutional knowledge, encourage collaboration within and outside, and maximise retention. This required careful selection of the future leaders – which in turn demanded an in-depth assessment and development of each candidate's capabilities.

To ensure an objective, fair, and robust assessment of capabilities, the institution decided to conduct structured assessment centres. A common understanding of desired skills and behaviours was first developed by creating a set of leadership competencies rooted in the institution's vision, values, and strategy.

Thereafter, a battery of activities – ranging from psychometric assessments to group case studies and role plays – was custom-designed to reflect scenarios typically faced by leaders at the institution. When played out in the assessment centre, each activity provided an opportunity to observe a distinct set of the leadership competencies. The number of participants was restricted to six, and an observer to participant ratio of 1 : 2 was maintained to enable in-depth observation.

As the institution conducted these centres, it obtained rich information on its leadership candidates. After the first round of centres, it emerged that only a handful of candidates demonstrated all desired leadership behaviours. However, this was as expected and, in anticipation, the institution had included a development aspect in the exercise as well. Based on the capability gaps observed in the centre, a targeted developmental plan was designed for each participant. Further, through the centre, the institution was able to identify some candidates as being less suitable for senior management roles. For these candidates, an alternative career path of technical expertise was charted, to appropriately tap into relevant skills.

As a result of these structured assessment and development centres, the institution has been able to make informed leadership decisions, such as:

- *Which candidates are 'ready now' to take on leadership roles, equipped with the competencies needed to achieve Strategy 2020?*
- *Which candidates need further grooming, and specifically, what targeted development is needed by each candidate?*
- *Which candidates are not suited for managerial leadership roles? Can the institution better utilise their skill sets as technical sector experts?*

Besides such individual decisions, the assessment and development centres provided an understanding of the organisational leadership capabilities as well as areas in which to focus for development. They enabled the institution to clearly understand the depth of its leadership pipeline and undertake developmental initiatives to align its leadership capability with business needs as defined by Strategy 2020.

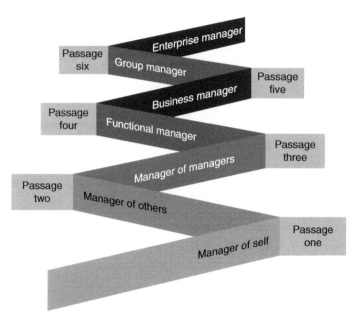

Figure 3.2 Developing a pipeline of leaders
Source: adapted from Charan, Drotter and Noel, *The Leadership Pipeline: How to Build the Leadership Powered Company* (Jossey-Bass, 2001)

Step III: Developing the pipeline of leaders

To develop a pipeline of leaders, companies can use a tailored approach that combines an organisation's leadership capability needs with the individual's learning requirements. In other words, the idea here is to blend different learning methodologies and customised content to implement an effective leadership development programme. This combining of learning experiences with a predominant focus on 'on-the-job' learning is an effective method for developing current and future leaders.

The centrepiece of this step is the creation of an individual development plan that underpins an effective leadership development process and which can act as a learning roadmap for current and future leaders. Key activities in this plan include:

- Identifying and providing challenging development opportunities;
- Providing 'breakthrough coaching';
- Delivering action learning programmes;
- Ensuring rotational experiences;
- Defining career paths;
- Delivering classroom experiences.

Providing continuous feedback to current and future leaders on progress also helps to reduce potential 'derailment'. Charan, Drotter and Noel identify six passages in the development of leaders, shown in Figure 3.2. Each passage represents a major career transition in terms of three things: skill requirements (new capabilities required to execute the new responsibilities), work values (what leaders believe is important, so it becomes the focus of their efforts), and time applications (new time frames that govern how one works).

The first passage is when an upcoming leader goes from managing him/herself to managing others. The second passage is when their progression takes them from managing others to managing managers. The third passage occurs when the person continues in their journey up the hierarchy and is entrusted to manage a whole area. The fourth passage is when the person is promoted to run a complete profit-and-loss entity. The fifth step occurs when the manager is raised to manage a group of related businesses. The last passage happens when the manager finally runs an entire organisation. At each passage the lessons learned at each prior stage are useful, but new and higher skills and competencies are required to be successful.

Of course, organisations can use all of these interventions to help leaders develop. However, of these, there are two that are important to get 'right': the first is expatriate assignments. There simply is no alternative to being there in a 'real job'. It is also the most expensive method. The keys to getting it 'right' are to select people who have the right attributes, making the experience real and challenging, providing the right support, and planning for their re-entry. The other practice is coaching and mentoring. Providing early career global leaders with other global leaders as coaches and mentors can support and help them develop as well as potentially avoid any pitfalls in their development and their effectiveness.

To summarise, an effective approach to develop the pipeline of leaders in an organisation would include:

- Aligning of individual leadership competencies around the organisation's leadership model;
- Differentiating the development of leaders by recognising that every stage of the leadership pipeline requires different learning strategies to develop and continually build leadership capabilities, skills, and behaviours;
- Equipping emerging leaders with specific tools to support business needs and goals;
- Focusing content on defined leadership skills and self-development;
- Determining the most appropriate learning methodology to achieve the leadership development objectives including:

- Workshop, classroom or web-enabled learning
- Individual (one-on-one) or group (peer-to-peer) coaching
- On-the-job training or business simulations;
- Using and embedding leading-edge adult learning principles and practices;
- Understanding that leadership development is not a one-off event but rather a continuous learning process.

CASE STUDY

Development programmes to nurture future leaders

A growing Asian electronics and power systems multinational was experiencing rapid change. Significant pressure from competitors and an increase in raw materials costs from suppliers was negatively impacting margin. At the same time, the company was struggling to integrate global acquisitions as differences in eastern and western work cultures were leading to a lack of trust. Even within the same region, collaboration across business units was lacking, resulting in lost opportunities for innovative idea generation and resource optimisation.

As they battled these multiple challenges, the company's leaders were suffering from a marked decrease in their own engagement. Moreover, while these leaders were technically strong, they lacked the management skills, experience, or mindset necessary to work in diverse situations and cultures. It was agreed that for the company to maintain its leadership position both within and outside Asia, drastic action would have to be taken to build leaders who could function well in an uncertain environment as well as respect and leverage the diversity and cultural differences reflected in their global workforce.

The company embarked upon a rigorous instructional design process to create a comprehensive, multi-module leadership development programme to address their key issues. The programme was rooted in the belief that the key to success would be introducing a 'mindset' change among leaders. Specifically, the company identified five critical mindsets (reflective, collaborative, worldly, analytical, and action) that the leaders needed to adopt in order to function in a dynamic and diverse environment.

Ahead of the actual leadership development programme, 360-degree feedback was collected to gain insights and observations into how leaders were perceived by key stakeholder groups. This revealed that:

- Mindsets had to change so that leaders were 'open' to managing and leading in an entirely new way;
- Fundamental skills had to be learned and practised in realistic yet safe action learning projects, and eventually applied in their day jobs;
- Participating leaders had to embrace an aligned vision and agree on how to embed the desired corporate culture throughout the organisation.

With this background, a nine-month, four-module leadership development journey, including an action learning component, was developed. The design of the programme was influenced by the leadership pipeline framework as well as significant research into models of mindset change. Programme content in each of the four modules was designed to address the specific challenges faced by participating leaders, as well as to help them acquire the fundamental skills and behavioural changes required. Given the global reach of this organisation, each module was held in a different country where the organisation had operations, exposing participating managers to different cultures, ways of thinking, and ways of doing.

At the conclusion of the final module, a second 360-feedback process was conducted to evaluate behavioural change among participating leaders. The results were very reassuring, demonstrating significant improvement across the five mindsets the programme was designed to address. Based on the impact of the first programme, key stakeholders have seen a material difference in how participating leaders approach their work both within and across borders.

Many leaders who took part in the first programme have been promoted, and have sent their direct reports to subsequent runs of the programme. Future programmes have been scheduled to continue the journey with other managers within the organisation.

Step IV: Managing performance and succession

As in other areas of business, leadership development is a series of processes that must be managed effectively. The two areas that merit detailed attention in this respect are performance management and succession planning. In Chapter 7 we will discuss in greater detail the components of these two.

For purposes of leadership development, the performance management process must strive to make employee appraisals constructive and productive, improve the quality and efficiency of evaluations, and chart the progress of individuals against corporate objectives. There are many useful software tools which can help to set and track goals, capture and retrieve performance data, and produce actionable information. In terms of succession planning, the key components are the ability to identify top performers early in their careers, help managers to develop leaders, identify talent gaps, build stronger bench strength, and engage and retain tomorrow's leaders.

The minimum outcome desired is threefold:

1. the identification of future leaders;
2. the creation of a slate of succession candidates;
3. the identification of the current talent gaps along with development actions.

World-class organisations however go beyond these three, including rigorous career plans, that include foreign assignments as a prerequisite, international mobility as a way of life, robust performance management systems that are consistent worldwide, and a strong corporate culture led by the CEO where acquiring and keeping talent is at least as important as acquiring and keeping clients. There is a new saying going around the HRF executives' circles: 'Competency trumps cost.'

CASE STUDY

Developing a strong bench of leaders

While domestic market share had been robust and growing over the previous years, this Korean cosmetics company started to experience a slowdown, given an increasingly saturated market. The company outlined an aggressive global expansion plan starting with China, the USA, France, and ASEAN countries to drive business growth. However, the execution of these plans was challenged by resource constraints – not financial resources but rather a lack of human resources.

More specifically, given its erstwhile domestic focus, the company lacked an internal leadership bench with sufficient experience outside the

Korean borders. Given this seeming lack of in-house talent, the company turned its attention to a 'buy' strategy and started recruiting for leadership roles.

However, owing to a poorly defined employee value proposition and the lack of a clearly defined success profile, the company found there were challenges in even attracting and evaluating suitable candidates. Without the necessary tools and experience to verify fit, they hired very experienced, very capable, yet extremely expensive leaders. This upset the company's internal equity and led to discontent among existing executives. And, unfortunately, as many of these new leaders did not share the company vision and values, they did not last long. Their exit caused even more disruption to the business and left behind succession gaps.

After a number of false starts, with tactical efforts such as foreign language training, the company decided to adopt a more holistic approach to global leadership development. This commenced with clearer understanding of global talent requirements. Through workforce modelling, the company clarified exactly *how many* global leaders were required – now and in the future – as well as *where* they needed to be deployed.

Simultaneously, the company articulated the desired profile of a global leader, captured in terms of five key competencies: adaptability, communication, leading change, global sensitivity, and technical expertise. Through enhanced clarity and consistent application of the desired profile, the company was able to improve its talent selection outcomes – both in terms of hiring more suitable external candidates, as well as identifying high-potential internal candidates.

To support the development of the high-potential candidates, the company created leadership development programmes, which balanced training with on-the-job development. Specifically, development activities such as global assignments and special projects were emphasised as the most suitable way to groom global experience.

Given the development of a more robust leadership development infrastructure, the global leaders improved capability and stability. The company has 'ready now' leaders and, when turnover does occur, they have been able to replace from within. Further, because development has been based on business needs, it has allowed the company to modify its global leader development plan to reflect various business changes, making it more flexible.

Internally, a healthy competitive environment has been created and engagement levels have increased, having a positive effect on performance levels. A greater awareness of globalisation and global markets has also been a positive side-effect. The development of a comprehensive strategy for grooming internal leaders has paid off. Business performance has improved, turnover is down, and engagement is up. Their efforts have resulted in a ready pipeline of capable leaders. The company's external employer brand has even benefited, boosting its attractiveness among potential leaders.

Techniques for leadership development

Keeping the principles above in mind, let us now turn our attention to a sample of specific techniques that will enable organisations to develop more and better leaders.

Many organisations embark on leadership development programmes and spend significant budget amounts on outside speakers, event planners, and travel costs. These are typically significant investments that yield very little in return as they tend to be one- or two-day 'entertainment' and good enlightenment events – but very limited in the actual job performance for leaders. Four techniques that have proven impact to developing leaders include coaching, team alignment, leadership development needs analysis, and action learning (Table 3.2).

Table 3.2 Tools and techniques for leadership development

Techniques for developing leaders	• Coaching
	• Team alignment
	• Leadership development needs analysis
	• Action learning
Tools to develop skills critical for leaders	• Emotional intelligence (EQ)
	• Right people in right job
	• Situational leadership
	• Performance management
	• Managing conflicts
	• Change leadership
	• Decision-making, influencing
	• Organisational leadership

Leadership coaching

Coaching is a process for equipping people with what they need to develop and be effective in their current role. The coach uses tools and his/her knowledge to provide feedback regarding how people can approach problems differently. Coaching helps people to enhance their own learning and development performance by providing opportunities they need to develop themselves and become more effective, pointing out how improved performance is possible and helping to set and achieve development goals. It is important to note that coaches do not develop people – they equip people to develop themselves.

There are many good reasons why coaching should be an integral part of every leader's skill set. Most importantly, when done properly, it helps to improve the performance of staff by supporting high performance, by raising good and acceptable performance to higher levels, and by helping to improve poor performance. Beyond developing staff, coaching can also be useful in delegation, bettering relationships with peers, and even in managing the boss.

If one accepts the premise that the most useful development, from a company's perspective, happens on the job, then it follows that coaching is also useful as it helps people to learn best by doing. The coaching process uses real work as the learning vehicle with the manager acting as the coach/facilitator of learning. To be an effective coach, the leader's role is about being a catalyst for development. This can be understood as doing the following:

1. **Advising** – communicating expectations and giving information;
2. **Instructing** – clarifying, teaching skills and knowledge;
3. **Facilitating** – assisting with the change planning and actions;
4. **Appraising** – providing ongoing feedback.

Often coaching, mentoring, and counselling are used interchangeably. However, these are distinct concepts, as Table 3.3 illustrates.

Effective coaching should be tailored to the individual's needs, abilities, interests, experience, and learning style and pace. A hands-off approach is usually more effective, but a direct approach is sometimes needed. The coaching process usually follows these steps:

1. **Agree on the topic.**

- *How did the coach and learner agree on the topic?*
- *How did they consider the learner's needs?*

Table 3.3 Coaching, mentoring, and counselling

	Coaching	**Mentoring**	**Counselling**
Focus	• Individual and organisational performance • Specific skill and capability development • Shorter-term	• Individual and organisational needs • Problems/difficulties and opportunities/possibilities • Learning and development	• Individual needs • May be entirely process • Overcoming a derailer
Outcome	• Specific action plans: who does what when • Timelines and measures	• Greater confidence and self-awareness • Career opportunities • Exposure	• Variable • Resolution of personal obstacle/block
'Leader' behaviour	• Situation-specific • More directive, takes charge • Follows up for results	• Mentors usually come from within the organisation • Facilitation and advice	• Unconditional positive • Less directive
Foundation	• Performance management	• Built on close relationship of trust and care	• Various counselling therapies

2. Identify the goals.

- *How did the coach and learner set goals for the whole coaching experience?*
- *How did they set goals for the particular session?*
- *Were the goals measurable and achievable?*

3. Promote discovery.

- *What is active listening?*
- *How did the coach draw out the consequences of the learner's behaviours?*
- *How did the coach share their experience?*

4. Set the parameters.

- *How did the coach and learner set parameters around the coaching?*
- *How specific were these parameters?*

5. Authorise and empower.

- *What did the coach do to authorise and empower the learner?*

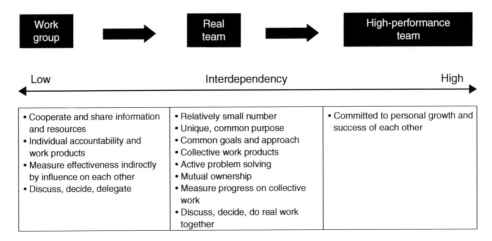

Figure 3.3 Teams versus groups
Source: Thomas and Kilmann, Thomas-Kilmann Conflict Mode Instrument (CPP, Inc., 2002)

6. **Recap.**
 • *What did the coach do to ensure consistency of expectations between learner and coach?*

Team alignment

In understanding leadership, we must not think leaders act alone; in fact, more often than not they must work in teams. A team is a group of people who work together for a particular purpose. Every *team* is a *group*, but not every *group* is a *team*. Although the terms are often used interchangeably, there are clear distinctions between teams and groups. As Figure 3.3 illustrates, at the most basic level of differentiation, groups have low interdependence. The level of interdependency is higher for teams.

It is important for leaders, teams and groups to be clear about how they want to work together and for what purpose. To be effective, teams ought to have clear goals that are understood and communicated; shared and agreed norms of behaviour; clear roles and responsibilities; effective processes and procedures; mutual trust and respect; high levels of empathy, listening and feedback; a strong desire for learning and continuous improvement; and high levels of adaptability and flexibility. This can be particularly complex when dealing with management across borders and working to establish trust between team members.[24]

Much of the above are procedural techniques, and training on these topics can easily equip managers at all levels with this knowledge. However, even if all the procedural steps are properly covered, it is highly unlikely that working in teams will always be smooth sailing. To effectively work in teams, leaders must necessarily learn how to manage conflict, a topic we will cover later.

Leadership development needs analysis

In an earlier section, we discussed the competencies required of a leader. To determine where each leader can improve, the organisation should periodically assess each leader against the desired competency levels and thus determine which area or areas the leader needs to work on. There are several tools for this purpose, from 360-degree appraisal to more formal assessments conducted by externally trained psychologists using tools such as Hogan or similar. By reviewing the collective results, the organisation can also determine if it needs specific programmes to improve its overall leadership.

Action learning

This is a popular approach for helping leaders improve. At its core it is simple: assign a 'live' project to a leader with the support of an external (or sometimes internal) facilitator or coach. As the developing leader goes through the process of solving the problem at hand, he or she may be tasked with leadership skills such as building a team, making decisions, resolving conflicts, etc. Action learning involves asking for, and acting on, feedback on how the developing leader addressed, and attempted to resolve, the leadership tasks involved.

For more on the tools to develop these leadership skills, once an assessment is made of the need to do so, let us turn to the next section. Please note that different developing leaders will have greater need of one over another of these skills.

Tools to develop skills critical for leaders

The techniques above show how we will address and interact with leaders to help them with development areas. Some of the areas that become the focus for these interventions include emotional intelligence, 'right people in right job', situational leadership, performance management, managing conflicts, change leadership, decision-making, and crucibles of leadership. Let us examine each of these areas in brief.

Emotional intelligence

There is conclusive evidence that emotional intelligence (EQ) is of the most importance in developing leaders. Ruth Jacobs and Wei Chen from Hay McBer conducted a study where they analysed competency data from forty companies. Of the competencies that separated effective leaders from the rest, one-third were cognitive (e.g. strategic analysis) and two-thirds were emotional (e.g. motivating others). Their colleague Lyle Spencer, Jr., studied 286 organisations globally at all levels of management. He identified twenty-one generic competencies that distinguished high performers from average performers: at the most senior level of management eighteen were emotional competencies, two were intellectual (analytical and conceptual skills), and one was technical. In a related study, Richard Boyatzis from the Weatherhead School of Management studied 2,000 supervisors, middle managers, and executives at twelve large US organisations. He was able to identify sixteen abilities that distinguished stars from average performers; all but two were emotional competencies. And Rossier, in a report from 1994, examined 181 different positions in 121 organisations worldwide and also found that 67 per cent of the abilities deemed essential for effective performance were emotional competencies.

EQ refers to the ability of leaders to work with others and to lead change. Daniel Goleman explains that EQ refers to the capacity for recognising our own feelings and those of others, for motivating ourselves, and for managing emotions well in ourselves and in our relationships.[25] Goleman goes on to say that 'Emotional intelligence is two times as important as technical skills and cognitive abilities for jobs at all levels and becomes more important at senior levels. It accounts for 90 per cent of the difference between average and star performers.' He explains the four areas that leaders must master to achieve EQ:

- **Self-awareness** – meaning deep understanding of emotions, strengths, weaknesses, needs, and desires; ability to be honest with self and others; recognition of impact of feelings on self, others, and job performance; a sense of direction and goals and a desire for constructive criticism.
- **Self-management** – meaning being in control of feelings and impulses; the ability to roll with and lead change; consistent honesty and integrity; high-achievement motivation; love of learning, desire for creative challenges, pride in a job well done, and drive for higher performance.
- **Social awareness** – meaning thoughtful consideration of employees, customers, and client feelings in decision-making; planned use of team development processes; understanding of cross-cultural dialogue and a focus on growing/retaining talent through coaching, mentoring, and effective feedback.

- **Social skills** – meaning moving people in the right direction through vision, influencing with or without position of power, a tendency to optimism, using persuasion rather than punishment, and capable of building network relationships.

The key implication of the above for effective leadership is clear: the higher a leader moves through the management ranks of an organisation, the more emotional intelligence contributes to success. The question then becomes – can EQ be learned? The answer is 'yes', but to eliminate old habits and create new ones requires a great deal of feedback (from coaches, supervisors, 360-degree feedback, and other means), introspection, action learning, and coaching. Some of the remaining tools in this section will support this learning.

Getting the right people in the right job

Bradford D. Smart makes a very interesting point: 'It is much easier to hire the right people to begin with than to try and fix them later.'[26] To do so, it is important to increase the probability of getting the right person in the right job using more than a gut feeling. The key to finding out how someone will perform in a job is to collect and analyse examples of how the person has performed in similar situations in the past through a technique known as structured behavioural interviews. In this type of interview, interviewees are asked to describe several specific behavioural events to demonstrate the extent to which they have certain behaviours or capabilities. The interviewer asks probing, but non-directive, questions to gain clarification and examples. The behaviours being sought can even be made known to the interviewee (e.g. *'Tell me about a recent time when you have given great customer service in a challenging situation'*).

The underlying assumptions underpinning this approach are that past behaviour is a good predictor of future behaviour, that superior performers demonstrate different behaviours compared to average performers, and that if a person truly has the capability, many different examples of that behaviour will be easily remembered.

The most important features of the structured behaviour interview are:

- **Critical behaviours** – asks the person to recount examples of a specific behaviour that is critical for successful job performance.
- **Based on real examples** – yields information about what the person did in a specific set of past examples. Deals with real events, not hypothetical situations.

- **Investigative** – uses a series of structured questions designed to 'dig' into the specifics of a person's capability.
- **Detailed** – elicits detailed accounts of specific events, and the individual's personal role in those events.
- **Consistent** – the same questions are asked of each person, so that all have the same opportunity to give examples of their competence.

Structured interviews allow for better prediction of future on-the-job success. They allow for greater alignment with organisational context and culture. They are relatively fast and easy to use by a trained interviewer. Finally, they reduce interviewer bias: vague generalisations are reduced significantly as interviewees are required to provide facts and recall actual situations. On the down side, this type of interview does not collect data on motivations or personality, so other approaches must be used to get at the individuals' values and fit with the organisation's culture.

Making better selection decisions is an important step in having the right leadership pipeline, in 'buying' the right talent, and in increasing employee retention and company performance.

Situational leadership

As mentioned earlier in this chapter, Hersey and Blanchard developed situational leadership with two primary principles in mind: the first is that each leader comes into any situation with a preferred leadership style. The second is that those whom the leader leads have a preferred way in which they want to be led. The corollary to these two principles is that the specific preferred style in each case may be different according to the circumstances (we explore this further in the section on managing conflicts, below).

There are several useful models to understanding these principles in practice: examples include the Wilson learning social styles model[27] and the learning styles (activist, pragmatist, theorist, reflector) model.[28] Many of these are based on a 2 × 2 matrix. For instance, Wilson learning uses two dimensions: the first is a 'people' versus 'task' orientation and the second is 'ask' versus 'tell' preference. A person whose preferred leadership style is high on task orientation and high on tell preference is a 'driver'; if high on task and high on ask, the resulting leadership style is 'analytical'; if high on people and also high on ask, the style is defined as 'amiable' and if high on both people and tell, the style is called 'expressive'.

Regardless of which model is used, the main ingredients for success in developing leaders are the same: increase the awareness of each leader of their own approach to situations; understand better the preferred styles to be used with those around them; understand these others' perceptions of the leader and his/her style; and make better choices of leadership styles to fit these others.

Setting objectives, delegation, and giving feedback

The secret of a good performance appraisal system is not how well the forms are designed or how automated is the process. The fundamental aspect of performance appraisals that work is strict cascading of objectives from the top and as far down as feasible. There are several tools and techniques commonly in use to determine objectives. From SMART objectives (specific, measurable, achievable, relevant, time-bound) to balanced scorecards, these are all useful aids. However, without alignment in objectives from the top down, there is little the tool or technique can do to help. What do we mean by 'alignment'? In simple terms, if every one of your direct reports accomplishes his/her objectives, you will have accomplished yours. The leader's role is then made clearer: help the team work together towards the achievement of interrelated goals.

The above sounds simple, but in practice many things go wrong. There was the example of the Asian real estate corporation whose CEO had forty-two key performance indicators (KPIs) in his balanced scorecard. Some of the KPIs had a weight of 1 per cent! As a result, the most important KPIs – growth, profitability, and operational improvements – collectively weighed less than 30 per cent. The idea was that the company was trying to follow the principle that '*What gets measured gets done.*' In practice, it was paying bonuses of nearly 90 per cent of target even though it was falling short of shareholders' expectations. There was also the case of the large logistics company in Latin America where objectives were audited to ensure they were 'SMART'. In truth, they were absolutely compliant with these principles but the objectives were not aligned. Each business unit and department created its own goals in isolation. Any coordination with other units was due only to enlightened leaders or pure chance! This organisation was also paying near target bonuses every year without actually achieving all its business objectives.

As with the real estate company above, it is important to measure all the relevant parts of the business, but the focus must be only on the ones that make the biggest difference. Much like an airline pilot has a great many instruments on the flight panel, but he only focuses on the ones that matter most at the particular point in the flight. As a rule of thumb, if any objective has a weight of less than 10 per cent, it should not be kept in the performance appraisal.

That limits the number of 'most critical' KPIs to a maximum of ten. In the same vein, SMART is a good principle, but it should be A-SMART, where the first 'A' stands for 'aligned' up and down the hierarchy as well as across the business and functions. This is very much what one of the largest brewers in the world does: three or four objectives at the top, which cascade down several layers of the organisation. At each layer, the incumbents can add a limited number of objectives to complement the top three or four. At this organisation, everyone works for the same results without any hesitation. And they have historically outpaced their competitors as a consequence. The role of leadership is to set the direction, encourage teams to work together, and set the policies to ensure all is done consistently.

Delegation is one of the most difficult challenges new leaders face in managing subordinates' performance. Many new managers want to 'do it themselves', because they feel the need to show their superiors that they are capable, or they want to have a say in how things are done by their subordinates, in the belief that their staff expects the manager to be the problem-solver and decision-maker. However, by definition, management is getting work done through other people and, therefore, a manager is one who delegates to others. When done properly, delegation supports the development of leaders in two ways: it allows for subordinates to learn substantial parts of the supervisor's job and, at the same time, frees the supervisor to spend more time learning parts of his/her supervisor's job! There are other benefits, such as enhanced motivation (and we saw earlier that engagement has a positive impact on business results), greater retention (less need to 'buy' talent as delegation allows you to 'build' talent), and increased productivity as tasks get done at a lower cost. Besides, in supporting their staff to learn and do higher-level work, managers also hone their leadership skills such as planning, organising, communicating, and monitoring.

The corollary to this line of behaviour is the actual performance appraisal interview. Even experienced leaders often sidestep this part of the process if they can. And yet, providing useful feedback is one of the most important things a leader can do to improve organisational performance. Useful feedback lets people know how they are doing, reinforces positive actions and behaviours, focuses attention towards something that does not work, increases awareness of the consequences of specific behaviours, builds on strengths and helps to address weaknesses, and generally helps employees know where and how to improve. In short, giving effective feedback helps to develop future leaders!

Managing conflict

Conflict is simply defined as any situation where your concerns or desires differ from another person's. Conflicts will often occur; in fact, sometimes they are inherent in the way business groups are set up. A common conflict in business occurs, for instance, when the customer service function strives to improve customer satisfaction ratings while, at the same time, the finance function is looking for ways to improve margins. One of the most useful interventions an HRF can have in the organisation is to provide leaders with the tools to manage through conflicts.

Before we look at this further, it is important to clarify a few myths about conflict:

- Myth I – conflict is a sign of a poor manager.
- Myth II – conflict is a sign of low concern for the company.
- Myth III – conflict is an impediment to creativity.
- Myth IV – conflict, if left alone, will take care of itself.
- Myth V – conflict must be resolved.

In fact, conflicts do not always have to be resolved but they do always have to be managed. In order to do so, the most important thing is to be sure that leaders are solving the right problem. In the customer service versus finance example above, the right problem is perhaps neither customer satisfaction ratings nor expense control (although each function may have these respectively in their KPIs and thus feel obligated to improve on them). The right problem may be customer profitability or sales productivity. By reframing the problem into a form both areas can agree on, the conflict can now be managed towards an agreed-upon joint solution.

Traditionally, conflicts are managed by having each person state their view briefly, then focusing on the common views but allowing new ideas to be introduced, exploring areas of disagreement for specific issues which can be resolved, having the opposing parties suggest modifications to their own and others' points of view, as well as having neutral team members reflect on areas of agreement and disagreement to find common solutions and, if no ideal answer can be found, ask opponents if they can accept the team's decision. It is also generally a good idea to formally summarise and record the decision.

Techniques which can be learned as a way to manage conflicts include having a structured way to handle conflicts. To do so, beyond relying on discussions alone, the HRF can provide leaders with other problem-solving methods.

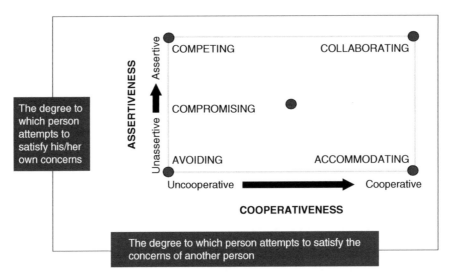

Figure 3.4 Five conflict-handling modes
Source: adapted from Roberto, *Why Great Leaders Don't Take No for an Answer: Managing for Conflict and Consensus* (Prentice Hall, 2005)

A useful way to understanding conflict management comes from Kenneth Thomas and Ralph Kilmann.[29] In this approach, conflict management relies on two main behaviours:

1. **Assertiveness** – the degree to which a person attempts to satisfy their own concerns; and
2. **Cooperativeness** – the degree to which a person attempts to satisfy the concerns of another person.

By examining these two dimensions together, we can see five conflict-handling modes as shown in Figure 3.4.

Competing is best when quick action is needed, when making unpopular decisions, when dealing with vital issues when you absolutely know you are right, or for protection where non-competitive behaviour may be taken advantage of.

Collaborating is an effective style when there is a need for integrating solutions or merging perspectives, as a means of providing learning opportunities or when it is important to gain commitment as a way to improve relationships.

Compromising is effective when dealing with issues of only moderate importance, when the opposing parties both have equal power and a strong commitment to their respective points of view, when temporary solutions are called for, when there are time constraints, or when you reach an alternative solution that, even if not ideal, both sides can live with.

Accommodating is most useful when showing reasonableness (after all, you cannot win them all), or when developing skills in delegation, creating goodwill, keeping the peace or retreating.

Avoiding is best employed when the conflict at hand revolves around an issue of low importance. It is also good when it is important to reduce tensions or to buy time. It also is useful when one of the opposing parties has low power. It is a good way to allow those who own the problem to handle it, or when problems are symptoms of a much larger issue (focus on solving the root cause).

The implication is that there is no universal right way to handle conflicts; each model is good in some situations and not so good in others. As we discussed in the section on situational leadership, leaders are to learn how to manage conflicts using the different modes according to the situation.

Leading through change

One of the true tests of leadership is the ability to mobilise entire organisations through the changes required, not only to adapt to but also to anticipate changes in the business environment. For each success story of leadership like Apple or GE, there is at least one other that illustrates insufficient adaptation, such as Kodak, which was the leader in the world of photography but which eventually filed for bankruptcy as it did not anticipate, nor adapt to, the world of digital photography.

William Bridges makes the point that managing change really is about managing transitions. Bridges argues that change is a situational, outcome-oriented event.[30] As such, it can be quick but, mainly, it has a before and an after. Transition, on the other hand, is the experience of making the change. It is inherently psychological, loss-based, and always gradual.

The Inventure Group explain that every transition goes through three phases: ending, neutral zone, and new beginning.[31] The basic tenet is that you must end before you begin anew. Endings are defined as what is left behind or what ceases to be. Endings can be experienced as gain (positive) or loss (negative). When the ending is experienced as gain, there is a more positive response. However, when the ending is experienced as loss, there is an ambivalent or negative response.

According to the model, there are several ways in which an ending might be experienced as a loss:

- **Loss of attachments** – friends, work groups, working relationships, mentor;
- **Loss of turf** – physical territory, field of responsibility, title, authority;
- **Loss of structure** – office, procedures, systems, reporting structure;
- **Loss of future** – plans, dreams, earning potential, career path;
- **Loss of meaning** – why things have to end, purpose of job;
- **Loss of control** – power, influence, freedom, autonomy.

After the ending and before the new beginning is an in-between hiatus called the 'neutral zone'. According to the model, people go through transitions at different speeds and in different ways and, often, it is easy to get stuck in the neutral zone as there is a high degree of uncertainty, mistrust or self-preservation at play. To move past this stage, people can no longer be experiencing the change as a loss.

Beginnings occur when the change is seen as gain and thus the energy shifts to proactive behaviours. The authors warn that leaders should not overemphasise beginnings at the expense of managing endings and the neutral zone. An insight gained from looking into this model is that leaders, as change agents, tend to move to beginnings before the rest of the organisation, which has the potential to cause conflict.

In the end, there is much to learn about change management and many ways to approach change. Management's role in this case is both to help select a process that suits the organisation and to develop leaders capable of managing and sustaining organisational change. More on managing change is covered in Chapter 7.

Making decisions

The one thing that will most mark a leader as a success or failure is their ability to make good decisions. The impact of poor decision-making on the organisation can be costly and so one of the main objectives to keep in mind when developing leaders is to develop the probability of leaders making good decisions.

What is a sound decision-making environment? Ram Charam suggests the following criteria:[32]

1. Leaders create a decisive culture through their words and actions.
2. Assumptions are challenged rather than not challenged.

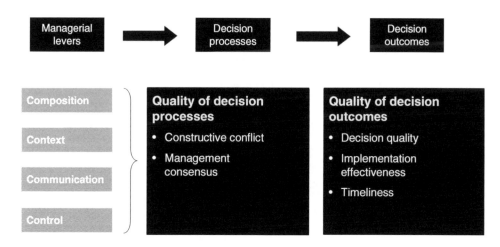

Figure 3.5 Decision-making process
Source: adapted from Roberto, *Why Great Leaders Don't Take Yes for an Answer: Managing for Conflict and Consensus* (Prentice Hall, 2005)

3. Information is shared rather than not shared.
4. Disagreements and conflicts are surfaced rather than not surfaced.

To create such an environment, the author points to the need for leaders to create an atmosphere of openness by balancing informality and formality. Then, drive for closure and later follow through and ensure feedback.

Will following this process enhance the quality of decisions? Michael Roberto explains that the quality of decisions depends on the quality of the process and that, in turn, the quality of the decision process depends on four levers, as shown in Figure 3.5.

The first lever is *composition* which addresses who should be involved in the decision-making processes. In general, managers should strive to involve multiple levels in the organisation, including different demographics as well as varying levels of expertise. A peer who is trusted by the people is very important.

The second lever is *context* or the type of environment and external factors where the decision takes place. Context refers both to structural (reporting relationships, monitoring, reward and punishment systems) as well as psychological (time pressure, sense of urgency, stress, anxiety, and risk).

Communication is the third lever and is focused on how people share ideas, thoughts and a dialogue together. It is important to define which information will be exchanged in a structured versus unstructured way. There is also a need to define rules for diverging and converging, as we saw in the conflict management model above.

The fourth lever, *control*, addresses how the leader will control the process and the content of the decision. There are various roles needed in change management and the leader needs to assign these according to the needs at hand and the profiles of the team members.

Influencing

Influence is the art or skill of getting work done indirectly without formal authority. This is an important ability in leaders as many business opportunities are not arranged according to the company's business silos. In fact, most dealers, suppliers, and customers are indifferent to our structure and, if anything, tend to be distracted and at times annoyed by it. For effective leaders, boundary breaking is a key to driving value creation since organisations often have a rich, broad, and diverse portfolio of assets which can be leveraged. HRF can support this effort not only by providing leaders with the means to acquire these skills, but by ensuring the organisation's culture is one of collaboration within divisions and across divisions.

For instance, in launching a new product, in most organisations this process will involve, at a minimum, individuals from engineering, marketing, procurement, and manufacturing. These individuals then need to work together to conceive, design, develop, manufacture, and market the new product.

Influencing then can also be seen as managing laterally in the organisation. The skills, values, and use of time required to develop and maintain lateral relationships are different than those used in vertical relationships. Leading laterally involves building networks based on trust and mutual respect – before you need them (we saw this point earlier), focusing on win-win (common objectives) solutions to achieve a greater goal, a clear understanding the business and the organisation, and being politically savvy to figure out and navigate critical interdependencies (up, down, and around the hierarchy) and to deal successfully with unintended consequences.

Being politically savvy does not have to carry negative connotations. In fact, on the way to the top, those leaders that rely heavily on expertise and not enough on their ability to influence others often find themselves passed over for promotions. In successful situations being politically savvy is a virtuous cycle whereby producing results leads to credibility, confidence, and trust in relationship partners. This increased trust and respect leads to partners being more willing and open to collaborate again and achieve results.

To build the ability to influence, it is important for the leader to identify potential networks, as the network determines the range of resources that can be drawn upon when needed. Therefore, relationships are to be built before they are needed, as by the time you need them, if you do not have them, it will be either too late or too expensive Also, being politically astute means developing goodwill. Since effective relationships are mutual, it is important to invest in the other person (think relationships, not transactions).

A good way to develop this skill in leaders is to help them find ways to volunteer or participate in committees, task forces, etc. A leader can also develop further by participating in external professional and not-for-profit organisations. But mainly, a leader builds trust and confidence based on delivering on promises.

Crucibles of leadership

As we have noted in this chapter, most leadership development starts with a strong understanding of one's self. This is a key aspect of authentic leadership as noted by Goleman as well as an important part of transformational leadership.[33] Improving self-awareness can come with feedback from assessments and 360-degree reviews as well as from coaching and self-reflection. The idea of crucibles of leadership was coined by Bennis and Thomas as they studied how leaders developed.[34] As it turns out, insightful leaders learn important lessons from difficult times in their careers where they were tested or even failed. Through these moments and the reflection of these moments, leaders can emerge with an even stronger set of leadership skills. This testing and learning in leadership has become known as the crucibles of leadership. With the combination of self-awareness, reflection, and testing, strong leaders can emerge with great future success. Organisations are helping their current and future leaders better understand how to learn from their own trials and tests as a leader through self-awareness and reflection to become a stronger leader in the future.[35]

Leaders must know themselves thoroughly before they can hope to lead others. This self-knowledge comes through listening to your inner voice, accepting responsibility for who you are, learning in greater depth than the average person, and reflecting on the unique experiences you have had throughout your life. Mistakes are inevitable, but they, too, contribute to your growth and development.

Warren Bennis

CASE STUDY

Motivating leaders to achieve higher performance levels

Disappointed by the returns it had captured from several recent acquisitions, a leading consumer products company with facilities in more than forty countries launched a new global business strategy intended to move the company toward a truly global manufacturing process and better business results. Realising that its aggressive change agenda depended on improved performance from its leaders, the company wanted to develop a new performance management process that would align its leadership talent with business goals, motivate them to achieve higher performance levels, and hold them accountable for their results.

The company faced a number of challenges in moving its leaders toward higher performance and greater accountability. As a result of its siloed approach towards managing individual business units, the company lacked clarity and consistency in setting performance expectations. Leaders across business units rarely understood how their goals linked to the overall organisational perspective.

Further, the absence of a consistent approach for performance management left the different business units making individualised decisions around performance management. It also meant that there were few consistent links between performance and pay or between performance management and other leadership management processes such as assessment, development, and succession planning.

As a first step, the company developed a globally consistent process for cascading organisational, business, team, and individual business goals. This process, supported by enabling technology, was designed to clearly define the results leaders are expected to contribute to business success and to ensure clear line of sight from the company's business planning process to its talent management processes.

The second step was to develop a competency model that translated the company's business goals into the distinct behaviours required of its leaders and a feedback process with multiple measures to ensure accuracy. Through a collaborative process involving many internal stakeholders, the company identified six differentiating leadership competencies – visionary, inspirational, innovative, decisive, collaborative, and building talent – and three fundamental leadership skills – critical thinking, tenacity, and learning agility – critical to achieving business goals. These competencies serve as the backbone of a multidimensional 360-degree leadership feedback process. Going forward, leaders will be measured on and held accountable for both specific business results and also this set of competencies, which not only provide consistency to the performance management process, but also link together all of the company's talent management programmes.

The third step was to develop a global process for calibrating decisions regarding performance, potential, compensation, and development needs. This was critically important, both because of the company's culture of fairness and to ensure the ultimate effectiveness of the programme. The final step was to ensure that leaders throughout the company had the skill and the will to implement the new performance management process. The company invested significant time and money in training and communication so that leaders would understand the business case for the new process and have the skills to use it.

Since the company launched its new global business plan four years ago, it has hit every milestone, enjoying considerable business success. Senior leaders believe that the performance management process, which clarifies leaders' roles and gives people clear guidance as to what they need to do, has been a key contributor to that success.

The programme has also enabled the company to gain a clear understanding of the capability gaps that exist among leaders – both as a group and individually. Based on this understanding, the company has created an implementation plan for company-wide and leader-specific development to address these gaps.

A leader is best when people barely know he exists, not so good when people obey and acclaim him, worse when they despise him. But of a good leader who talks little when his work is done, his aim fulfilled, they will say: 'We did it ourselves'.

Lao-Tzu

Summary

The basic premise of this chapter is that leadership can be learned and consistently improved. While there are a number of leadership theories and approaches, there are also a number of common elements and steps to developing leaders in organisations today. We reviewed leadership concepts, ways of developing leaders, and several tools and techniques to enhance leadership as a means to improve business results. Which specific model, tool or technique is applied is not as important as the understanding of how leadership affects culture, structure, and policies and using the situational leadership approach to best fit each occasion.

Key questions for consideration:

- *Is the leadership team aligned around future talent priorities?*
- *Does the organisation have the talent to fuel current and future growth opportunities?*
- *Which talent programmes need to be implemented, eliminated or modified?*
- *Is there sufficient leadership bench strength to drive business outcomes in the future?*
- *Have you defined the quality, quantity, location, and cost of your future workforce needs?*
- *Is it clear where to make future talent investments? Can you calculate the return on investment (ROI)?*

FURTHER READING

Bass, B. M., and Bass, R. (2008) *The Bass Handbook of Leadership: Theory, Research, and Managerial Applications.* New York, Free Press.

Cooper, R. K., and Sawaf, A. (1996) *Executive EQ.* New York, Berkley Publishing Group.

George, B. (2007) *True North: Discover Your Authentic Leadership* (Vol. 143). San Francisco, Jossey-Bass.

Harvard Business Review (2011) *HBR's 10 Must Reads: On Change.* Boston, MA, Harvard Business Review.

Northouse, P. G. (2013) *Leadership Theory and Practice.* London, Sage Publications.

Thomas, R. (2008) *Crucibles of Leadership.* Boston, Harvard Business Press.

REFERENCES

[1] Maister, D. H. (1997) *Managing the Professional Service Firm.* New York, Free Press Paperback.

[2] Bennett, M., and Bell, A. (2004) *Leadership and Talent in Asia: How the Best Employers Deliver Extraordinary Performance.* Singapore, John Wiley & Sons (Asia) Pte Ltd.

[3] Hexter, E. S., and Young, M. B. (2011) *Managing Human Capital Risk.* The Conference Board, Inc.

4 Favaro, K., Karlsson, P.-O. and Neilson, G. L. (2010) *CEO Succession 2010: The Four Types of CEOs* [Online] Available from www.booz.com/media/file/BoozCo-CEO-Succession-2010-Four-Types.pdf [Accessed: June 2012].

5 Fiedler, F. E., and Chemers, M. M. (1967) *A Theory of Leadership Effectiveness* (Vol. 111). New York: McGraw-Hill.

6 Burke, W., and Litwin, G. (1992) 'A Causal Model of Organisational Performance and Change', *Journal of Management* 18(3): 523–545.

7 Goldberg, L. R. (1993) 'The Structure of Phenotypic Personality Traits', *American Psychologist* 48(1): 26.

8 Judge, T. A., Bono, J. E., Ilies, R., and Gerhardt, M. W. (2002) 'Personality and Leadership: A Qualitative and Quantitative Review', *Journal of Applied Psychology* 87(4): 765.

9 Goldberg, L. R. (1990) 'An Alternative "Description of Personality": The Big-five Factor Structure', *Journal of Personality and Social Psychology* 59(6): 1216.

10 Bass, B. M., and Bass, R. (2008) *The Bass Handbook of Leadership: Theory, Research, and Managerial Applications.* Free Press.

11 Mumford, M. D., Zaccaro, S. J., Harding, F. D., Jacobs, T. O., and Fleishman, E. A. (2000) 'Leadership Skills for A Changing World: Solving Complex Social Problems', *The Leadership Quarterly* 11(1): 11–35.

12 Blake, R. R., and McCanse, A. A. (1991) *Leadership Dilemmas – Grid Solutions.* Gulf Publishing Company.

13 Maccoby, E. E. (2007) 'Historical Overview of Socialization Research and Theory' In J. E. Grusec, and P. D. Hastings (Eds.), *Handbook of Socialization: Theory and Research* (pp. 13–41). New York, NY, Guilford Press.

14 Hersey, P., and Blanchard, K. H. (1969) 'Life Cycle Theory of Leadership', *Training & Development Journal* 23(5): 26–34.

15 Blanchard, K., Zigarmi, P., and Zigarmi, D. (1999) *Leadership and the One Minute Manager: Increasing Effectiveness Through Situational Leadership.* New York, William Morrow.

16 Bryman, A. (1992) *Charisma and Leadership in Organizations* (p. 198). London, Sage.

17 Hater, J. J., and Bass, B. M. (1988) 'Superiors' Evaluations and Subordinates' Perceptions of Transformational and Transactional Leadership', *Journal of Applied Psychology* 73(4): 695.

18 Greguras, G. J., Daniels, M. A., and Diefendorff, J. M. (2013) *The Overlooked Role of Individual Identity in Transformational Leadership Processes.* Paper presented at the 28th Annual Society for Industrial and Organizational Psychology Meeting, Houston, TX.

19 Sendjaya, S., and Sarros, J. C. (2002) 'Servant Leadership: Its Origin, Development, and Application in Organizations', *Journal of Leadership & Organizational Studies* 9(2): 57–64.

20 Greenleaf, R. K., and Spears, L. C. (2002) *Servant Leadership: A Journey Into The Nature of Legitimate Power and Greatness.* New York, Paulist Pr.

21 George, B., and Bennis, W. (2008) *Authentic Leadership: Rediscovering the Secrets to Creating Lasting Value.* John Wiley and Sons.

22 Avolio, B. J., Avey, J. B., and Quisenberry, D. (2010) 'Estimating Return on Leadership Development Investment', *The Leadership Quarterly* 21(4): 633–644.

23 Conger, J., Mahtre, K. H., and Mercer (2011) *New Insights on Global Leadership Development.* Mercer.

24 Tan, H. H., and Chee, D. (2005) 'Understanding Interpersonal Trust in a Confucian-influenced Society: An Exploratory Study', *International Journal of Cross Cultural Management* 5(2): 197–212.

25 Goleman, D. (2000) *Working with Emotional Intelligence.* New York, Bantam Books.

26 Smart, B. D. (1999) *Topgrading: How Leading Companies Win by Hiring, Coaching, and Keeping the Best People.* Paramus, NJ, Prentice Hall Press.

[27] Wilson, L. (2004) *The Social Styles Handbook: Find Your Comfort Zone and Make People Feel Comfortable With You*. Herentals, Belgium, Nova Vista.

[28] Honey, P., and Mumford, A. (1992) *The Manual of Learning Styles*. Maidenhead, Berks, Peter Honey Publications.

[29] Thomas, K. W., and Kilmann, R. H. (2002) *Thomas-Kilmann Conflict Mode Instrument*. Palo Alto, CA, CPP, Inc.

[30] Bridges, W. (2009) *Managing Transitions: Making the Most of Change*. Philadelphia, Pa, Da Capo Lifelong.

[31] The Inventure Group (1992). *Managing Aftershock*.

[32] Charan, R. (2001) *What the CEO Wants You to Know: How Your Company Really Works*. New York, Crown Business.

[33] Goleman, D., Boyatzis, R. E., and McKee, A. (2002) *The New Leaders: Transforming the Art of Leadership into the Science of Results*. London, Little, Brown.

[34] Thomas, R. J. (2008) *Crucibles of Leadership*. Harvard Business School Publishing Corporation, Boston.

[35] Bennis, W. G., and Thomas, R. J. (2002) *Geeks and Geezers: How Era, Values and Defining Moments Shape Leaders*. Harvard Business Press.

4   Structure

Every company has two organisational structures: the formal one
that is written on the charts; the other is the everyday relationship
of the men and women in the organisation.

Harold S. Greneen

In this chapter we will explore the area of organisation structure. The reporting lines, allocation of activities, and clustering of departments are all ways
of thinking about structure in an organisation. Structure is the form that the
organisation takes in executing processes, decision-making, and working
towards the business strategy.

Of course, there are many types of structures and the topic of how to organise an entity can be complex when considering the variety of factors such as
market orientation, size of firm, types of discipline, nature of work activities,
location of operations, cost profiles, risk factors, regulatory impacts, and the
like. We will review some of the key areas in designing an organisation as well
as the component parts such as jobs and teams.

Organisation design is the process of determining the structure or architecture
of the firm. The goal in organisation design is the creation of a strategy-aligned
operating model and structure at the enterprise, business unit, or function level
that enables the unit or business to run efficiently and effectively as a high-
performing firm.

Over the last several years more attention has been placed on corporate
governance due to the rising complexity of business ownership, global business models, the financial crisis, and changing expectations for board members. It is important to note that governance generally refers to the work of
the board of directors or other governing body of the organisation.[1] Structure

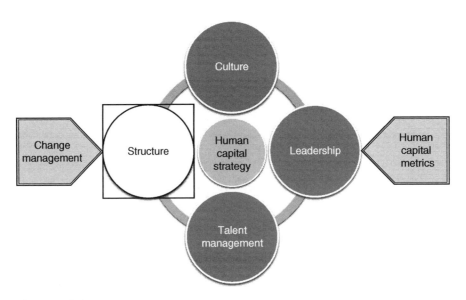

Figure 4.1 Structure
Source: McGee, Thomas and Wilson, Strategy: Analysis and Practice (McGraw-Hill, 2010)

relates to the management of the firm (running the business), not the corporate governance.

A structure that is well aligned with the business strategy helps to facilitate the strategy execution. Imagine a large firm like General Electric (GE) trying to run with a single centralised organisation structure across their many wide-ranging businesses types. The structure would be an impediment to executing on the strategy. Instead, GE runs autonomous business units, which allows decision-making, reporting, and management oriented in a way that creates a market-sensitive structure. In this way, each of the GE business units can aggressively compete in their market segments independently from the rest of the corporation.

In this chapter, we will review types of organisation structure, ways of designing teams, trends in the design of jobs, and also consider some of the informal structures in a firm. Of course, the structure must also fit well with the other elements of the 'human capital strategy' and we will review the potential links between structure and the culture, leadership, and talent components.

Organisation structure and business

Organisation structures in business have evolved over time as the complexity has often increased and needs of business have changed. The industrial revolution introduced the concept of division of labour to increase productivity and allow for mass production. This notion of grouping by functional specialisation gave rise to large firm structures with formal and more mechanistic ways of operating.

Alfred Chandler's work on strategy and structure in the 1960s illustrated the changing nature of large organisations from more of a functional orientation to a multi-divisional orientation.[2] We saw this illustrated by companies such as General Motors, DuPont, and Sears Roebuck in the 1920s and 1930s. This multi-divisional structure created operating units or profit centres that were organised by product, brand, or geography. After the Second World War, the multi-divisional structure spread so much that by 1969 less than 20 per cent of *Fortune 500* companies were not using this type of structure.[3] This type of structure continues to be the most common structure across multinational enterprises today.

The important shift in thinking about structure and organisations came about during this time when researchers realised that structure follows strategy. Companies need to continually adapt to meet the strategy or they will not survive. Thompson noted this in his work on organisation strategy, which has since been the topic of several research studies.[4]

Henry Mintzberg's research and papers on organisation structure in the 1970s and 1980s helped form the modern-day thinking for designing enterprises. His notable and simple 'structure in 5s' approach includes five basic parts of the firm (operating core, strategic apex, middle line, technostructure, and support staff) along with five basic mechanisms of coordination (mutual adjustment, direct supervision, standardisation of work processes, outputs, and skills).[5] During this time, it became more accepted that structure must be considered with other elements for success. McKinsey and Company introduced the '7S model' (structure, systems, style, staff, skills, shared values, and strategy) and helped practitioners consider multiple factors when designing organisations.[6]

Jay Galbraith's work on organisation structure in the 1980s and 1990s provided a basis for linking structures with strategy and organisation planning.[7] His recent work to help meet the needs of leaders to address structures in light of globalisation, customer-centricity, and new business models has furthered the work of organisation design practitioners. Research in the area of structure is continuing to examine the impact of structure on strategy, the use of complexity theory, and the notion of virtual networked organisations.

As we consider the structure of business organisations today, we are faced with a myriad of business complexities with globalisation, new business structures, internet-enabled virtual teams, new employment trends, global strategic alliances, outsourcing, and intertwined ownership structures. As we examine the concepts of structure we will start with a macro-level view, reviewing several considerations in designing structures; and consider the design of teams and jobs, and the informal structures of organisations today.[8]

General organisation structure types

The way a firm is structured is important because it directly impacts on how work gets done and how teams work together to share information and outcomes. The structure of the firm also communicates the strategic emphasis for the business. For example, a company that structures its work and teams around customer segments says to employees that understanding and servicing customers well is of primary importance to achieving business outcomes. In the same way, the personalised attention that customers receive as a result of this structure and behaviour tells the customer that their satisfaction and their success are important to the business.

Another business that believes developing innovative products at a sustained pace is central to its success may structure itself around different product types. In this case, it is less important that employees understand a specific customer segment only, and more important for them to understand how the needs and wants of different customer segments could be considered in a new product. Such decisions and examples highlight the importance of designing a structure alongside the strategy of the business.

One of the primary structure determinants is centralisation versus decentralisation. Centralisation is generally an advantage when tight control is needed from the top with clear accountability. This is common in a start-up or single proprietor operation where the owner or founder makes all the important decisions. A centralised structure can be appropriate when decisions should be made centrally due to the critical phase of the organisation or nature of activities. The disadvantages of the centralised organisation are the potential response time for decision-making, limited level of responsibility and accountability at lower levels, and potential buy-in for the top-down central decisions and direction. The size of the firm will have an impact on the structure as the performance of the firm may be affected if the structure is not managed to the appropriate scale.[9]

A decentralised structure encourages lower-level leaders and employees to take the initiative and make prudent decisions. It can speed response times for taking action while promoting empowerment and involvement of employees in the activities of the business. The drawbacks of decentralisation are that it could create coordination challenges across parts of the business if there are inconsistencies and it could create risk if lower-level leaders make bad decisions. Of course, there are ways to mitigate these risks and it is important to recognise the trade-offs with any structure decision.

Enterprise-level structures

At a macro or enterprise level, organisation structures can be grouped into a few types: functional, holding, multi-divisional, and functional holding. As noted by McGee, Thomas, and Wilson in their overview of business strategy, these basic structures can be compared in terms of centralisation of strategy and decentralisation of operations.[10] Figure 4.2 illustrates the basic concepts.

Functional structures tend to be centralised around the essential elements of the business. This allows for maximum control and efficiency within each function. Of course, the drawbacks of difficult coordination and limited local decision-making can create challenges as the enterprise grows in scale and complexity. Figure 4.3 shows a typical functional structure.

The multi-divisional structure will have strategic functions such as research and development (R&D), finance, and marketing centralised, while other areas operate in a decentralised fashion (operations and sales). This is often the case

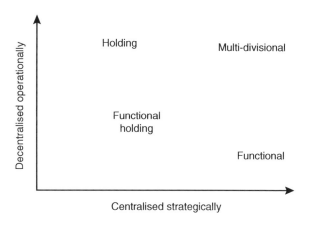

Figure 4.2 Enterprise structural types
Source: adapted from Mcgee, Thomas and Wilson, *Strategy: Analysis and Practice* (McGraw-Hill, 2010)

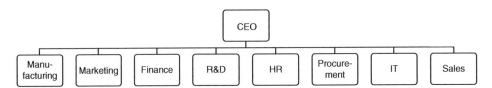

Figure 4.3 Functional organisation structure
Source: based on Apple, Inc.: www.apple.com

with multinational enterprises that allow business units to operate in their industries, yet selected functions remain centralised to either encourage some level of corporate standardisation, take benefits from economies of scale, or utilise scarce resources. Some form of multi-divisional enterprise structure is relatively common in global organisations that wish to have some level of local decision-making while maintaining a level of global standardisation.

Investment or venture capital firms that look to maximise returns with a portfolio of companies typically use the holding company structure. This structure keeps all functions within a business unit to allow easy acquisition and divestiture of companies in the portfolio. Each unit runs in an autonomous manner and the true costs of operation are reflected within each business. While management is not taking advantage of any synergies across businesses, the priority is the ability to run the enterprise as a portfolio of separate companies.

Similarly, the functional holding company structure runs in a primarily decentralised state, but keeps some functions (typically finance) centralised for control. This allows some level of standardisation, management control, and visibility by the enterprise leadership.

While these primary structures may exist at an enterprise level, typically we will see many variations of organisation structure within these four general models. Let us look now at business unit structure varieties. While enterprise and business unit structures are not mutually exclusive, it is important to note that we generally see greater variety of structures within a business unit as each works to shape the structure in a way that fits with business strategy and goals.

Business unit structures

Depending on the nature of the business and the strategy, several organisation designs are possible and even combinations of designs. While an exhaustive review of structure is beyond what we can cover in just one chapter, we will review some of the essential designs and considerations. As with any organisation structure consideration, it is important to start with the business strategy. Of course, it is difficult to address structure in isolation from the other human capital elements. It is important to note that each strategy and structure will have implications on leadership, talent, and culture as well. Here we will review some of the most common organisational unit structures: product leadership, customer intimacy, functional efficiency, matrix management, process efficiency, and project orientation.

- **Product leadership** – if the business intends to compete on a platform of product leadership where the products and services have the latest features and the best performance in the industry, then it will be important to have a structure that fits and supports this strategy. In this case, a structure that allows product engineering and product marketing teams to work together might be important. A strong centralised marketing function with emphasis on brand management may be critical in global reach. Product and account teams may need to work closely together to stay close to the marketplace and current trends to stay ahead in product leadership. Apple Inc. is a good example of a company that competes with product leadership.

CASE STUDY

Blended structure – Apple, Inc.

Apple is using the typical functional enterprise structure, which is organised on the basis of its core functions. Under the CEO's leadership, eight divisions (Figure 4.4) – finance, product marketing, software engineering, design, application, general counsel, operating, and retail – look after their own responsibilities.[11]

As one of the leading electronic devices providers, Apple has core competencies in both innovative products with superior design and performance, and the strong brand recognition through effective marketing strategies. In order to maximise its core competencies, Apple's structure is oriented toward R&D and marketing functions. Through their organisation structure, Apple can expect several benefits that support the strategy. First, Apple can create innovative products more efficiently. If Apple tried to focus on individual processes or projects, it could not expect economies of scale in R&D

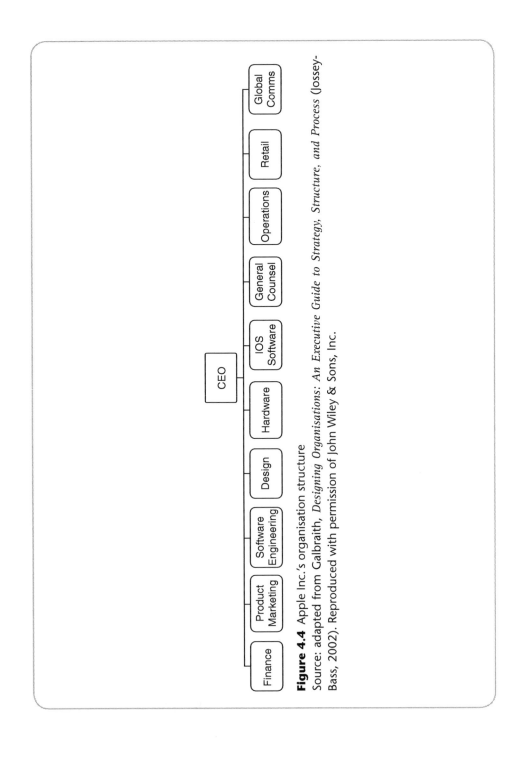

Figure 4.4 Apple Inc.'s organisation structure

Source: adapted from Galbraith, *Designing Organisations: An Executive Guide to Strategy, Structure, and Process* (Jossey-Bass, 2002). Reproduced with permission of John Wiley & Sons, Inc.

and operations. Through the functionally divided divisions of design, software engineering, application, and operation, Apple is able to launch the more evolved products (e.g. evolution from iPod to iPhone) every time.

Secondly, Apple also creates strong brand equity through the company structure. Integrated marketing and retail activities enabled its customers to recognise Apple's identity more easily. Further, consistent marketing strategy created a number of Apple followers who are not likely to switch to competitors if the product leadership continues.

Of course, there are trade-offs with this structure. First, it can cause difficulty in coordination between key functions. Second, functional structure can cause bureaucracy in the organisation. Each function has boundaries that can limit horizontal information flow and hurt the company's overall performance. Finally, the independent financial function can cause inefficiency because it may not clearly understand the necessity of some new or existing projects.

To prevent these types of inefficiency in the functional organisation structure, Apple works aggressively to manage cross-functional communication and has established a culture of collaboration and teamwork. At the same time, Apple is oriented towards customers through an account management structure that allows geographic and segment orientation. This blend of product leadership with customer intimacy creates a powerful combination that fits with the corporate strategy.

- **Customer intimacy** – with a business that has a strategy centred on customer intimacy, it will be important to stay close to customer needs, market insight, and customer relationships. The organisation structure will need to support this with account teams oriented on customers or customer segments, linkage between sales and service teams, and potentially strategic alliances. While there are many potential nuances of this type of structure, we may find that the design starts with the customer (segment, geography, account type, etc.) and how the organisation unit can best stay close to the needs and the relationship.

The increased buyer-power influence in many industries is driving an increase in organisations working to be more 'customer-centric'. Globalisation, partnerships/alliances, increased visibility through the Internet, and more emphasis on solutions is increasing the desire to structure around the customer.[12] An organisation that is structured to be customer-centric would typically have set up separate units that are aligned to different customer types or groups. For example, a mobile device company may create separate teams for large multinational corporations, small businesses, and individual customers. While the products and services are largely the same, the buyer values and customer needs are likely different in both sales as well as service.

This structure is useful if the needs of distinct customer groups are very different, and therefore, the solutions and/or services that cater to such needs are unique. It is also a relevant structure if the expectations of the different customer groups differ. However, customer-centric or customer-intimate organisation does present challenges. As products are positioned separately (and possibly differently) to the various customer groups, this may lead to confusing messages to the consumer. There is also a high chance that there is duplication of effort and, therefore, redundancies in the organisation.

- **Functional efficiency** – a business that is oriented on operational excellence may have goals related to product reliability, competitive prices, and volume distribution. In the case of this strategic intent, it will be important to emphasise operational standards; team accountability for end-to-end process efficiency, and centralised functions that maximise business efficiency and purchasing power. As discussed earlier, an organisation that is structured functionally sets up separate units performing distinct business functions (e.g. sales, manufacturing, and distribution). This structure is particularly suitable when specialised skills are required in one or more functions, when product lines are limited, and there is a stable business environment. This structure is likely to promote expertise within each department for its function, but may create some challenges. A functional-based organisation can tend towards silos, as departments concentrate on doing what they do well, and have limited opportunities to see how their work is interlinked with the work that other departments perform in order to achieve the larger business outcome. A functional-based organisation can also lead to conflicting performance measurements if the key performance indicators (KPI) for each department and individuals within the department do not align with how the organisation as a whole needs to work to achieve business outcomes. Finally, a functional-based company can be inflexible and slow to respond to changing market conditions and customer needs.

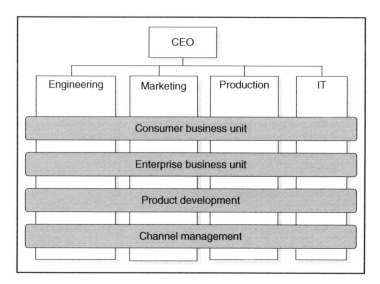

Figure 4.5 Matrix organisation structure
Source: adapted from Galbraith, *Designing Organisations: An Executive Guide to Strategy, Structure, and Process* (Jossey-Bass, 2002)

- **Matrix management** – to counter-balance the challenges with a functional structure, many firms will set up a matrix structure. This is particularly popular in services firms where there might be an organisation based on customer type as well as by function.[13] The matrix structure is common across several multinational enterprises that must take into account several dimensions of business (e.g. product line, geography, function, etc.). This type of structure is needed when strategic factors demand simultaneously strong business units and countries[14], as illustrated by Figure 4.5.
- **Process efficiency** – another model of organising with efficiency, but not necessarily within a function, is a focus on processes. This structure comprises units aligned to specific, market-driven business process outcomes. This structure attempts to break down barriers of the functional organisation, by combining multiple functions into logical customer-impacting processes. This model, reflected in Figure 4.6, is suitable for businesses that are highly customer-driven, and the firm needs to be responsive and flexible such as for call centres or other customer processing centres.
- **Project orientation** – some parts of businesses may operate in project teams in industries such as construction, consulting, or engineering when a project-oriented structure becomes critical. When project teams are put together, clear accountability can be established and decision-making streamlined based on the project scope. This structure allows more flexibility in the use

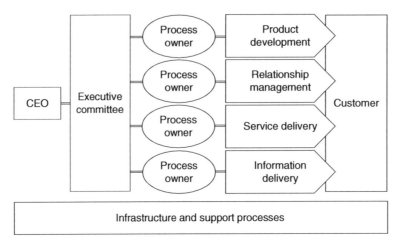

Figure 4.6 Process efficiency structure

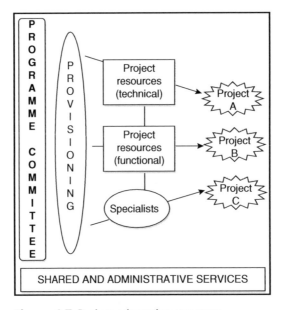

Figure 4.7 Project orientation structure
Source: adapted from Galbraith, *Designing Organisations: An Executive Guide to Strategy, Structure, and Process* (Jossey-Bass, 2002). Reproduced with permission of John Wiley & Sons, Inc.

of human resources and provides an often-needed interface between departments. It has some important impacts on the development and career path management of people, which must be taken into consideration. It can create an increased cost structure as it limits economies of scale while making communication patterns erratic. Yet, this structure, shown in Figure 4.7, fits well with the organisation unit that operates with a strategy centred on projects.

While each of these structure types can be found in an array of different forms in practice, it is important to consider how each fits with the strategy that the business is working towards and to what degree the trade-offs make the chosen structure better or worse than alternatives. Of course, the type of structure does not exist independent from other human capital elements and we must take care to understand the dynamics and considerations.

Structural considerations

With every type of structure, there are trade-offs. Each structure can help bring emphasis in some dimensions, but may result in suboptimal issues such as inefficiencies or reduced coordination. When considering an organisation structure, there are several considerations that should be reviewed such as cross-unit coordination, vertical hierarchy, geographic coverage, spans of control, and sizing.

- **Cross-unit coordination** – structures of many types may lead to silos, as invisible (and visible) boundaries form around groups of individuals who deliver discrete pieces of work. These silos typically lead to some level of internal competition, with a lack of an end-to-end perspective about what the business is, and more importantly, what it takes for the business to succeed. When communication is top-down, collaboration can be difficult to embed as people in different departments can be oriented toward self-interests.

There are also often artificial delineations of responsibilities that can become focused on protecting individual or group interests, rather than on what it takes to achieve an outcome. This may impact on the speed at which decisions can be made, and the accountabilities that people feel for these decisions. These ways of working will continue if insufficient attention is given to breaking down these boundaries and putting in place the necessary processes, infrastructure, and culture for people who work in different departments to interact and work with each other.

To counteract the natural creation of silos or organisational boundaries, many companies work on cultural elements to improve communication and coordination. Certainly the availability of data and communications has helped with the ability to share information and ideas across internal borders in many firms. Many firms are encouraging cross-unit work teams on special projects to help foster a sense of community and collaboration. These actions help bring a balance to any structure that will naturally create potential barriers or silos within the firm.

CASE STUDY

Retail pharmacy coordination

A large retail pharmacy company in the USA grew at a rapid pace through acquisition. The retail stores had two distinct areas, the pharmacy and the over-the-counter retail shop. In the early years of retail pharmacy stores, the pharmacist ran the pharmacy as was required by the US regulations but did not have a role in managing the retail operations. Pharmacists are specially trained with certifications and licences to practise. As a result, the pharmacy manager for a retail store ran that pharmacy and reported to a regional manager who was also a pharmacist, who then reported to the geographic leader who was also a pharmacist. This same structure was then replicated for the retail shop managers.

With the growth of the retail pharmacy business, store sizes and number of locations increased dramatically. As such, the management structures also increased in size. With more than 3,000 stores, this organisation also had more than 300 pharmacy regional managers, 300 retail regional managers, 25 pharmacy area managers, 28 retail area managers, and 3 geographic vice presidents for each who all reported to the chief operating officer.

The traditional structure was creating challenges in communications across the pharmacy and retail boundaries. The pharmacists and retail managers were not working together, goals were not aligned, and the 'two stores within a store' feeling in each location confused customers.

To improve the cross-unit coordination, the leadership team began to align goals between pharmacy and retail operations. They created mutual incentives for each location in total to help support teamwork, and eventually collapsed the management structures to create a more seamless experience for the customers. As a result, the same store sales began to grow as pharmacists took more interest in the retail side of the business and customers became more satisfied with the employee teams who were interested in their needs.

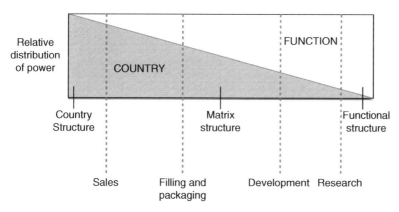

Figure 4.8 Differentiated country-functional structure
Source: adapted from Galbraith, *Designing the Global Corporation* (Jossey-Bass, 2000)

- **Geographic coverage** – the idea of creating silos or borders within an organisation can especially be true when considering geographical boundaries and regions where the physical distance can create silos or islands of independence. As Jay Gailbraith notes in his book, *Designing the Global Corporation*, there are several models that have been evolving over the last decade of rapid globalisation.[15] Often times we will see a differentiated country and functional structure evolve based on what is important to have globally coordinated and what is important to have sensitive to the market. As shown in Figure 4.8, Galbraith notes the relative power changes based on the organisation structure. In a country-based structure, the power lies primarily at a local level while in a functional structure the power in the firm is much less focused on geography. Typically we will find that the sales and distribution functions are driven by the local markets while development and research are driven more centrally from a functional standpoint. While this varies based on industry and organisation type, the tension between geographic and functional power within a firm can create challenges.

Geographic coverage and management continues to be a challenge for many organisations that operate around the world. With real-time data and new modes of communication such as video-conferencing now commonplace, the degree of coordination between locations has been increasing. Of course, in some cases language barriers can be a challenge; however, the interconnection across borders continues to improve as more companies become global in nature.

- **Vertical hierarchy** – during the rise of the multi-divisional firms in the 1960s and 1970s the number of vertical levels in organisations became quite high as companies grew in size and yet kept a tight view on spans of control or number of direct reports. Over the last decades, spawned by economic challenges, many companies have delayered levels of management to create a more streamlined or flat structure.

In a more vertical structure, there is often a very clear chain of command and very clear reporting relationships. Levels of authority and accountability are quite clear at each level of the chain of command. In a top-down driven firm, this can be quite effective in execution of orders from the top. The military organisations typically operate this way to create clear and decisive communications from the top of the hierarchy. In organisations such as this, career paths are generally quite vertical and clear for people, as are the responsibilities.

A flat structure on the other hand relies heavily on empowerment and teamwork. While levels of accountability exist, they can often be blurred as people in the same level work together to made decisions and set direction based on their vantage points. A flat structure requires people to potentially grow in their careers by moving horizontally or through special assignments. This can allow people opportunities to build a broad understanding of the business from various perspectives. A flat organisation can help in handling customer issues more directly, but can cause inconsistencies across the enterprise. With the current trends towards flat structures, additional efforts are often needed to help define career paths and opportunities for people who may be accustomed to the traditional vertical advancement paths.

- **Span of control** – the span of control measures the number of workers who each supervisor manages directly. The word 'directly' warrants emphasis. Imagine the CEO of a company, who has thousands of employees working for him in the company. Although thousands ultimately report to him, his span of control is never likely to be more than twelve to fifteen people.

Until recent years, practitioners believed that the most effective span of control was five or six employees. Today, the trend is double these numbers.[16] This increase in span of control is due to multiple factors: improved communications, information systems, empowerment, and fewer layers of management. What happens if companies have smaller or greater spans of control? It appears that companies with spans of control less than six are saddled with a heavy cost structure and inefficiency. Likewise when spans of control are quite large, the performance of the organisation could be at risk.

There is no magic number for the 'best' span of control. The right span of control for an organisation is largely driven by the nature of the work, and the nature of the direct reports. The maturity of the team, the competencies of the employees in the team, and therefore, the level of autonomy and independent work that team members can perform directly impacts the number of direct reports that a supervisor can effectively manage. Work that is more complex would generally require smaller numbers of direct reports as the supervisor is required to provide more guidance depending on the use and practice with knowledge management systems and processes.[17]

- **Organisation sizing** – depending on the nature of the organisation, some type of capacity planning may be used to determine the size of departments or units. The detailed calculation of full-time equivalents (FTEs) required for each job typically follows after there is sufficient level of clarity about what work needs to get done and how this work will be divided among roles and jobs. This can be a critical factor in budgeting and planning. Yet, few companies outside the manufacturing sector fully engage in the practice of organisation sizing.[18]

Sizing depends on the business, industry, and geography. At the most basic level, sizing answers the question: 'How much work needs to be done and how many people are required to do it?' The data required as input for capacity planning typically includes the design of the roles and jobs, the estimated volume of transactions or work over time, and current estimates of production throughput. This can be true in manufacturing as well as service functions. The data for transaction volume and time to complete can be collated in different ways – through activity-based studies, extraction of data from IT systems, or surveys of people who perform these activities.

When considering the time available for work, managers should think about the expectations that each firm (or country) has about the length of the working day, the number of working days in a month, the vacation entitlements, as well as seasonality of the business (and social) cycle. Another factor is culture. This is uniquely company specific, and refers to the 'downtime' that is often associated with business activities that do not directly drive output. Examples of such business activities include continuous improvement meetings, internal communications, and organisation events. This is applied as a percentage to decrease the available time for work. A quick way to arrive at the right culture factor loading is to ask managers how much time they want someone to spend doing the task in a day, and what are the other things outside the transactional aspects of the job that they want people to do.

All the practices above would impact sizing, and some of these practices may need to be addressed by senior decision-makers of the business if the headcount outputs will be compromised. Once an FTE number is determined, it must be rationalised for the expectations and potential changes that may be coming in the organisation. The FTE number may be an end-state workforce number, but more effort may be needed for learning and stabilisation as the firm transitions to new ways of working. Many businesses will create flexibility in their workforce size by using contingent workforce (e.g. contractors or temporary workers). This will allow flexibility in addressing the variations that come with business cycles and volatility.

Team design

Teams are usually built around work that needs to be completed. Each team member fulfils their individual role that contributes to the larger team outcome. This is the interdependence of task responsibilities. An individual may complete his assigned task successfully, but if this is not aligned with where the team is headed and what the team needs to accomplish, then the individual is still not successful. Teams also often have an interdependence of decision-making.[19] Each decision that is made in the team has an impact on everyone in the team, and therefore, each person needs to understand and appreciate how everyone is connected, and how decisions impact downstream and upstream activities.

There are several types of organisational teams, and yet practitioners often neglect the importance of designing the team.[20] Too often, team members are left to determine what type of structure makes sense given their goals – or simply become less effective due to the misalignment of desired outcomes versus the team structure. As a result a newly formed team typically goes through an evolution from the early formation to an eventual model that makes sense for the work. While maximising team performance with the best design and dynamics is a broad topic, we will cover three types of team design that are commonly used in practice in businesses today.

Manager-led teams – these groups are relatively common as managers look for ways to create a sense of teamwork within a department while also maintaining control over processes and outcomes. In this case, the team members have responsibility for the execution of work activities while the leader will generally monitor progress, help address issues, and make decisions.[21] This type of team is common in hierarchical organisations or with managers who simply wish to gather their direct reports into a team-like structure.

Self-directed teams – in this case, the team takes control of decisions such as the allocation of tasks, the monitoring of performance, routine decision-making, and external interfaces. A leader will help coach the team and address issues that extend beyond the team's parameters. Project teams can often operate in this structure when groups are set up to address an organisational challenge. Task force teams, cross-functional teams, or other ad-hoc groups that have a clear purpose and some level of autonomy to accomplish a specific goal are examples of this type of team.

Self-managing teams – these groups are accountable for their work, generally share in a common team incentive, and have authority to design the structure and working arrangement of the team and the interfaces within the firm. The team can also decide on membership, overall plans, and needs for the success of the team. Self-managing teams have been successfully used in manufacturing settings and in service settings; however, there has not been widespread use of self-managed teams due to the need for formal authority-level identification and accountability limitations required in many companies.

Katzenbach and Smith brought new light to the topic of high-performing teams in their research on teams and teamwork.[22] They point out that, while teams and teamwork have become commonplace in many organisations, very few teams actually achieve a high level of performance. Their review of teams showed that firms with strong performance standards create more effective teams than firms that promote teamwork. In other words, only focusing on the idea of being a team and fostering teamwork is not sufficient for actually creating team results.

As discussed earlier, team structures are an effective way of working across organisational boundaries. Cross-functional teams for the review of programmes and solving complex issues are common in many high-performing enterprises. While there is a widespread belief in the power of the team as the collective knowledge and ability of a team is greater than that of an individual, there is sometimes a reluctance to fully utilise teams as they can be a threat to managers, create a level of uncertainty, or be inconsistent with the individual performance measurement.

When designing a team, it is important to consider both the context and the composition for the team. Architects of teams should consider both the case and surrounding context for the team as well as the internal composition and workings of the group.

Example considerations for the context of the team:

- **Management support and commitment** – *do leaders support people spending time as a team versus other priorities in the organisation? How have the leaders demonstrated their commitment?*
- **Sufficiency of resources** – *will the team members have the information, time, budget, and tools to perform what is expected?*
- **Team authority** – *can the team execute the plans with the current levels of authority?* (This is especially important when working across functions.)
- **Clarity of outcomes** – *what is the goal or what are the outcomes expected with this team?*
- **Need for change** – *is there a sense of urgency for the outcomes for this team and a genuine need for the investment in this team?*

Example considerations for the composition of the team:

- **Expertise and skills** – *what skills are needed and can we populate this team with the right competencies and experience to achieve the results?*
- **Preference for teamwork** – *how do we select members who would be effective in working together as a team?*
- **Diversity** – *how do we ensure we have the diversity of team members to help optimise team results?*
- **Team size** – *how can we design the team with an optimum size for collaboration and team management?*
- **Training** – *what development and orientation will be required for the team to get started?*
- **Complexity and expectations** – *how should the team be structured, given the complexity and level of expectations of the output?*

Of course, designing the team structure is just one element in making teams effective. Team dynamics, external factors, and personality challenges must all be managed to make the team arrangement a high-performing experience. With more attention to the design of team structures, more business teams will be set for success before they get started.

Job design

Job design is the art of creating job families and differentiating jobs based on the type of work done and the capabilities required for success. Effective job design is needed to classify and categorise jobs to ensure process tasks and responsibilities have been well assigned. Generally, a job is considered a collection of responsibilities or roles that have been grouped together.

A role represents one specific aspect of an individual's contribution to the business process (scheduler, designer, etc.). We typically classify roles by competencies and/or complexities as we will cover in Chapter 5 on talent management. An individual may perform multiple roles; hence a role can be one of the several responsibilities of a jobholder. A job represents the entirety of the jobholder's participation in the business process (technician, expediter, area manager, etc.).

Early studies on job design came from an engineering perspective with the focus on scientific principles such as task breakdown, logical sequencing for efficiency, and work simplicity. While this approach became popular in many manufacturing settings, it often lacked the human elements of individual needs, recognition, and growth.

Hackman and Oldham developed a job characteristics approach based on their research finding which linked job satisfaction and several key characteristics.[23] These include skill variety (utilise skills and develop new skills), task identity (identifiable work is completed), task significance (perceived importance of the job), autonomy (degree of independence), and feedback (acknowledgement or recognition).[24]

Generally accepted job design strategies include job simplification, job enlargement, job enrichment, and job specialisation. Efforts in job design are moving away from job simplification to job enlargement. Through job enlargement, companies are able to provide greater opportunities for fulfilling work by expanding the variety of activities that an individual is able to experience in the job. Job design that is heavily career-centred in building specialist skills may stifle an employee's opportunity to learn transferable skills from outside their chosen trade that would improve their performance.

There are many factors to consider when designing jobs, as noted in Table 4.1. By centring on outcomes and performance measures, many firms are linking jobs not only with processes in the firm, but also with performance outcomes. A clear cascading set of measures from enterprise goals down to each unit, team, and job can be a powerful tool in aligning the organisation for optimum performance. While these factors continue to be important in the design of work, new insights based on the globalisation of manufacturing and use of specialised skill centres continue to evolve in today's work environment.[8]

Table 4.1 Job design strategies

Strategy	Approach	Application	Result
Job simplification	Break a work process down to the task level and assign small components of the process to individual members	• Workforces have low competencies • The organisation provides limited training • When organisations have increased the level of automation in the work environment • When organisations have increased the number of repetitive tasks contained within a process	• Allows jobholders to develop expertise • Repetitive and less challenging work
Job enlargement	Increase the number and variety of tasks assigned to a given position	• Used where there are few exchanges between/within organisational units in a process flow • When organisations invest substantially in training and retraining	• Reduces the boredom factor • Increases the meaningfulness of work
Job enrichment	Expand employee involvement in decision-making, specifically in vertical processes such as resource allocation, controls and rewards	• Used when organisational changes have increased the autonomy required for one or more organisation units • Used when organisational changes have increased the flexibility of the culture of an organisation or its units • When organisations invest substantially in training and retraining	• Increases motivation through a sense of ownership of own and organisation performance • Increases motivation by expanding career opportunities through increased leadership skills and decision-making

Job specialisation	Narrow the focus of employee tasks to enable a deeper, specialised area of expertise	• Used when an opportunity exists to build specialised skills or is required as a result of segregation of duties • When organisations see the possibility of economies of skill for specialised roles/skills	• Allows jobholders to utilise their deep expertise • Allows organisations to focus skills • Deeper and more specialised work

Evaluating organisation structures

Organisation design is an iterative process and must continually be reviewed in light of evolving business challenges. There is no single 'right' structure that will continue to take a business through changing social and economic environment. The structure must not be considered in isolation from the business strategy as the form of the organisation follows the function or plans of the business.[25]

As business strategies change, so do structures. When changing organisation structures, people can become anxious due to the potential for change in status or perceived loss of power. It is important to employ solid change management approaches when making this type of change. Organisation structure must also be closely linked with the other elements of human capital strategy. The culture, leadership, and talent of the firm will have an impact on how effective the structure operates in achieving the business strategy.

Goold and Campbell outlined several questions to consider when evaluating the effectiveness of an organisation structure.[26]

- *Does the design address and help maintain sources of competitive advantage in the markets in which the business operates?*
- *Have the strengths, weaknesses, and motivations of the firm's people been considered in designing the organisation?*
- *Have constraints to the implementation of the organisation design, such as culture, leadership, and local capabilities, been taken into account?*
- *Does the design identify and protect units that require specialist subcultures?*

- *Has consideration been given to aligning business units that have historically been difficult to coordinate?*
- *Are the number of parent levels and units optimised to ensure that processes can be executed efficiently?*
- *Does the architecture help the corporate parent add value to the organisation?*
- *Have effective governance and internal controls been put in place?*
- *Does the design facilitate the development of new strategies and provide the flexibility required to adapt to a changing economic context?*

Of course, it can be difficult to evaluate a structure in isolation, but it is important to continually review and adjust the organisation structure in a way that fits the current and future needs of the company.

The organisation network

While there has always been an understanding that firms operate both within the structure as well as through informal mechanisms, this has often been difficult to capture and understand. With the age of social networking and advances in understanding social networks within organisations, new tools and methods are now available for understanding the informal structure of a company. While network analysis is not new, the tools and analytics have now allowed theory and general understanding to be put into practice in companies. In his work on social networks, Rob Cross outlines simple tools and approaches for practitioners to analyse the informal networks within an organisation.[27] Social networks have been found to be a useful mobilising factor in making organisation designs work most effectively, especially in complex global matrix structures. As shown in Figure 4.9, a network analysis looks much different from an organisation chart as it can actually identify who is connected and communicates in the firm, regardless of affiliation or departmental lines.

By understanding the organisation network, organisation architects can better understand where there might be opportunities to improve collaboration, address areas that could improve affiliation, and point out strengths in operational coordination. New research studies show that the social network can impact trust and relationships.[28] As research and analytical data become more prevalent in this area, we expect to see new ways of working and perhaps structuring work based on organisational networks.

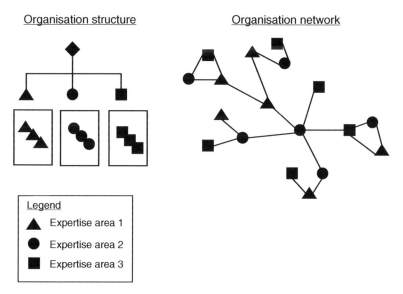

Figure 4.9 Organisation network diagram

Summary

Structure is a critical part of human capital strategy as it provides clarity on how the firm will execute against the business plans. The clustering of groups, alignment of responsibilities, and formalising of jobs and teams are an important signal to the organisation about what is valued and expected in the formal sense of the company.

While there are many types of firm structures, many large organisations use several types of structure in different parts of the business. We may see process-based teams in call centres, project teams in engineering, and a matrix structure in R&D. As we noted, centralisation plays an important part in determining the enterprise architecture as well as the design of business units. Various models of reporting such as matrix, process, and project can all support the organisational operating model in the right situation.

The design of teams and jobs is often an afterthought in some businesses, yet comprises a powerful part of the organisation that helps shape the employee experience. Developing a cascaded organisation design where the teams and jobs are in alignment with organisation unit goals and objectives can result in a powerful architecture.

In the future, we expect to see more networked organisations and designs that incorporate the natural networks within and between companies and communities.[29] New models of organising work may help incorporate risk management, healthy lifestyles, and global networks which will likely continue to evolve.[30] As analytic data and research become more advanced, new types of organisation models may emerge.

Key questions for consideration

- *Given the business strategy, what implications are there for the organisation structure?*
- *How do the customers experience the structure of the organisation?*
- *In what ways does the organisation structure facilitate growth and expansion?*
- *How does the organisation foster collaboration and innovation?*
- *What are the mechanisms in the organisation that help overcome boundary silos?*
- *How does the company set up and design teams?*
- *Is it clear how teams are measured and aligned to goals?*
- *What job design strategies are employed across the organisation?*
- *How do the job designs fit with the organisation culture?*
- *When do top leaders review the effectiveness of the organisation structure?*

FURTHER READING

Galbraith, J. R. (2001) *Designing Organisations: An Executive Guide to Strategy, Structure and Process.* San Francisco, John Wiley & Sons.

Katzenbach, J. R., and Smith, D. K. (1993) *The Wisdom of Teams: Creating the High-Performance Organisation.* Boston, Mass, Harvard Business School Press.

Mintzberg, H. (1993) *Structure in Fives: Designing Effective Organisations.* Englewood Cliffs, Prentice Hall.

Tricker, R. I. (2009) *Corporate Governance: Principles, Policies, and Practices.* Oxford, Oxford University Press.

REFERENCES

[1] Tricker, R. I. (2012) *Corporate Governance: Principles, Policies and Practices.* Oxford, Oxford University Press.

[2] Chandler, A. D. (1962) *Strategy and Structure: Chapters in the History of the American Industrial Enterprise.* Cambridge, MA, Massachusetts Institute of Technology.

[3] Hill, C. W. L. (1994). *Diversification and Economic Performance: Bringing Structure and Corporate Management Back into the Picture.* Cambridge, MA, Massachusetts Institute of Technology.

[4] Thompson, J. D. (1967) *Organizations in Action: Social Science Bases of Administrative Theory.* New York, McGraw-Hill.

[5] Mintzberg, H. (1993) *Structure in Fives: Designing Effective Organizations.* Englewood Cliffs, NJ, Prentice Hall.

[6] Waterman, R. H. (1982) 'The Seven Elements of Strategic Fit', *Journal of Business Strategy* 3: 167–185.

[7] Galbraith, J. R. (1995) *Designing Organizations: An Executive Briefing on Strategy, Structure, and Process.* San Francisco, Jossey-Bass Publishers.

[8] Grant, A. M., and Parker, S. K. (2009) '7 Redesigning Work Design Theories: The Rise of Relational and Proactive Perspectives', *Academy of Management Annals* 3(1): 317–375.

[9] Gooding, R. Z., and Wagner III, J. A. (1985) 'A Meta-analytic Review of the Relationship Between Size and Performance: The Productivity and Efficiency of Organizations and Their Subunits', *Administrative Science Quarterly* 30(4): 462–481.

[10] McGee, J., Thomas, H., and Wilson, D. (2010) *Strategy: Analysis and Practice.* Maidenhead, Berkshire, McGraw-Hill Higher Education.

[11] Apple, Inc. (2012) *Organization Chart* [Online] Available from: www.apple.com [Accessed: June 2012].

[12] Galbraith, J. R. (2005) *Designing the Customer-Centric Organisation: A Guide to Strategy, Structure, and Process.* San Francisco, Jossey-Bass.

[13] Burns, L. R., and Wholey, D. R. (1993) 'Adoption and Abandonment of Matrix Management Programs: Effects of Organizational Characteristics and Interorganisational Networks', *Academy of Management Journal* 36(1): 106–138.

[14] Galbraith, J. R. (2002) *Designing Organizations: An Executive Guide to Strategy, Structure, and Process.* San Francisco, Jossey-Bass.

[15] Galbraith, J. R. (2000) *Designing the Global Corporation.* San Francisco, Jossey-Bass.

[16] Dalton, D. R., Todor, W. D., Spendolini, M. J., Fielding, G. J., and Porter, L. W. (1980) 'Organizational Structure and Performance: A Critical Review', *Academy of Management Review* 5(1): 49–64.

[17] Myers, P. S. (1996) *Knowledge Management and Organizational Design.* Routledge.

[18] Johnson, G. L., and Brown, J. (2004) 'Workforce Planning Not a Common Practice', *Public Personnel Management Volume* 33(4): 379–388.

[19] Medsker, G. J., and Campion, M. A. (2007) 'Job and Team Design'. In Salvendy, G. (ed.) *Handbook of Industrial Engineering: Technology and Operations Management.* John Wiley & Sons, Inc., Hoboken, NJ.

[20] Morgeson, F. P., and Humphrey, S. E. (2008) 'Job and Team Design: Toward a More Integrative Conceptualization of Work Design', *Personnel and Human Resources Management* 27: 39–91.

[21] Guzzo, R. A., and Dickson, M. W. (1996) 'Teams in Organizations: Recent Research on Performance and Effectiveness', *Annual Review of Psychology* 47: 307–338.

[22] Katzenbach, J. R., and Smith, D. K. (1993) 'The Discipline of Teams', *Harvard Business Review* 71(2): 111–120.

[23] Oldham, G. R., and Hackman, J. R. (2010) 'Not What It Was and Not What It Will Be: The Future of Job Design Research', *Journal of Organizational Behavior* 31(2–3): 463–479.

[24] Hackman, J. R., and Oldham, G. R. (1976) 'Motivation Through the Design of Work: Test of A Theory', *Organizational Behavior and Human Performance* 16(2): 250–279.

[25] Child, J., and McGrath, R. G. (2001) 'Organizations Unfettered: Organizational Form in an Information-intensive Economy', *Academy of Management Journal* 44(6): 1135–1148.

[26] Goold, M., and Campbell, A. (2002) 'Do You Have a Well-Designed Organisation', *Harvard Business Review* 80(2): 117–124.

[27] Cross, R. L., and Thomas, R. J. (2009) *Driving Results Through Social Networks: How Top Organizations Leverage Networks for Performance and Growth*. San Francisco, CA, Jossey-Bass.

[28] Ferrin, D. L., Dirks, K. T., and Shah, P. P. (2006) 'Direct and Indirect Effects of Third-party Relationships on Interpersonal Trust', *Journal of Applied Psychology* 91(4): 870.

[29] Gulati, R., Puranam, P., and Tushman, M. (2012) 'Meta-organization Design: Rethinking Design in Interorganizational and Community Contexts', *Strategic Management Journal* 33(6): 571–586.

[30] Parker, S. K., Wall, T. D., and Cordery, J. L. (2001) 'Future Work Design Research and Practice: Towards an Elaborated Model of Work Design', *Journal of Occupational and Organizational Psychology* 74(4): 413–440.

5 Talent management

If you want a year of prosperity grow wheat, if you want 10 years
of prosperity grow trees, if you want 100 years of prosperity grow
people.

Old Chinese proverb

Introduction

Talent is a key ingredient for most organisations today, yet there is much room
for improvement in the way that companies manage their talent. In fact, it
could well be that retaining talent is harder than retaining clients. According
to a recent Conference Board Inc. research in the US, human capital risk ranks
fourth out of eleven risks in terms of potential business impact.[1] When The
Economist Intelligence Unit asked risk managers to rank thirteen key risks,
human capital topped the list.[2] Effective human capital may become the single
most important driver of long-term financial success and shareholder value
creation.

When human resources professionals were asked how effective they were
at addressing critical talent issues, the number of 'very confident' responses
was only in the 20 to 30 per cent range.[3] Another survey found that approximately 50 per cent of organisations do not have a talent strategy.[4] On the other
hand, organisations with superior talent management practices have realised
significant advantages including 26 per cent higher revenue per employee,
41 per cent lower turnover among high performers, 17 per cent lower voluntary turnover, as well as having a 156 per cent greater ability to develop great
leaders.[5]

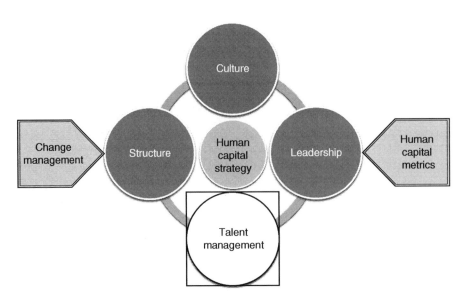

Figure 5.1 Talent management

Let us look, for instance, at the case of the Panama Canal. In 1999, the canal came under the control of the Panamanian government. When it took over the canal, there were several immediate changes. The first was a shift in strategy: whereas before the Panamanians received rent from the USA, it had to shift its sights to one of maximising profitability. To the latter point, early on, the canal started the process of investing in additional capacity to ease the passage of today's mega-tankers. Its initial investment plan was for a project to expand capacity (the third lock). Another additional immediate change was that the transfer of the Canal to Panama was done in part by a law passed by the Panamanian Congress. Among other things, the law permits only Panamanian citizens to be employed by the canal.

In order to traverse the canal, a vessel must allow a Panama Canal Captain to take command of the ship from one end of the canal to the other. The canal trains its captains on canal waters and it takes seven years to train an individual to become a captain. It became readily apparent that the expansion plan had to be tempered by the seven years it takes to train captains as the canal could, by law, only employ Panamanians and thus perforce had to build its talent!

Leaders understand the need to continually focus on talent. In fact, economic intangibles, such as organisational capabilities, can sometimes represent up to 50 per cent of the market value of the modern company.[6] Yet, in practice, when the economy is good, companies tend to invest in talent programmes and in training and developing their people. But when the economy goes into a down cycle they hold back investments in people as they focus on cost-cutting and reductions. This is a short-sighted approach. Since talent is a long-term company asset it stands to reason that it should be managed under a long-term strategy. The shift in focus through economic cycles can be counter-productive.

Talent development is a long-term proposition which requires a systemic approach and a sustainable set of interrelated practices. A sustainable approach is one which balances employee engagement with company results. The ultimate objective of talent management is to have an engaged workforce that is motivated and capable to achieve the organisation's goals.[7] It means gaining better insights into what drives and motivates each segment of the workforce and then testing existing policies and culture to see how well they address these drivers.

This is not an easy task given today's geographically and generationally diverse workforces. Take a look, for instance, at Table 5.1, where the top five drivers of engagement are shown to differ by country.[8] Note that the same study shows difference in drivers by gender as well as by age. To create sustainability also requires having the right tools, processes, and HR support to deliver 'best-fit' solutions to various groups within the organisation.

In this chapter we will focus on the fundamental strategies for managing talent including selection, development, performance management, and rewards. While each of these topics deserves more attention, we will provide some highlights that become critical in the overall human capital strategy.

Talent and workforce planning

To deliver business results through people, many leaders will view the organisation's workforce as a portfolio of talent, with different parts of the portfolio requiring different levels and types of investment. The 'portfolio' or segment view of talent is gaining in popularity as it allows for organisations to better allocate scarce resources, redistribute benefits to the key segments, and align investment to sources of value.

However, most talent practices in a company start with a focus on a 'new' programme, like performance management or succession planning. The 'results' are given in the context of the specific programme in isolation ('*the programme was rolled out in time*' or '*we trained all our new managers*') and, when results are not achieved, they look at the programme or practice versus the issues that

Table 5.1 Top five drivers of employee engagement by selected countries

Rank	1	2	3	4	5
Australia	Base pay	Type of work	Flexible work schedule	Working for a respectable organisation	Bonus or other incentives
Brazil	Career advancement	Base pay	Training opportunities	Working for a respectable organisation	Type of work
China	Career advancement	Base pay	Supplemental retirement savings plan	Training opportunities	Bonus or other incentives
Germany	Base pay	Type of work	Bonus or other incentives	Flexible work schedule	Working for a respectable organisation
India	Career advancement	Base pay	Training opportunities	Type of work	Working for a respectable organisation
Mexico	Base pay	Career advancement	Training opportunities	Bonus or other incentives	Retirement savings or pension plan
Netherland	Base pay	Type of work	Retirement savings or pension plan	Working for a respectable organisation	Paid time off
Spain	Base pay	Type of work	Flexible work schedule	Training opportunities	Career advancement
UK	Base pay	Type of work	Bonus or other incentives	Retirement savings or pension plan	Flexible work schedule
USA	Base pay	Retirement savings or pension plan	Type of work	Low health care costs	Bonus or other incentives

Source: Mercer Survey, What's Working™ (Mercer, 2011)

may exist within the workforce. This non-systemic approach is unlikely to deliver results. A more effective way is to start with identifying (segmenting) the unique employee populations that are critical to success, determining the size of the gaps that need to be filled, and then targeting investments on the specific segments or practices that require it.

Talent issues are often driven by a gap in the workforce that is due to a size, performance, engagement, or capability gap, or a combination of two or more of these. Therefore, investments need to be targeted to solve these gaps. A gap in size relates to whether more or fewer people are needed in the role going forward based on different revenue and growth assumptions. A performance gap examines whether the people in the role are focusing on the right things and performing at a high enough level. An engagement gap is about whether more discretionary effort, more retention or more commitment from the role are needed. It also addresses attraction and retention issues. A capability gap investigates whether the people in the role need more, deeper or different capabilities to meet future business needs.

Segmenting employees in this way and reviewing gaps against each critical segment provides a level of specificity needed to take action. For example, a manufacturing company recently completed a workforce planning exercise where they projected future business growth and compared it against expected turnover and hiring rates. They determined they needed to hire 5,000 new employees over the next five years. Just knowing this was not enough to drive actions, and thus they got very specific in terms of which jobs/skills were expected to experience shortages, and in which specific locations they should place people based on customer demand and labour force availability.

Another organisation trying to improve the talent in a unit assumed the issue was a lack of training and spent hundreds of thousands of dollars on designing and delivering a new training curriculum. When after a year performance had not improved, they took a deeper dive and were able to determine that skill levels within the unit were already quite high. Their issue was that managers were not setting adequate performance standards.

In the distribution of outcomes achieved by talent management efforts from different organisations, there is a wide range of results from the very high to the very low.[9] Yet when evaluating the distribution of practices, there is a relatively small variation in what organisations actually do. In fact, most companies' talent programmes are fairly similar. There are relatively few truly unique or different practices. So the idea of driving higher levels of performance by benchmarking and adopting more and more 'best practices' may be a fallacy.

Alignment of talent management practices is important for driving consistent messages and practices with employees. The correct alignment of different talent initiatives is critical to ensuring that employees are productive and successful. If you implement a performance-differentiated rewards programme with highly differentiated performance driving all pay levers, and alongside it a career deployment programme that incorporates stretch assignments and experiential development, the two counteract each other and, as a result, few of your employees are going to take stretch roles or assignments for fear of losing their performance-related rewards. These two are pulling against each other and will cause major issues for your organisation. On the other hand, if an organisation implemented a roles and competencies programme with tightly defined roles and narrow competencies scoped alongside a capabilities development programme that focuses on training based on the specific roles that you have defined, then these two should work well together.

The human resources function cannot change talent management within an organisation alone. Talent management is an essential part of leading an organisation. HR helps to shape the leaders, and it is the leaders who change the organisation. Managing talent needs to become a skill and an accountability shared by leaders at all levels. To do this, leaders need three things: accountability for talent across the organisation, a shared mindset, and the right capabilities.

If there is no accountability for talent, there is no talent management. Accountability needs to go beyond process compliance – it is not the accountability to follow the process or complete the forms or participate in the talent review. It is the accountability to manage the talent, to grow the assets, to make the tough but right decisions on who to promote, who to move out, and who should lead which efforts.[10]

Leaders must participate in and manage the talent processes. But to do so effectively, they must learn how to make better decisions about talent. Leaders must be proficient at using talent data, such as assessments or feedback. They must also know what to look for in making a promotion, how to build development into a person's daily job, how to set stretch goals, and how to weigh a missed stretch goal versus a met non-stretch goal. Talent decisions are informed by data but involve a considerable amount of judgement, which can be learned via leadership development programmes (covered in Chapter 3) and experience. Having the right governance by establishing the right policies, decision-making guidelines, and an environment where formal and informal feedback on whether individuals have made good talent decisions is a key tenet of talent management.

A frequent challenge when considering the need for talent is the question of whether to 'build' or to 'buy' future talent. In other words, is the right approach to always build from within? Or should the organisation go out to the market to buy the talent it needs when it needs it? There are proponents on both sides of this argument. One very successful company which practises 'build' is Procter & Gamble (P&G).[11] As a rule, P&G only hires employees at entry-level positions and grooms them from the selection process all through their career. Such a practice demands high alignment among the talent programmes in order to select those individuals with a higher probability of success, develop them for many years from day one, retain the ones most likely to perform well and climb up the hierarchy, and engage them along the way.

There are other organisations much more prone to buy talent when needed or available. Service organisations and investment banks in general are notorious for this practice. As business improves or revenue-generating talent becomes available, they buy the talent. Conversely, they are generally quicker to discard this talent when results turn sour.

Many organisations in turn opt to build *and* buy. Ideally, such a practice would involve building the most promising and productive talent and buying talent opportunistically or to close an existing immediate gap. The leaders of these organisations often actually prefer the idea of periodically 'bringing new blood with fresh ideas' into the fold. However, in order to do so, it is important to be able to identify the 'most promising' and the 'most productive' employees. It is also important to identify the critical roles in the organisation, the ones that must always be filled with the right people. In Pepsi Co. or Coca Cola, a key role is that of the people who know 'the formula', and go to the various plants around the world in order to mix the ingredients. In other consumer goods companies, a key role is the person that takes the input from marketing focus groups and translates it into product design and characteristics that can be manufactured by the factory and sold by the sales force. We will address these questions below.

Let us have a closer look at the three major groups of talent management processes: recruitment and selection of talent; training and development of the workforce; and performance management and rewards.

Creating a 'best-fit' talent strategy to close skills gaps

Faced with a serious succession issue and a lack of technical skills in the external market, this critical business division within a large utility company in Greater China was facing severe talent management issues which were directly impacting its business viability. Maintaining high levels of service was dependent on staffing projects with the right calibre of technical capability as well as maturity of experience. Both of these were in short supply, internally and externally.

Three factors contributed to this unsustainable situation:

1. An aging population and retiring senior technical staff made succession management a significant business continuity risk.
2. The pace of progression and promotion offered was too slow for a younger workforce compared with talent competitors.
3. An improving business environment had also created an additional demand for talent and numerous competitors in the labour market – including the government – which offered better pay.

The division realised it needed to establish a talent strategy to deliver the right capability, at the right time, in sufficient quantity to support its business objectives both in the short term and longer term. Most importantly, it realised that a unique talent strategy was needed to address the challenges specific to this division, as opposed to a generic, company-wide strategy. This unique strategy was required to define how the division would build the bench strength to meet business needs and staff its projects, including sourcing the right talent into the division, training employees to develop the right skill sets, developing a career path to groom technical talent from within, and building leaders to manage the division in the future. The division also identified the need to create an attractive employment deal to attract and retain the right talent, including creating a total rewards offer of pay, benefits and careers, offering employees opportunities to grow, and actively communicating an attractive employment proposition to target employees.

Through a rigorous process, this division developed a comprehensive talent strategy to address its unique challenges while still working within the parameters of the wider corporate HR policies. The talent strategy, rooted in the division's business objectives and key success factors, focused on four core areas illustrated by Figure 5.2.

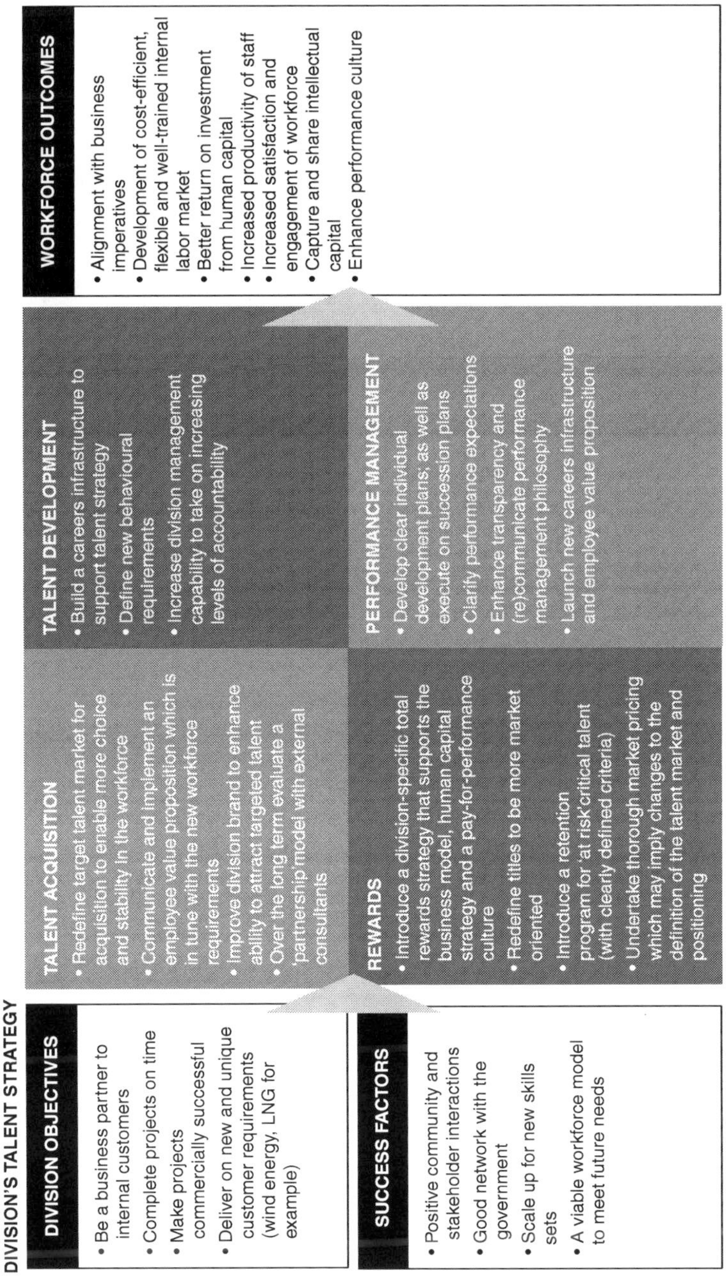

DIVISION'S TALENT STRATEGY

DIVISION OBJECTIVES

- Be a business partner to internal customers
- Complete projects on time
- Make projects commercially successful
- Deliver on new and unique customer requirements (wind energy, LNG for example)

SUCCESS FACTORS

- Positive community and stakeholder interactions
- Good network with the government
- Scale up for new skills sets
- A viable workforce model to meet future needs

TALENT ACQUISITION

- Redefine target talent market for acquisition to enable more choice and stability in the workforce
- Communicate and implement an employee value proposition which is in tune with the new workforce requirements
- Improve division brand to enhance ability to attract targeted talent
- Over the long term evaluate a partnership model with external consultants

REWARDS

- Introduce a division-specific total rewards strategy that supports the business model, human capital strategy and a pay-for-performance culture
- Redefine titles to be more market oriented
- Introduce a retention program for 'at risk'/critical talent (with clearly defined criteria)
- Undertake thorough market pricing which may imply changes to the definition of the talent market and positioning

TALENT DEVELOPMENT

- Build a careers infrastructure to support talent strategy
- Define new behavioural requirements
- Increase division management capability to take on increasing levels of accountability

PERFORMANCE MANAGEMENT

- Develop clear individual development plans; as well as execute on succession plans
- Clarify performance expectations
- Enhance transparency and (re)communicate performance management philosophy
- Launch new careers infrastructure and employee value proposition

WORKFORCE OUTCOMES

- Alignment with business imperatives
- Development of cost-efficient, flexible and well-trained internal labor market
- Better return on investment from human capital
- Increased productivity of staff
- Increased satisfaction and engagement of workforce
- Capture and share intellectual capital
- Enhance performance culture

Figure 5.2 Developed talent strategy for a division

As a result, the division was able to develop a customised 'best-fit' talent strategy and corresponding tactical plans for closing the talent gap. These plans included a focus on the detailed steps, the rationale behind the recommendations, as well as internal and external constraints. In addition to key benefits, necessary resources and suggested measures of success were also defined. An implementation roadmap was designed to communicate the timeline of activities. Finally, the estimated level of investment was calculated to ensure budgets were properly allocated.

Recruitment and selection of talent

Creating an effective and efficient recruiting strategy is the first step to support the talent needs of organisations. By recruitment strategy we mean a comprehensive vision of how hiring practices will help attract, recruit, and hire the talent needed when it is needed. The recruiting plan identifies the vacancies and job opportunities in the company, as well as defining the skills and capabilities required for a role, and the approach to find suitable candidates from the appropriate channels. To do so, the company should have metrics for each relevant market regarding availability and cost of specific skills needed, along with metrics to identify upcoming/recruiting/retention issues and a clear picture of its internal labour market analysis, which is covered in Chapter 6.

Effective staffing begins with the first recruiting contact and carries through selection, hiring, and orientation and is reinforced by the experience of the first 180 days. Figure 5.3 illustrates a simplified staffing model

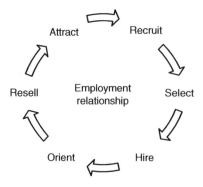

Figure 5.3 A simplified staffing model

that incorporates this view. In the sections below we look at each element of this model.

- **Attract** – the key question here is how and why top candidates will choose your specific organisation. This requires a thorough understanding of labour market opportunities, the organisation's relative position vis-a-vis other alternatives for employment, and knowing how the talent market perceives your company. For instance, does the company have a differentiated employee value proposition? One quick way to check this is to go into your own company's website as if you were seeking employment there. What does it say about your organisation? Does it portray what working in your company would be like? Does it clearly stipulate leadership values? Will it motivate prospective employees to send their résumés?
- **Recruit** – identifying the most effective sources for talent and focusing the recruiting organisation and processes accordingly. There are many channels for recruiting: college campuses, executive search firms, recruiting agencies, the Internet, employee referrals, etc. Which one is the most efficient and effective (defined as cheapest and quickest but also as the channel most likely to bring employees who will be productive and stay the longest)? Is it the same by location, job family or level?
- **Select** – after finding the best talent, managers must make the best choice to ensure a good fit and avoid bad hires. Ideally, you want to go beyond 'gut feel' and rely on tested methods for decision-making. By tested we mean tested within your company. Which source has proven more effective and efficient? Are the competency profiles and testing methods of candidates accurate in predicting future success? Have referrals proven to be useful? Is the process well-oiled and able to gain commitment from desired candidates consistently? When analysed as a systemic process, recruiting and selection can yield enough data about which practices work best. Not every candidate is a fit for every company and vice versa.
- **Hire** – complete the process of securing the chosen candidate into the company. It entails defining the job offer, presenting it to the candidate, ensuring their commitment, and completing the contract formalities. In particular, the job offer can be quite elaborate and may require substantial negotiation in cases where the employee is being 'bought out' from an existing job.
- **Orient** – ensure a smooth and successful transition into the new role. The induction of the candidate into the new role or team needs to be closely managed so that the new employee can quickly reach the desired level of productivity. Orientation also does not end with the induction meeting: it

should also include short- to medium-term (at least 1, 3, and 6 months) checkpoints to support the employee's integration.

- **Resell** – once inside the company, it is important that the candidates find that the reality experienced in the job matches the promise delivered during the recruiting process. A well-branded new hire experience requires periodic management monitoring, detailed feedback from candidates/employees who have gone through the process, and decisive action to swiftly correct any discrepancies. For instance, a semiconductor company found that one of the major reasons they were experiencing 'quick' turnovers (new recruits leaving the company within the first year) had to do with these new employees finding that the promise made during the recruiting process of broad learning opportunities did not materialise once in the job, as the company's promotions were slow and tended to be in a single job family.[12]

A well-executed recruiting strategy will ensure the organisation always has access to the talent and skills it needs to achieve business results. The strategy helps to identify and source talent. It should also address the recruiting process workflow and sequence and decision-making protocols. The results of the process can be permanently monitored via analytics to ensure no slippage on recruitment targets.

CASE STUDY

New recruitment strategy and workforce plan for rapid growth

Located at a major aviation hub with rapidly growing traffic, a leading air carrier was keen to capitalise on the growth opportunity through rapid business expansion. On average, the airline was adding one new aircraft arrival every month and new flight destinations were also being frequently added as the airline expanded its network and reach.

The air carrier wanted to maintain its accelerated speed of expansion, but was concerned over the availability of key talent – both in the immediate as well as the longer term. The market was ripe for expansion; however, with not enough manpower to fly the aircraft, the air carrier was finding it difficult to capitalise on opportunities. Moreover, since the company had proceeded with its programme to acquire aircraft, the manpower shortage was posing a serious drain on capital expense as well.

The company's workforce planning was managed in reactive mode, without standards, with no focus, and with many changes made throughout the year. It realised that to cope with the talent demands, it needed to establish a robust workforce planning discipline and adopt a recruitment strategy and processes that aligned with and reinforced the business strategy as a fast-growing, full-service airline.

The company recognised that effective staffing begins with the first recruiting contact and carries through selection, hiring, and orientation – and is reinforced by the experience of the first 90–180 days. The air carrier identified that it needed to address a number of areas in its recruitment approach – starting from establishing more robust processes for workforce planning and recruitment, to broadening sourcing options, strengthening its employee value proposition, and adopting an online recruitment system, to ramping up capabilities of its own recruitment staff.

The air carrier first established its talent priorities and defined the workforce planning and recruitment processes at a global level. These processes were tailored to accommodate specific requirements of key talent segments, including cabin crew, flight deck, network operations, ground handling, engineering, maintenance, retail, and corporate functions. Key considerations included determining how to plan the workforce taking into account large turnover, roster/staffing ratio, diversity, flight destinations, aircraft types, service/language requirements, and best locations to hire. Through this approach, recruiting was enhanced to include non-traditional sources of labour with greater emphasis on developing talent from within, such as occupation transitions and promotion. Analyses of outside labour markets helped the recruiters target sourcing locations with the greatest supply of – and least competition for – talent.

To support the effective rollout of the recruitment processes, the air carrier assessed the capabilities of its recruitment staff, and invested in training all relevant employees in the new approaches. The existing structure was also reorganised to ensure delivery of required processes. Finally, the company invested in setting up an online recruitment system to support its growing volume and discipline in recruitment.

As a result of the initiatives, the air carrier was able to significantly diminish gaps in the recruitment pipeline, and planes spent less time being grounded and were utilised to deliver enhanced revenue. At the same time investments in capability building reorganisation and technology yielded benefits as costs relating to hiring times were reduced by 40 per cent.

The development of the workforce

Organisations with highly effective development plans significantly outper-form organisations without these plans by double the revenue per employee.[13] Developing employees with training and other means of personal growth can bring positive results.[14] Key elements of development include learning, competency management, career management, and succession management.

Learning implies giving employees the means to learn skills, competencies or even behaviours to increase their productivity, customer service, and effect-iveness. The first step in designing learning programmes is to determine if training is needed. A needs assessment involves at least two kinds of analysis: organisational and individual. From an organisational perspective, the needs assessment involves understanding what are the learning-related activities that a company needs to take to achieve its business strategy and identifying the budget, time, and resources to provide the required training. The individual analysis assesses the specific areas which will improve performance, correct behaviours or increase the competencies of each employee. It is important to ensure that both the organisation and the individuals are ready for training.

An important consideration in instituting learning is to make sure each employee actually uses the newly learned competencies in the work setting. This requires self-discipline as well as support from supervisors and others. Without this, training becomes merely acquisition of knowledge but not change in behaviour.

The training channels employed will make a material difference in the effectiveness of training. While instructor-led classroom training is generally the method used (and it is an effective method), there are other ways of deploy-ing training throughout the organisation. Teleconferencing and webcasts are increasingly in use as more people can be reached at a time. Videos are also popular, as are online programmes. There are also training programmes that can be installed on iPads and similar portable devices, which can then be stud-ied at the employees' own pace and preferred location. On-the-job training (OJT) is also an effective method as new employees learn by watching others and having the chance to try out these behaviours and skills in a work set-ting. Other ways to implement learning involve apprenticeships, simulations, e-learning, computerised business games, and blended learning involving two or more of the above simultaneously. As technology continues to evolve, no doubt new ways of deploying training will be developed. The choice of a learning method lies in the learning objectives sought, the speed required for deployment, costs, number and locations of employees to be trained, and the complexity of the material.

Measuring the effectives of training is part of the data-driven approach we discuss throughout this book. In particular, each programme should have a positive return on investment (ROI) measure to ascertain if economic value was derived from the programme. In addition, training programmes should be evaluated around how well they succeed in achieving the learning objectives set. This means measuring immediately after the programme and perhaps six months later to see if the person did learn the concepts taught and is implementing them in their work environment.

Competency management

Competencies are bundles of skills, knowledge, attitudes, and experiences that are required for performance in a given role. A competency model is the combination of a group of competencies that are required for superior performance in a given role or organisation. Position profiling is a process of documenting the specific competency model requirements.

The use of competencies and competency models allows organisations to identify distinguishing behaviours that are predictive of outstanding performance. As such, these behaviours need to be linked to business plans. To be effective, the model must be sound, but more importantly, competency models should be integrated with HR systems as part of an ongoing process of effective talent management.

Typically there are two types of competencies: behavioural and technical. Behavioural competencies are often divided into common competencies (critical behaviours aligned with organisational values which are expected of everyone across the entire organisation, such as customer service or teamwork) and leadership competencies (critical behaviours expected of someone who leads people, such as decision-making and people management). Technical competencies are made up of the knowledge and skills required to perform a certain type or level of work effectively, which is unique to a job/functional area (such as market research or database management). To be effective, competency proficiency levels must identify the critical differences between top and average performers.

When developing competency models, it is important to focus on critical behaviours that are directly relevant to organisational values and strategy. The use of well-specified, observable indicators of the competencies that can be reliably assessed in proficiency-level terms or anchors allows for an improved level of consistency in application. By then defining competencies using clear descriptors of behaviours, knowledge, skills, abilities, and outcomes for different employee levels, managers will have a strong set of tools to help manage their workforce.

Each job in the organisation can be described in terms of the proficiency level of common, leadership, and technical competencies required to perform the roles required. Assessments are then used to determine the level of competencies each incumbent or potential incumbent has to perform these roles. The gaps identified then serve to guide the developmental needs required by individuals to progress in the company and collectively by the organisation to improve performance.

Competencies can also be used in recruiting, performance management, career planning, promotions, job design, and rewards, as illustrated by Table 5.2.

With the competency models in place, the next step to close the gap is to assess employees. There are a variety of tools to do so. Some of the most common ones are assessment centres, multi-source feedback, behavioural event interviews, and expert technical panels.

The principle behind this approach is simple: if employees improve their levels of competency, overall organisational performance will improve as well. HR professionals can help by embedding competencies into practices and using a combination of the tools above to institutionalise competency improvement. For instance, in embedding the competencies into career and promotion decisions, the results of the assessments can be used to facilitate career discussions between an employee and their manager. By employing competency assessments, companies can achieve consistency in promotion decisions by making the promotion criteria explicit. In addition, assessments can assist in attracting and retaining talented employees by defining career opportunities within the company and in this way assist in general workforce planning.

Specifically, if the organisation knows what competency levels are expected of each employee in their current job, what it will take to perform at the next level, and their current level of competencies, then it is easy to decide what to train the person on, either to improve their performance in the current job, or to help them get promoted to the next level. In fact, the assessment results of several employees who are in line for a given promotion may yield information about who among them is most prepared for the increased responsibilities.

Table 5.2 Potential applications of competency models

HR policy	Potential application	Tools
Performance management	How should performance be planned, coached and assessed?	• Performance indicators • Objective setting • Performance review training • Performance and development reviews
Selection/staffing	How should qualified staff be identified?	• Performance indicators • Objective setting • Performance review training • Performance and development reviews
Development and training	What are the development requirements for the job?	• Resource guide • Multi-source feedback • Personal profile • Gap analysis • Training strategy • Skills matrices
Succession	What are the succession requirements for staff?	• Career mapping • Group profiling
Job/career plan design	How should career paths be structured for staff?	• Competency dictionary • Core competencies • Organisational review
Rewards	How should staff be valued and rewarded?	• Job banding • Position profiling • Role evaluator

Another good example of the use of competencies is in performance management. Typical 'pay-for-performance' models focus on the results (the '*what*') to determine pay levels. Competency assessments can help understand the '*how*' of performance and influence pay decisions. For instance, would you promote your best salesperson to be the next sales manager? Sales results (the '*what*') should be rewarded, but to be promoted the skills required are different. Sales may require high negotiation skills but people management skills are not as needed. The latter, however, are most important in supervising staff. Following the same logic, if two salespeople have similar results and similar negotiation skills, but one has higher people management skills, the latter will be more valuable to the company in the long run. Therefore, the company would do well to reward him/her better than the other.

An important way to use competencies is the determination of 'high-potential' employees. A useful way to think of high-potential employees is to define them as those who are capable of developing their competency skills to the degree required for at least two levels above their current level.

Career management and mapping

Organisations would do well to focus on the importance of career management and the impact of career mapping. Career management refers to the tools and activities in place to influence employees to make the career decisions that match with the organisation's talent management aspirations. As employees come to points at which they make career decisions, the career management tools and processes guide them toward those decisions that the organisation would like people with those skill sets to consider.

In considering career management, it is important to note that careers themselves are seen differently today than in the past. The metaphor for a career has traditionally been the 'ladder', which is rigid and vertical and comprises a series of rungs. But the metaphor that is more appropriate for today's organisation is the climbing wall, which is a broad face that is generally vertical, but also horizontal, and has a series of handholds and toeholds by which you can manoeuvre across the rock face. You may go straight up the rock face, or you may go at an angle, or you may go up for a while, move over to find a different path and then continue on. In a career context, each one of these hand- and toeholds can be thought of as a two-to-five-year experience on a particular project or assignment, or in a role. We clearly specify 'role' rather than 'job' because careers are better defined not necessarily by permanent jobs but by roles that might be an aspect of a job or a temporary assignment.

Historically, careers happened within silos with distinct hierarchical layers. As individuals progressed in their careers, they simply took their manager's job or moved up a few points on a grading scale. But today, as organisations have become more complex, more matrixed, and much flatter, it has become harder for employees to see where the career prospects lie and how to work their way through the organisational maze. It has also become harder for organisations to ensure that people reach certain stages in their careers with the right experience and skill sets. As a result, some organisations find that they have to 'buy' senior management from outside because it is so difficult to 'build' talent to get the right experience inside. In addition, when employees get lost in the organisational career maze, they may decide to advance their careers elsewhere.

Another challenge is providing a career velocity that is acceptable to the individual. In the past, people expected to get promoted every five or more years and would wait in line until it was 'their turn'. But people today want to experience change every two or three years, and companies are struggling to match the velocity of career changes to people's expectations. Mature companies with fairly stable work simply may not be able to offer people a rapid-enough career progression. These companies have to be honest with employees about career options and think about how they manage the careers of the many people who will plateau or pass through the organisation rather than advance to senior levels.

For some organisations, career management has become much more of a priority, either because they want to emphasise careers as part of the employment value proposition, or because it has become even more important for companies to know where their talent is in career stream terms. This helps companies identify their talent weaknesses and determine how they want to influence career decisions in order to achieve organisational goals. The challenge facing companies, particularly since they want to use careers as a stronger part of the employment value proposition, is to create career opportunities in other ways, such as by restructuring the work, by moving people out if they have reached a plateau or are underperforming, or through proactive churn.

We expect to see more organisations emphasise career management approaches in the future, which will require changes for many processes and the orientation of management. Organisations need to be clear about what they want to influence employees to do with their careers. It is as basic as thinking about whether there are careers they specifically want to manage and, if so, what types of tools and processes they should put in place to influence people when they are making career decisions.

In addition, organisations need to have the data to understand actual career movement. They can then compare how people are moving through the organisation against how the company would like career movement to happen in order to uncover particular career flow problems or blockages. By looking at these flows, companies can identify the places where they need to intervene to help employees make the right career decisions. Organisations can also use the data to shorten the cycles employees must go through to attain key roles

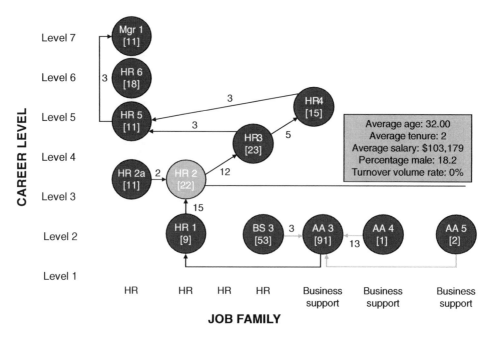

Figure 5.4 Career maps

by making sure that identified talents are not going off on career tracks that go in a loop or end up in strange places.

Companies also need to carefully manage the processes by which roles and assignments are made. In most organisations, individual managers often make those decisions with little oversight and little understanding of the company's career strategy. While the manager may be thinking about what he or she needs from that role today, the organisation needs these decisions to be based on what will best build the company's capabilities and retain the most people.

Finally, companies need to start proactively managing the number and types of opportunities that, according to the data, have the biggest impact on people's careers. One tool that will allow additional focus on career management is the use of career maps.

One type of career map is the *pro forma* career map, which shows how the organisation wants people to progress. It is designed by working backward from a destination job to identify the feeder jobs that will allow a person to get there. The other type of career map is built on data about how and how quickly people move through roles to reveal the pathways people actually take to get to that destination job, as demonstrated in Figure 5.4. This type of career mapping often reveals pathways the organisation was not aware of. It also provides information about how long it takes to follow a particular career path. If an organisation knows it will need 20 more plant managers in the next 10 years, for example, it can look at how long it has taken historically to get from entry point to plant manager and then determine if this progression is sufficient to meet the needs of the business. If it is not, the company can design interventions to alter or speed up the process.

With reference to Figure 5.4, consider an HR manager currently at level 2 in his or her organisation. They can compare where they are in that particular point in their career against the averages provided in terms of age, pay, tenure, etc. They can also look ahead to see what types of roles lie in the future and how long they should expect to take to reach them. For instance, understanding that it should take two to three years to move from the current level to the next, the next step would be an HR 3 role (of which there are currently 23 incumbents in the company). Twelve people from HR 2 are expected to make it to HR 3. From there, the next step could be HR 4 or HR 5 and from there HR 6 or Mgr 1. In this way the employee can visualise what their career could be like and what they need to do to progress.

This type of career mapping often looks completely different from traditional models of career development. By mapping how people are actually moving through the organisation, the company can gain insights that will help it make interventions that will benefit the business. This type of mapping may uncover bottlenecks where people get stuck or leave the organisation and where the organisation needs to take special care to make sure the right employees get through. Any career strategy needs to be underpinned with this data-driven understanding of how people actually move through the organisation.[15]

Career opportunities and career-related incentives are valuable tools to help organisations engage both their managers and their employees, and share in the future value of business growth. Developing careers within an organisation can help to build an internal talent pipeline, grow talent capabilities, and enhance the employee's value both within the organisation and in the marketplace.

Succession planning

Succession planning is defined as the practice of identifying, assessing, and selecting talent to succeed incumbents in critical roles.[16] This is a key aspect of talent development and yet the majority of global companies do not have clearly defined succession planning processes in place.[17, 18, 19, 20, 21, 22] This situation can lead to a host of problems, including high turnover as employees do not believe there is a high enough probability of being promoted (more '*buy*' than '*build*'), higher enterprise risk if key employees leave, and lower perceived employer brand by potential future hires. A well-developed succession planning process will help to avert these problems by being an integral part of the organisation's talent management programme, based on implemented processes for strategic selection and development of candidates in accordance with business strategy and with clear accountability for the development of the annual succession plans (in case of CEO succession, accountability lies with the board's nomination committee).

Making succession planning an integral part of executive talent management means carrying out annual assessment and development of the corporate talent pipeline to provide the basis for successful plans around replacements, succession planning, and talent development, illustrated in Table 5.3.

In all cases the starting point is an evaluation of the company's requirements in terms of future leaders and critical roles, given the business strategy, risk profile, and people strategy. With these data in hand, there is an iterative process of assessing the current bench strength, providing development in the needed areas for those that require it, and ensuring there is enough of a pipeline to be able to replace any key role in the organisation at short notice.

In practical terms this is done by evaluating the competencies required for each job with the competencies the candidates or incumbents have (similar to recruiting for a role). If there are individual gaps, then the executive can be placed in the right type of development programme to close the gap. If the organisation as a whole is found to have similar gaps (e.g. innovation) then the choices are broader in terms of development programmes or bringing in new talent for key roles.

Typically, the HR professionals will determine which tools to use to determine the required competencies for each key job as well as to assess individual competencies. The HR function will also do the gap analysis and, jointly with line management, make the selection decisions.

In the case of succession planning for CEOs, the process is more elaborate as the risk associated with a wrong decision is higher. Ideally, board/CEO discussions on long-term succession planning should begin no less than two to three years prior to the time a CEO transition is expected. The full board (not just the nominations committee) should be involved in the CEO's succession plan

Table 5.3 Selecting and developing the high-potential pool for succession

Dimension	Replacement planning	Succession planning	Talent development
Purpose	Risk management	Succession and development	Succession, development, retention, diversity, performance culture
Target	Key executive jobs	High-potential pool	Critical talent pools, including multiple leadership levels
Assessment	Performance track record	Performance trend and leadership competencies	All outcomes and capabilities that matter, including performance, potential, and learning capability
Outcome	Slates and replacement lists for critical positions	Development and staffing plans for high-potential pool	Development and deployment system fully integrated with HR processes
Career path	Linear, mainly within function	Cross function, some geography and division movement	Opportunistic, cross function, geography and business
Implementation	Yearly review	Yearly review, include development planning	Ongoing activities aligned with other HR processes
Ownership	Executives	Corporate HR	Board, CEO and executive team, senior management, HR partners
Participation	Compliance-driven and completely confidential	Understood and accepted by senior executives	Transparent and participative

via formal annual open discussions and with the CEO on the topic of succession planning. The main topics of conversation in these sessions are the CEO's future plans, possible internal candidates, criteria for selection of candidates, agreed-upon selection processes and transition plan to ensure that any succession be staged (and horse races avoided), including a comprehensive emergency CEO succession plan (which should be in place at all times). Developing internal candidates is typically preferable to external recruitment,[23] thus it is important that board members be given opportunities to interact with internal candidates in various settings.

Performance management and rewards

Arguably, compensation can have the biggest impact in attracting, retaining and motivating employees. Earlier, in Table 5.1 we saw that base pay is either first or second in importance as a driver of engagement in all the selected countries. However, not getting pay right can also have a seriously detrimental effect on the organisation. According to Rick Guzzo et al. at the University of Maryland, of all the HR interventions in an organisation, financial incentives can provide the highest boost to productivity, but if not well designed, they can actually be damaging to the enterprise.[24] One only needs to look at how, as a reaction to the implicit blame laid on variable pay for the recent global financial crisis, a number of governments, from the UK to Australia, and from India to the USA, want to implement regulations to control the amount of variable pay and thus total pay that any one executive can receive. The main point in all these discussions centres on the link of pay to performance, a subject we turn to next.

To execute business strategy, firms will often work to align people and plans by ensuring the plans are translated into individual objectives. The achievement of these objectives is assessed at the end of the stated period, and the employee is then ranked in terms of the achievement of the objectives, either against the objectives themselves or relative to the performance of other employees (or organisations). Pay and performance are linked by tying the amount of rewards to the level of achievement of the objectives. Performance management, in its most basic form, is the process that allows for performance to be measured, rewards to be allocated, and developmental opportunities identified. Figure 5.5 illustrates the link between pay and performance. Once the company has determined its strategic direction and overall performance targets, these targets need to be broken down into individual objectives for each employee. At the end of the performance period, there should be an evaluation of how well each employee achieved their targets. From this review there should be at a minimum two outcomes: one is the developmental needs the employee may have to improve their performance in the future. The other is an assessment of how much pay increase, bonus and/or long-term incentives the employee should receive to reward them for their performance.

Another form of performance management is competency-based. Generally, compensation programmes are based on a job evaluation of the position each employee has in the company. We also analysed how performance needs to be tightly linked to pay. However, there is still a need to differentiate individual pay. Competencies can be used to determine a person's salary relative

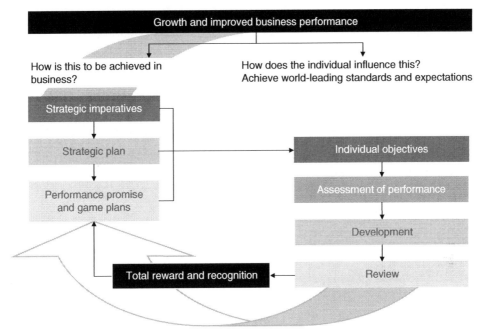

Figure 5.5 The link between pay and performance

to the market level of salary. In simple terms, any individual whose level of competencies is below the level required for the job is considered to be 'In development' and therefore should have a pay level perhaps 10 to 20 per cent below the market. If the person has the level of competencies required, then pay should be closer to the market, perhaps within 10 per cent above or below. If the person has capabilities above those required for the job, then he or she should be paid at least 10 per cent above the market as they are likely ready to be promoted soon and must be protected. Additionally, competencies in high demand receive a market premium pay. Volkswagen[25] and Reebok[26] are two well-known companies which have used competency-based pay.

Considering strategies for performance management and rewards, it is important to keep in mind the frame of reference, as rewards can look very different from the point of view of employers, employees, the market, and the shareholders.

From the employers' perspective, the company is mainly looking to opti-mise its workforce (skills, demographics, and location) while at the same time ensuring compliance, supporting the culture, and managing costs. In this vein, the company looks to design and deliver rewards programmes that will help to secure the desired workforce outcomes.

The employees from their part, and judging again from the importance placed on base pay as per Table 5.1, want to maximise their earnings. They can do so by earning more base pay, thus their focus would be on 'the market'; by earning more variable pay, thus their focus would lay on the fairness of the process; or by being promoted, thus their focus would fall on career opportunities. From this perspective, the company needs to create a compelling place to work and differentiate the organisation from its competitors by better understanding the value employees place on the various rewards elements.

From the market perspective, the firm must consider where it would like to pay in relation to the average in the marketplace. Typically the company usually defines 'the market' as the pay received by people in similar jobs in the companies where they recruit or in the companies to whom they lose people. Another consideration is the mix of pay (incentive, benefit, variable, base, etc.) which may vary by geography or by industry.

Finally, from a shareholder perspective, there needs to be a balance between the need for prudent cost management with the requirement to improve productivity and enhance business value. To invest or to reduce? When seen from the shareholder's perspective, the company should always invest in people who have improved results, or who clearly have the potential to do so. Conversely, it should reduce investment in everyone else. With the trend towards 'say on pay', shareholders are likely to demand that these principles be followed. The end game from this perspective is to create a rewards strategy to support the desired strategy at an affordable, sustainable cost.

A rewards strategy should be explicit in terms of resolving the apparently conflicting views in the above four perspectives. A well-formulated strategy includes the companies or industries which the organisation wants to use as its 'market', the weights to be assigned to salary, bonus, long-term plans, benefits, development, and careers, and the specific competitive level it wants to set against this market. The strategy should also be clear in terms of the segmentation of employees and how each group is to be addressed, for instance, plans which are only for top performers or for high-potential employees.

CASE STUDY

Designing a global reward strategy to align management systems and realise growth opportunities

The merger of two sister companies, one primarily US-based and the other global, represented an opportunity to gain cost and scale synergies and capitalise on underrepresented market segments in high growth areas. The companies had a loose partnership in the past and complemented each other's capabilities and interests.

However, differences in the management styles, reward strategies, and global management experience represented potential obstacles to achieving the desired benefits of the business combination. In order to realise the integrated value, a balance needed to be struck between enabling local flexibility and ensuring global control. Each organisation had a different operating model for compensation and HR: the acquiring company operated under a centralised system while the sister organisation operated independently in each global location. The future organisation's pay strategy needed to be aligned with the company's overall business strategy, while striking a balance between integrated and locally flexible strategies.

One of the first tasks was to understand and analyse the differences between the two organisations in terms of management structure, rewards systems, and human capital needs. A series of extensive interviews and discussions were conducted with leaders of both companies, across various locations, to determine the level of integration needed to support the balance between global synergies and local flexibility. These discussions provided valuable management perspectives on the current and desired future state of business and human capital needs, and on the types of reward strategies required to support the same.

Furthermore, there were also some significant issues to address, such as managing global mobility programmes and the complexity of equity and tax laws in the different regions. Because the US-based company had limited overseas operations and minimal experience with international compensation management, achieving the right balance to retain and attract employees represented a significant challenge. Employee perspectives were sought to ascertain key elements of compensation which would help retain and attract required talent. These internal perspectives were complemented by market data, such as global research reports, compensation levels, mobility practices, etc. to assess best practices and define the appropriate talent and rewards strategies.

Armed with these perspectives, compensation plans from both organisations were analysed in-depth to understand and address issues specific to the two entities. In addition, Mercer's International Position Evaluation system (IPE) was used to create uniform job levels for senior executives and provide a basis for a global mobility framework. Ultimately, the integrated organisation established the right mix of base and incentive pay among global leaders, and created the appropriate incentive vehicles to support a consistent focus on driving performance with associated reward opportunities. Importantly, they also identified high-priority areas and developed a transition strategy that decreased organisational challenges in the integration process.

The transition and subsequent integration of the two organisations were a success. The governance plan established upfront helped leadership manage the balance between local and global business needs, while maintaining a focus on the overall company strategy. The executive compensation programme facilitated the retention of key executives that enabled value delivery in the combined organisation.

Managing performance

Most organisations engage in performance management to evaluate performance and to align goals across the organisation. By better aligning goals among the various levels and functions, organisations want employees to focus on the activities that will create the greatest value for the business. This focus allows employees to understand how their goals link to the goals of the business. On the other hand, from the employee's perspective they want to know that their efforts are recognised and, eventually, rewarded.[27]

Effective performance management is based on a simple premise: the sum of individual and team performance equals organisational performance. It is about aligning talent to execute the business strategy – ensuring that people know what they have to do and then holding them accountable for doing it. As such, performance management is a core business process that impacts optimal organisational success by driving results, building capability, and linking performance to decision-making.

Successful performance management starts by aligning individual performance expectations with organisational mission and values. Specifically, the performance management process can be differentiated from one company to another in terms of individual versus team performance, degree of centralisation or freedom to act, and whether the company only measures performance or if it is also interested in measuring skill acquisition and modelling of the company values.

A challenge in many cases is the alignment of key performance indicators (KPIs) with the organisation's overall goals. In our opinion, this is the most important step in the process. We have seen many performance management processes that are impeccable in terms of the forms and timelines, but that lack clarity in terms of the objectives being set. To the contrary, other companies may lack sophisticated forms of software to drive the process, but are very clear in terms of objectives being set and they derive much more from performance management.

A case in point is told by Marcel Telles, Chairman of Anheuser-Busch InBev when he was CEO of Brahma Beer in Brazil (the original company which eventually grew to acquire Anheuser-Busch): 'We try to keep things down to three operational priorities per year. I always keep the company's three priorities on a sheet of paper on my desk, and these are translated into performance objectives for every employee in Brahma.'[28] The message is clear: keep performance criteria simple and focus on the mission-critical performance measures that can be cascaded as far down in the organisation as possible. This high degree of alignment certainly had a great role to play in Brahma's growth from the number two beer company in Brazil to eventually become the largest brewer in the world!

The performance management process must provide managers with the guidelines and tools to distinguish levels of employee performance across their business units or departments. At the same time the organisation must require managers to give honest feedback and provide them with the training to do so effectively. The underlying principle is that employee performance should improve if they receive regular performance feedback and coaching.

Another key tenet is to ensure performance management is well integrated with other management processes. In particular, the yearly review of the company's strategy and budgets should drive the cascading of objectives tied to the overall goals and strategic direction set by top management. Performance appraisals should drive promotion as well as pay decisions. They should also play a key part in determining training needs of individuals and of the company as a whole. To be able to link to development decisions, the performance management process should use a blend of results and behaviour-based measures to evaluate each employee.

Finally, it is important to evaluate periodically if the performance management system is simply seen as a process to be complied with or as a way to truly focus employees on the right goals and the right behaviours. Performance must be noticeably improving and career decisions should also be better, otherwise the process is not delivering the expected results. Performance management is an ongoing process that should reflect the current and emerging business priorities and company values. As the business and workforce change, modify the performance management process. Constantly assess and improve as needed, but resist the temptation to change everything every year.

While many companies find standardised scoring in a performance appraisal to be a useful way to determine pay increases and bonuses, not everyone believes performance appraisals are helpful. There are many who criticise performance scores on the premise that these are subjective and prone to rater bias. There are studies that support many employees' belief that, had they been rated by another rater, they would have received a different rating. As these perceived biased ratings are used to decide on salary, promotions, and bonuses, they can undermine trust in management and erode employee engagement. In fact, as most employees will end up rated as 'meets expectations', the perception of the majority is that hard work does not pay off except for a minority.[29,30] Companies including Juniper, Medtronics, and Kelly have eradicated performance scores altogether.

Another highly charged argument is the need or not for forced distribution of performance scores. Many support the idea, most famously espoused by General Electric's Jack Welch, that it is necessary to clearly differentiate top performance from average and certainly from low performance. The argument goes that the organisation must ensure all top performers stay and grow with the company, whereas low performers should not be rewarded and in fact should be encouraged to leave the company. Whereas these are good ends, the argument is on the means: Welch and his supporters propose relative measures of performance. That is, the top 10 to 20 per cent of performers are to be considered 'high performers' whereas the lowest 5 to 10 per cent of performers are considered 'low performers'.

Levine and O'Neill make a strong case against forced distribution being useful as a way to promote high performance.[31] Forced distribution ensures managers do not abuse the highest ratings and ensures that true low performers are assessed as such. So, forced distribution at the very least succeeds in identifying the outstanding employees as well as the underachievers. In general, managing out the underachievers and replacing them with new employees (who theoretically will have a 'normal' distribution of performance) should yield benefits; however, studies have shown that the gains from replacing low performers with new 'normal' employees tends to zero within a few years.[32] Levine and O'Neill argue that forced distribution can generate a perceived lack of 'due process' and thus be demotivating even to top talent. Furthermore, leaders could retain or even recruit underperformers in order to protect their 'star' performers, which would then bias the intent of the policy. In the case of one Japanese manufacturing site, supervisors divvied up the high and low ratings among employees on a yearly basis (e.g. *It's his turn for a low rating*) to ensure that all employees, over time, were treated 'fairly'. By the way, whoever received the highest ratings would then allocate a portion of the bonus received and 'donate it' to the lowest rated employees as a means of demonstrating appreciation for 'taking one for the team'!

An organisation concerned with retaining key talent may want to think carefully about using a forced distribution.[33] In analysing causes of turnover, researchers found that high performers were more likely to leave following the implementation of a forced distribution. Additional analysis has shown that larger incentive payouts are also associated with increased attrition.

Abolishing forced distribution or even performance scores might not be the right decision for every company. However, it is important to evaluate whether the performance management process is delivering the right results. At the same time, it is useful to think of testing possible changes in pilot programmes to assess if they could benefit the organisation as a whole. By subscribing to the evidence-based approach we advocate throughout this book, each company can determine if its performance management process is identifying high and low performers.

Executive compensation

The notion of human capital as an investment to be cultivated, as opposed to a bottomless resource that can be tapped on demand, represents one of the most significant shifts in business thinking in recent years. Executive retention is one of the top talent issues for most companies and this concern is increasing.

Executive pay for CEOs in many countries is fairly transparent and readily available via the Internet in company annual reports. This allows boards to determine what competitive pay levels are for the talent they seek to attract and retain in terms of fixed salary, annual bonus, and long-term incentives (LTIs), along with other executive benefits. The most difficult decision a remuneration committee needs to make in this respect is about the group of companies to choose for appropriate comparisons. This is not always straightforward in all markets, as often there are a limited number of large organisations within the same industry in each country (for instance, Singapore has only three locally listed banks), making comparisons more art than science. Many remuneration committees opt for choosing companies of a similar size, even if in different industries, under the premise that a CEO in one industry could be poached by a company in another industry.

Good practice suggests that an executive's pay should have both fixed and variable components. The fixed component is designed to pay a competitive wage for the accountability of the position, and the variable component should be linked to both short-term and long-term performance periods. In addition, companies often have more than one plan to balance their need for performance with their need to retain executives. Pay mix then becomes an area for attention regarding market competitiveness. In Asia, for example, we find that companies provide a greater amount of variable pay than their Western counterparts in the region.[34] The fact that the fixed pay element for Asian companies has fallen from 60 per cent in 2009–2010 to 41 per cent in 2011–2012 highlights the trend that Asian companies prefer more flexible pay structures which can be adjusted – up or down – based on business performance. They are also less likely to use shares than cash. However, this is a trend that should wane as more Asian companies become global. For instance, AIA, which is the world's fifth largest insurance company, headquartered and listed in Hong Kong, has long-term programmes that are aligned to global market practices.

Companies often use a combination of internal financial metrics (typically some measure of profits such as return on equity and total shareholder return) with external validation of performance against peers in their pay programmes. Such external calibration is often both retrospective, to assess how the company actually performed compared to its competitors, and prospective, to ensure that performance targets include an appropriate degree of 'stretch'.

A well-aligned programme with a rigorous performance evaluation process means little if, at the end of the year, individuals are not held accountable for meeting agreed-upon goals. While this notion of 'black and white' results is common, sometimes companies also use non-financial measures in their incentive plans. This can take the shape of a formal 'balanced scorecard' in which performance is evaluated in specific areas such as people management, customer satisfaction, or process improvements. These measures can give a more appropriate picture of overall performance than rigidly adhering to financial metrics alone.

Annual incentive plans are commonplace, but many companies also have multi-year plans to ensure that key executives do not lose sight of their longer-term objectives. A recent trend, spurred by the links between executive pay schemes and the global financial crisis in 2008–2009, finds companies moving away from stock options to other types of plan as the use of stock option plans can lead to both excessive risk-taking as well as retention difficulties in a volatile market. Instead, companies can use more restricted shares to aid retention and connect pay to performance.

Corporate governance around pay has also received recent attention. Shareholders have a right to know the financial decisions a company makes, and executive remuneration is effectively an expense that should be disclosed in more detail. Several countries have made strides in the direction of greater transparency, partly spurred by the Financial Stability Board's guidelines for financial institutions.[35] Variations of these good corporate governance practices have been adopted by financial regulators and organisations and they have had a spillover effect in other industries. Disclosure leads to greater information which helps regulate and control pay but it has the side effect of potentially inflating pay, as nomination committees find they need to go beyond median levels of pay to attract CEOs externally.

Sales compensation

Sales compensation design links goal setting with pay – in other words, the objectives required of the role as defined by the sales force structure and the sales methodology, with the results achieved by each salesperson. The approach in designing sales compensation thus begins with understanding the systemic nature of sales effectiveness in connecting strategy and execution. Roles, competencies, and goal setting must come together and pay reinforces this system with the client at the centre. That also means that to increase sales productivity, improve retention, and reduce turnover, the answer may lie in modifying several factors and not just compensation.

For instance, if a company is strategically aiming to increase cross-selling, it may be tempted to create an additional bonus to reward sales representatives who open opportunities for other salespeople who sell different products. This may drive a short-term gain in introductions, and perhaps an increase in cross-sales. But this is likely not enough. In the long term, sales representatives are likely to spend more time in the activities that would provide the highest bonus, and these are likely not cross-selling activities. These campaigns have short-term effects but generally not a long-term impact. To change behaviours permanently requires a change in sales methodology (more team selling?), perhaps a change in the profile of salespeople required (more team players?), and then a change in compensation programmes (more team rewards?).

A main tenet of sales compensation is how much of the pay should be fixed or variable. Sales compensation pay mix should be decided based on the influence of the sales role on the customer's buying decision. Prominence of the sales role is defined by the extent to which personal selling skills – to the exclusion of other external marketing factors – can influence the customer's buying decision. In other words, the more the buying decision is based on the sales representative's influence, the higher the level of variable pay that should go into the sales compensation plan design. As an example, a fast-moving consumer goods salesperson for the traditional trade channel can be placed on a very high commission structure (say, 70 per cent variable) whereas a process controls salesperson for industrial accounts, where the sale is defined by the product characteristics, after-sales service, and the like, may have a much lower level of variable pay, say 20 per cent.

Ironically, the higher the level of variable pay, the less control supervisors have over the sales behaviours of the sales representatives. Hence the point made earlier about cross-selling. So, while it is often true that the sales force will do what it is paid to do, it is also often just as true that a sales compensation programme is not a substitute for supervision.

In designing a sales compensation programme, it pays to keep in mind two important principles: one we have already mentioned, which is that the objective of the plan is to drive behaviours that are consistent with the role design and the sales strategy. Will the salesperson sell primarily the most profitable products (as opposed to the easiest ones to sell)? Will he/she open new accounts, control days of sales outstanding, visit all clients with the frequency required, introduce new products, maximise gross profits, etc.?

The other principle is to align pay with the market in a way that the top performers will receive top levels of pay, and low performers wll receive low levels of pay. This should result in a much higher turnover of lower performers who, when replaced even by new employees, overall will achieve average results (some better and some worse), so overall performance is increased. For example, a consumer goods company created a plan that they called 'lions and gazelles' which is covered in the box. In this plan, sales representatives were measured against quotas that were set for each sales route. At the end of each month, the sales representatives that ended at the top 25th percentile of performance received an extra 25 per cent of commission. This placed them above the 75th percentile of the competitive compensation market. The next quartile of performers received an extra 10 per cent of commission, placing them above the median pay level of the market. The third quartile of performers saw their 'earned' commission reduced by 10 per cent, putting them behind market median pay, and the lowest quartile of performers had their commission reduced by 25 per cent, placing them close to the market 25th percentile of pay. They had a turnover rate of approximately 20 per cent, but over 80 per cent of those who left the company were on the lower quartile, and none were from the upper quartile.

The story of the lions and the gazelles

Every morning in the jungle, a lion wakes up knowing that it has to run faster than the gazelles, otherwise it will go hungry and eventually die.

And at the same time, every morning a gazelle wakes up knowing that it has to run faster than the lions, otherwise it will be caught and die.

The moral of the story is this: every morning lions and gazelles must outrun each other to survive!

CASE STUDY

Motivating a sales force with a customised and innovative employee proposition

Having grown through acquisition, a large financial services company planned to leverage its critical mass by setting up branches where it previously had no presence. Leadership knew the firm would be coming up against tough competition; rivals were already well-established in most of the target markets. It would take a lot more than opening its doors to establish a vast network of branches; if anything, the company would have to focus on service delivery to succeed. The firm needed a fresh approach to distinguish itself in the market: more customer-focused, retail operations in contrast to the traditional systems prevalent in the industry. A new breed of high-calibre candidates was needed to establish the operations and execute the growth strategy.

Hiring the large number of employees needed in the new branches was no easy task; further, in a tight labour market, it promised to be especially difficult. The organisation had to hire about half its new workforce from the retail and the rest from the traditional financial sectors to serve customers. Just having a good reward programme would not suffice; a holistic employee proposition is what would eventually retain the desired employees. The compensation arrangements would therefore need to be tailored to the different groups, commensurate with local pay practices, and at the same time be equitable with the organisation's general policies. Moreover, the employees with the non-financial services background would need appropriate training programmes to achieve the business objectives, and this investment needed to be factored into the hiring proposition. In addition to these challenges, the company also had to secure government approval to implement its expansion plan. The workforce is unionised, and implementing new systems that affected employees' working conditions added yet another layer of approvals and potential obstacles.

To address the various aspects of building its workforce, the organisation decided to focus on salaries and incentives, performance management and recognition schemes; more importantly these different elements were looked at holistically to develop a suitable remuneration programme. For the sales staff, base salaries were lower and incentives formed the greater part of remuneration. This aggressive stance taken on total target reward was unusual in this industry. Versatility was fundamental in designing the incentive structure: a variety of plans such as recognition rewards, flexible working hours, specialised training, and career development programmes helped attract and motivate sales-focused staff. All these elements enhanced the employment proposition, greatly reducing the possibility of turnover.

The company successfully entered its targeted markets and is already well on its way to reaching revenue projections. The recruitment of desired sales employees has been very successful. A high-calibre and driven sales staff has helped overachieve the sales target within the first few weeks of the first branch's opening. This initial response shows that the organisation is on track with the business strategy, and positive customer response proves beyond a doubt that the organisation is perceived as a dependable financial service provider.

No longer dependent on anecdote and instinct to manage its workforce, the company is now actively planning for its future. Management adopted the recommendations of the workforce planning team, holding a workforce planning 'summit' to share lessons across business units and integrating the recommendations into their yearly planning cycle. Managers are using newly developed workforce planning handbooks that reflect the unique needs and challenges of their businesses, as well as a new forecasting tool that will enable them to conduct rigorous, measurement-based workforce planning in future cycles.

Summary

The various talent elements impact multiple systems in the organisation. Leaders must make sure that talent systems are aligned internally and to the business and people strategies, so that they pull and push the organisation and people to a common goal or vision rather than diffusing or diluting efforts. Misalignment builds friction into the system and slows the talent engine, thus hurting company performance.

Specifically, a robust selection and recruitment process is necessary to acquire the right talent in terms of quality and quantity. Training and development can be used not only to improve productivity and enhance culture and values but also to drive motivation and engagement. Pay is instrumental in retention and motivation. But it is the seamless working of these programmes as a system that truly represents the means to manage talent as a way to achieve competitive advantage.

Key questions for consideration

- *Does the organisation have good talent?*
- *Does it have the right integrated talent management systems?*
- *What populations should the organisation invest in to achieve what kind of return?*
- *How are roles and competencies structured?*
- *How is performance measured and rewarded?*
- *How is capability developed?*
- *How are careers and deployment managed?*

FURTHER READING

Cannon, J. A., and McGee, R. (2007) *Talent Management and Succession Planning*. London, Chartered Institute of Personnel and Development.

Cappelli, P. (2008) *Talent on Demand*. Harvard Business School Press, Boston, MA.

Cheese, P. (2007) *The Talent Powered Organization: Strategies for Globalisation, Talent Management and High Performance*. London, Kogan Page.

Scullion, H., and Collings, D. G. (2010) *Global Talent Management*. New York, Taylor & Francis.

Ulrich, D. (2009) *HR Transformation: Building Human Resources from the Outside In*. Chicago, McGraw-Hill.

REFERENCES

[1] Hexter, E. S., and Young, M. B. (2011) *Managing Human Capital Risk*. The Conference Board, Inc.

[2] Economist Intelligence Unit (2007) *Best Practice in Risk Management: A Function Comes of Age*.

[3] Mercer (2011a) *The Future of Talent Management Survey*.

[4] O'Leonard, K., and Harris, S. (2010) *Talent Management Factbook 2010: Best Practices and Benchmarks in U.S. Talent Management*. San Francisco, Bersin & Associates.

[5] O'Leonard, K., (2011) *The Corporate Learning Factbook 2011: Benchmarks, Trends and Analysis of the US Training Market*. San Francisco, Bersin & Associates.

[6] Ulrich, D. (2009) *HR Transformation: Building Human Resources from the Outside In*. Chicago, McGraw-Hill.

[7] Scullion, H., and Collings, D. G. (2010) *Global Talent Management*. New York, Taylor & Francis.

[8] Mercer (2011b) *What's Working™ Survey*.

[9] Lewis, R. E., and Heckman, R. J. (2006) 'Talent Management: A Critical Review', *Human Resource Management Review* 16(2): 139–154.

[10] Cheese, P. (2007) *The Talent Powered Organization: Strategies for Globalization, Talent Management and High Performance*. London, Kogan Page.

[11] Cooper, R. G., and Kleinschmidt, E. J. (1996) 'Winning Businesses in Product Development: The Critical Success Factors', *Research Technology Management* 39(4): 18–29.

[12] Diez, F. (2009) 'Using An Analytical Approach to Increase Retention in High-Growth Countries: An Example in India', *World at Work Journal* 18(2).

[13] O'Leonard, K. (2009) *2009 Talent Management Factbook: Best Practices and Benchmarks in Talent Management*. Bersin & Associates.

[14] Aguinis, H., and Kraiger, K. (2009) 'Benefits of Training and Development for Individuals and Teams, Organizations, and Society', *Annual Review of Psychology* 60: 451–474.

[15] Greenhaus, J. H., Callanan, G. A., and Godshalk, V. M. (2009) *Career Management*. Sage Publications, Inc.

[16] Soransen, A., and Jacobs, D. (2011) 'A Practitioner's Guide to Succession Planning', *Workspan* 18(2).

[17] Grawybow, M. (2007) CEO Succession is Lacking at Many Big Companies. *Reuters*. [Online] 19 January. Available from: www.reuters.com.

[18] Society of Corporate Secretaries and Governance Professionals (2006) *August Survey of 113 Publicly Held Companies*.

[19] Center for Board Leadership and Mercer Delta Consulting (2007) Public Company, Private Company and Not-for-Profit Governance Surveys.

[20] Lublin, J. S. (2006) No One to Turn To: When CEOs Fall Ill, Boards are Often Caught Unprepared. *The Wall Street Journal* [Online] 9 October. Available from: http://online.wsj.com.

[21] Forbes.com Staff (2008) Why Succession Planning Matters [Online] 7 January. Available from: www.forbes.com.

[22] Hay Group (2007) *Fortune Most Admired Companies.*

[23] Favaro, K., Karlsson, P.-O., and Neilson, G. (2011) 'CEO Succession 2010: The Four Types of CEO', *Strategy and Business:* 38–41.

[24] Guzzo, R., et al. (1975–1985) *330 HR Interventions Which Impacted Productivity.* University of Maryland (Updated 1996 by Mercer).

[25] Pavard, P. (1998) 'Human Resource Management International Digest', *Bradford* 6(3): 8.

[26] Waters, P. (1998). 'Human Resource Management International Digest', *Bradford* 6(3): 4.

[27] Garr, S. (2011) *High-Impact Performance Management: Part 1 – Designing a Strategy for Effectiveness.* Bersin & Associates.

[28] Escobari, M., and Sull, D. (2005) Brahma Versus Antarctica: Reversal of Fortune in Brazil's Beer Market, London Business School.

[29] Murphy, K. R. (2008) 'Explaining the Weak Relationship Between Job Performance and Ratings of Job Performance', *Industrial and Organizational Psychology* 1: 148–160.

[30] Nickols, F. (2007) 'Performance Appraisal: Weighed and Found Wanting in the Balance', *The Journal for Quality & Participation* 30(1).

[31] Levine, B., and O'Neill, C. (2011) 'Abandoning Pay-for-Performance Myths in Favour of Evidence', *WorldatWork Journal* 20(1).

[32] Scullen, S. E., Bergey, P. K., and Aiman-Smith, L. (2005). 'Forced Distribution Rating Systems and the Improvement of Workforce Potential', *Personnel Psychology* 58(1): 1–32.

[33] Nalbantian, H. R., Guzzo, R. A., Kieffer, D., and Doherty, J. (2004). *Play to Your Strengths: Managing Your Internal Labour Markets for Lasting Competitive Advantage.* New York, McGraw-Hill.

[34] Mercer (2012) *2011/2012 Asia Executive Remuneration Snapshot Survey.*

[35] Financial Stability Forum (2009) *FSF Principles for Sound Compensation Practices*, 2 April 2009.

6　Human capital metrics

Evidence-based management can help managers and leaders do
a better job of learning and practicing their profession, and make
these difficult jobs a bit less taxing and more successful. There
are no simple, easy answers, but there are answers: better ways of
thinking about business knowledge and more fact-based ways of
understanding management practices.

Jeffrey Pfeiffer and Robert I. Sutton

Introduction

In the previous chapters we covered the critical components of human capital
strategy. Culture, leadership, organisation, and talent must all work together
to execute the strategy of the firm. To help ensure that these components are
generating the right results and aligned on intent, it is important to develop
human capital metrics.

In the last decade, increasing efforts have been made to move towards an
'evidence-based management' approach.[1] Borrowing from the field of medicine,
the idea is that proven approaches or practices with known results are adopted
by practitioners so that managers begin to take actions based on proven practices. While there are good ideas and theories in this area, actual metrics in the
field of human capital are at a nascent stage as the quantification of 'people
practices' has been an elusive area for many companies.[2] While the benchmarking of the human resources function has been commonplace, this generally

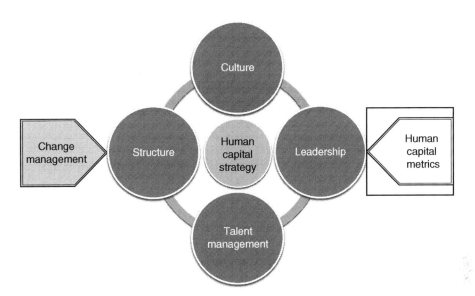

Figure 6.1 Human capital metrics
Source: adapted from Nalbantian, et al., *Play to Your Strengths: Managing Your Internal Labour Markets for Lasting Competitive Advantage* (McGraw-Hill, 2003)

only deals with the efficiency of the processes and general headcount ratios rather than the actual impact on business results of human capital practices in the line organisation. New approaches to more strategic views of human capital measures have started to take shape and will provide managers with valuable insight on their human capital effectiveness. As this area evolves, many practitioners look forward to a time when the human capital metrics will sit alongside the financial performance metrics as key indicators of company performance.

Unfortunately today, many organisations lack adequate measurement systems and spend considerable time and money guessing or copying human capital practices from other organisations. For example, if a manager thinks that Google has the best culture he/she may decide to copy it, even though it may be quite misaligned with the company strategy. The same may be true with reviewing market studies on human capital. When managers learn that the average turnover rate in China is 14 per cent, they might deduce that they are in line with the average and have nothing to worry about, without understanding more about how this may impact the strategy or perhaps the missed opportunity for competitive advantage. Still other examples exist when looking at industry data. A manager who learns that the median bonus paid for managers at a competitor is 20 per cent might automatically decide that they should adjust the pay policies to match that number, without any context or consideration for the holistic view of the employee value proposition. There are numerous examples of management actions or assumptions that are not anchored with appropriate human capital measurement.

Author Jac Fitz-Enz explains in *The New Human Resource Analytics* that most organisations have well-honed financial strategies to hedge against market fluctuations, but have very little in the human capital arena to offset future surprises. Staffing managers are unsure which source will yield the best applicants. Training managers are unsure of the best sales training programme to launch a new product. 'They could not give you an answer based on anything other than anecdotal, obsolete experience', claims the author.[3]

To be fair, many other organisations have heard the call over the years and much has improved in linking people, strategy, and performance.[4] New advances in technology and analytic tools have made it easier to look into predictive models for human capital (HC). Research is starting to link the human capital practices to business results and we expect that this trend will continue.[5] This chapter addresses the use of analytics related to human capital. For a deeper dive into the specific tools, we suggest you go to the books noted at the end of the chapter. To clarify our focus, it is important to differentiate the types of related measurements:

- **HR function measurement** – efficiency measures and benchmarks (started by Saratoga Institute);
- **HR function effectiveness measures** – employee and manager satisfaction along with general capability in meeting the needs of the organisation;
- **HC metrics** – measuring the components of the frameworks for this book (each chapter has a section on measurement);
- **HC analytics** – using data related to HC to improve decision-making and business results (the subject of this chapter).

Workforce management that works

Tools to measure the workforce often seem primitive in comparison to the sophisticated methods and metrics commonly used by other areas of business such as logistics, manufacturing, and finance. However, as we have discussed earlier, workforce management can be a driver of business performance.[6] It can be argued that competitive advantage can be created from the ability to align the workforce with business requirements to serve complex customer requirements across multiple economies and markets.[7] Thus, management must ensure the collective skills, knowledge, and experience of people are best put to use in the pursuit of sustainable performance. This chapter explores methods and tools that can provide ways for business leaders for securing, managing, and motivating a workforce to achieve business goals.

Since human capital is an asset, it follows that human capital strategy is a form of asset management. Most organisations lack an explicit human capital strategy. Without an explicit strategy, human capital assets are seldom managed carefully. Without an appropriate approach, human capital management is often fractured and inconsistent. The workforce does not achieve its full potential and neither does the business.

To measure the effectiveness of human capital strategy, it is necessary to look into all required workforce characteristics and management practices needed to optimise business performance.

Workforce characteristics have three dimensions:

1. **Workforce capabilities** – these are the mix of knowledge, skills, competencies, and experience that determines what the workforce can do.
2. **Workforce behaviours** – these include the specific actions of the workforce as reflected in its work intensity, diligence, cooperation, teamwork, and adaptation to change. These reflect what the workforce does.
3. **Workforce competencies** – the term 'competencies' in this context refers to psychological propensities concerning risk-taking, initiative, commitment, teamwork, and flexibility – what the workforce believes and values.

The relationships among workforce capabilities, behaviours, and competencies are complex. Moreover, they are contingent on the broader business context and environment (system of management practices) in which they play out. Research has shown that the capabilities and productivity of the workforce play a key role in firm performance.[8] Thus, it is important for managers to find ways to gauge the capabilities and performance of the workforce in their organisation.

Ownership for all workforce practices clearly extends beyond the human resources function, with many practices being the direct responsibility of operations leaders and top executives. By aligning core activities of talent acquisition, talent development, performance management, and rewards management which is covered in Chapter 7, the organisation can create a significant opportunity to help operational leaders shape and influence its workforce.

Methods for making workforce decisions

To properly assess the impact of workforce characteristics and management practices it is necessary to link decisions about people with productivity and financial objectives.[9] Applying the principles of value-based decision-making and using relevant facts about an organisation's human capital system, top management should be able to answer this question: *'What needs to change to secure, manage, and motivate a workforce that can execute the organisation's business strategy?'* To answer this question, leaders should apply the same rigour as when answering other strategic questions:

1. Understand the current state of the human capital system influencing the workforce.
2. Articulate the ideal state, via strategic business priorities.
3. Analyse the gaps and create a plan for closing them.
4. Use metrics developed along the way to measure progress.

The combination of employee profiling, risk assessment, and an analysis of workforce dynamics is the key to identify the sources of (and obstacles to) workforce productivity.[10] This approach can often mean a great deal of change, since it requires collecting and interpreting employee data in new ways, using a mix of qualitative and quantitative information. An overview of such a process and data sources is shown in Figure 6.2.

Strategy is no place for benchmarking

Because organisations seek to distinguish themselves from competitors, their workforce requirements will reflect the uniqueness of their business goals. That is, a unique business strategy will have a direct counterpart in a unique human capital strategy. Copycat workforce practices derived from benchmarking have little chance of motivating workforce behaviours tailored precisely to business needs.[7]

In isolation, workforce management practices do not constitute a strategy. They are simply instruments for influencing workforce characteristics – a means to an end. To be effective, these practices must be consistent with each other; ideally, they are mutually reinforcing. The true value of these practices is their impact on the workforce, not how well they conform to external benchmarks or best practices.

While benchmarking plays a valuable role in programme design and implementation, it has no place in strategy

Founded on the careful identification of current and desired workforce characteristics, a well-documented workforce plan can distinguish the degree to which a single workforce characteristic or management practice helps or hurts an organisation's ability to perform. When the process is approached with the same level of rigour as other functions, the organisation can assign quantitative values to workforce planning investments.

Unfortunately, the most common source of workforce performance measures [is] benchmarking ... focuses on commonality, implicitly taking the industry standard as the appropriate measure of success ... in firms with the right perspective ... key workforce measures are not taken from a list of Ten Best Measures or copied from an industry competitor.

Mark Huselid, Brian Becker, and Richard Beatty[7]

development. Executives run the risk of unleashing unintended consequences when they rely solely on the successes of other organisations without considering what is unique about their own organisation.

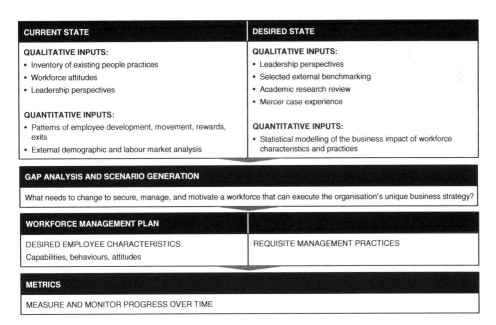

CURRENT STATE	DESIRED STATE
QUALITATIVE INPUTS: • Inventory of existing people practices • Workforce attitudes • Leadership perspectives **QUANTITATIVE INPUTS:** • Patterns of employee development, movement, rewards, exits • External demographic and labour market analysis	**QUALITATIVE INPUTS:** • Leadership perspectives • Selected external benchmarking • Academic research review • Mercer case experience **QUANTITATIVE INPUTS:** • Statistical modelling of the business impact of workforce characteristics and practices

GAP ANALYSIS AND SCENARIO GENERATION
What needs to change to secure, manage, and motivate a workforce that can execute the organisation's unique business strategy?

WORKFORCE MANAGEMENT PLAN	
DESIRED EMPLOYEE CHARACTERISTICS Capabilities, behaviours, attitudes	REQUISITE MANAGEMENT PRACTICES

METRICS
MEASURE AND MONITOR PROGRESS OVER TIME

Figure 6.2 Overview of the workforce analytics process and data sources
Source: adapted from Nalbantian and Jeffay, *New Tools for Talent Management: The Age of Analytics* (McGraw-Hill, 2003)

Analytics shed insight on human capital

Evidence-based management is defined as a movement that recognises the power of making practical decisions rooted in fact-finding methods and theories normally associated with academia.[11] In addition, evidence-based management emphasises cause-and-effect connections, isolates variations that measurably affect desired outcomes, and fosters a culture of evidence-based decision-making. This approach has significant implications for human capital management practices. Namely, evidence-based management relies less on benchmarking and presumed 'best practices' by relying more on employer-specific facts to set policies. Specifically, there is greater use of statistical models for determining causality and for forecasting.

A successful talent strategy needs to be fact-based and aligned with business goals. A successful talent strategy needs to be specific to the organisation, taking into account the specific skills and capabilities required for successful execution. A successful talent strategy must also be adaptable to changing market and business conditions. Making these fact-based decisions requires solid analytic tools.

Because each organisation will have differences in how they approach talent strategy, the result is that even firms that compete with each other do not manage their talent in the same way. Legendary are the differences for instance between Coca-Cola and Pepsi employees, or between Apple and IBM. As a result, it is necessary to clearly understand – via analytics – the internal and external circumstances involved in creating an organisational talent strategy.

From anecdotes to analytics

According to Haig Nalbantian and Jason Jeffay in their chapter entitled 'New Tools for Talent Management: The Age of Analytics',

Analytics allow decision-makers to test specific hypotheses about talent management and its role in business performance and to project the likely consequences of specific actions, in order to produce actionable insights, prioritise and size the impact, and set the yardstick to measure progress.[12]

The authors go on to explain that there is a wide spectrum of analytics, from simple to sophisticated, as illustrated by Figure 6.3. Many organisations mostly operate at the lower left end of this curve, making workforce decisions based on

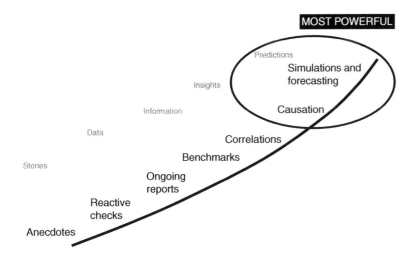

Figure 6.3 The analytics value curve
Source: adapted from Nalbantian and Jeffay, *New Tools for Talent Management: The Age of Analytics* (McGraw-Hill, 2003)

anecdotes, gut feel, reactive checks, and simple descriptive statistical reports. To the extent analytics are used, they rely more on external benchmarks and so-called 'best practice' comparisons.

The results of these comparisons, even sophisticated ones, are generally insufficient. Benchmarking inputs can be misleading in that they fail to recognise the unique organisational context that influences how well talent management practices will play out. Imagine if both Coca-Cola and Pepsi looked at the same benchmarking data and both wanted to implement the same 'best practice' espoused by a third company. The outcome will likely be that one or both of them will fail!

Many companies have been accelerating their implementation of workforce analytics modules in human resources information systems (HRIS). Some of these organisations are also undertaking more sophisticated statistical analyses aimed at identifying cause-and-effect relationships and allowing them to project likely outcomes of implementing certain policies. At the high end of the spectrum, organisations are combining perceptual and archival data in statistical models to better understand the interplay of perception and actual events as well as the mechanisms by which management practices influence results. While there are some barriers to moving up the analytics value curve – such as cost, complexity, and the capabilities of HR departments – easier access to data and statistical modelling packages are overcoming those barriers.

CASE STUDY

Robust analytics to resolve attrition issues in a supermarket chain

The manufacturing and distribution operations of a large supermarket chain were experiencing high turnover across diverse and geographically dispersed labour markets. Particularly acute was the problem of 'quick quits' – employees who voluntarily left within the first year of employment. Roughly half of the company's distribution hires and one-third of its manufacturing hires left in the first year, resulting in lost productivity as well as higher recruiting, hiring, and training costs.

The head of manufacturing and distribution operations recognised that the company had to find a way to improve retention. The cycle of 'quick quits' was not only costly but also was presenting other serious long-term challenges, such as jeopardising succession planning and widening generational gaps. While the company had a large number of employees at either end of the tenure spectrum – those with either more than 25 years' experience or with less than 1 year – it had very few employees in between who were moving up the ranks and would be prepared to assume greater responsibilities in the future (Figure 6.4).

The supermarket chain sought answers to a few critical questions: '*What were the key drivers of employee turnover? How competitive was the company's total rewards package relative to the employment deal offered by other local employers? Which elements of the package did employees value most?*'

The company adopted a holistic approach to diagnose the causes of turnover – by measuring both employee perceptions and the direct impact of people practices on retention. First, to get an accurate reading of employee perceptions, it conducted a conjoint survey that assessed the relative importance and satisfaction employees had with various elements of the employee value proposition. This analysis revealed that, while wages, profit sharing, pension plans, and health care benefits were most important to employees, satisfaction levels for their wages and health coverage were low.

So was the answer simply to raise wages or offer more health coverage? To help further examine this question, the company then benchmarked its compensation and benefits programmes against the market to assess their

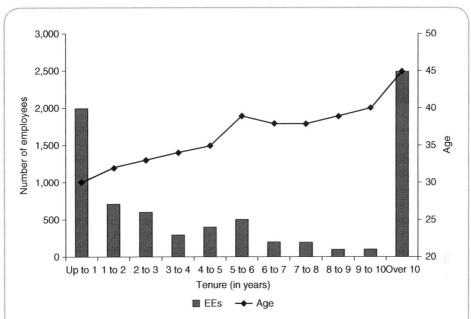

Figure 6.4 Distribution of the workforce by age and tenure

competitiveness. This analysis revealed that while pay was fairly competitive, health care fell short and retirement savings programmes were well above the market in terms of competitiveness.

Before taking any action, one critical question remained: to what degree were employee perceptions and the relative competitiveness of various elements of the 'deal' actually influencing turnover behaviour? As a final, critical step, statistical modelling was applied to examine the connection between actual levels of total rewards and voluntary turnover patterns. By analysing HRIS and payroll data, it emerged that certain key elements, including higher pay and more shift and overtime hours, consistently and significantly lowered the incidence of voluntary turnover.

With this analytical approach that combined perceptual data, benchmarking, and statistical modelling, the company obtained a comprehensive picture of the drivers of turnover. This analysis showed that while compensation levels were competitive, high employee contributions to health care were directly affecting workers' cash flow. Further, lower-wage workers did not value the rich retirement savings programmes because they did not have sufficient cash at the end of the month to make meaningful contributions to these plans. This offered interesting insights into the company's unusual tenure pattern: while generous retirement programmes were highly valued by older, long-tenured employees, these benefits were not effective retention tools for the younger workers.

Based on these complementary analyses, the supermarket chain implemented a targeted strategy to improve retention, through a rebalancing of total rewards with a greater emphasis on pay. Armed with the right evidence to reduce 'quick quits', the company has been able to work on developing a stable and productive workforce for tomorrow.

Using analytics to drive talent planning

The success of any talent strategy should be measured against its ability to help the organisation secure the talent required to meet business goals, optimise the performance of the workforce, and establish a culture that facilitates high performance and adaptability to market changes.[13] In addition, specific workforce goals relating to diversity, compliance, etc., must be measured.

Nalbantian and Jeffay point out that HR metrics and analytics can help in answering key talent strategy questions such as the following:

- *What are the critical talent segments in which we need to be strong?*
- *What are the critical operational roles where the best talent matters?*
- *What are our leadership requirements and what kind of leaders do we need?*
- *What are our performance requirements?*
- *What is our employee value proposition?*

Let us consider these questions in turn.

Segmenting the workforce

Some workforce segments are more important to current and/or future business success than others. This could be because they are top talents, have a critical or hard-to-find skill, or are filling critical roles, as shown in Figure 6.5.

But isn't every role critical? Every role that contributes to the business is important, but some roles are more critical because they have greater impact on the organisation's success. Mission criticality weighs both the role's impact and contribution and the quality of potential successors for the role. In addition,

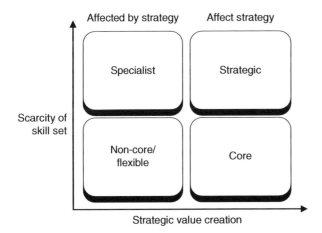

Figure 6.5 Employee segments according to criticality

highly mission-critical roles are considered more difficult to fill if the current incumbents leave the organisation.

In addition to the above, some segments (age groups, gender, function, etc.) may find different parts of the employment value proposition more or less appealing and thus may respond differently – in actual performance and engagement behaviours to various elements of the value proposition.[14] Organisations with multiple business lines may need to have varying degrees of emphasis of one segment over others.

A case in point is that of a leading telecommunications firm that faced stronger competition from new entrants in the market due to deregulation and the advent of new technology, requiring changes in its business model and organisation structure. To continue growing, the company needed very different skill sets, experience, and capabilities in its workforce. Veteran analogue-technology technicians, the mainstay of its formerly highly profitable business, were no longer the only important employee segment. The new cadre of younger engineers with knowledge of digital and network technologies were now the key employees. For a culture that was team-oriented, with a one-size-fits-all approach to talent management, this was a challenge. The company needed to segment its talent carefully to enhance the ability to transform the workforce without undermining a culture that historically had been very effective and to which there was strong allegiance among employees and throughout the leadership ranks. To do this well, the company needed to know not only which segments were critical, but to what extent workforce segments differed in the way they responded to elements of rewards and other management practices. They also needed to determine whether current talent management practices supported or impeded the required workforce transition. In an environment where resistance to change was strong, nothing less than hard facts would enable senior leadership to make the business case for change.

Given the swift shifts in the business, it was quite obvious which talent segments were becoming increasingly important. But more quantitative analytics were required to address some of the other key questions. For example, a review of raw turnover data showed exceedingly low rates of turnover among low performers. To understand to what extent talent management practices were driving these outcomes, the company analysed its labour flow (incoming, outgoing, and promotions) and associated rewards to quantitatively describe the workforce dynamics and explain what drives them. In their case, they wanted to understand their internal labour markets; that is to say, what factors influence promotions, career development, and pay. Or to what extent do specific practices help retain high-performing talent to effectively manage this labour flow and shape its outcome? One simple, purely descriptive analysis mapped the annual flow of compensation dollars to those in different performance quartiles. The analysis showed that the lowest performers were absorbing a larger share of bonus and other 'pay for performance' dollars than all but the highest quartile of performers. In fact, the company was valuing its low performers more than many other employees who delivered better results. With that kind of subsidy, it was then not surprising that turnover of the lowest performers was low. In addition, statistical modelling of pay revealed that employees' years of service dominated other skill and performance factors as a driver of individual pay. This result showed again that the company was not rewarding for the factors that were becoming most essential to its future success. Furthermore, the strong emphasis on seniority (with back-loading of pay and benefits) effectively became an obstacle to hiring from the outside market. Ironically, in the past this emphasis had allowed the company to invest efficiently in the training and development of employees required to support its old business model – in other words, those trained could be counted on to stay and deliver a return on this investment. But now this had become a liability. It prevented external market signals of pay levels to adequately influence how its internal labour market was functioning and thus induce adjustments in the relative prices to deliver the new mix of talent the business required. The analysis drove the company to introduce significant changes in talent management – emphasising talent segmentation – to remove these roadblocks to workforce transformation.

Critical operational roles

Certain roles in organisations are more important than others, but which? And how much more important? If pay markets were 'perfectly competitive' (borrowing a term from finance), market pay should reflect the marginal productivity of specific jobs. But even if this were the case, it might not capture the value of specific roles in a given company.

In the case of a retail bank, analytics helped reveal the answer by looking at the actual business impact of turnover in different jobs. The assumption is that the losses resulting from turnover would be more costly to an organisation if it occurred in more important roles. The bank analysed this hypothesis by measuring the correlation of turnover in specific roles with the business outcomes associated with the units in which it occurs. Looking across all branches, the bank examined whether turnover among branch managers correlated more strongly with outcomes such as customer retention or growth in accounts than turnover among tellers and back-office personnel. In its analysis, the bank was cognisant that a simplistic approach could be perilously misleading; thus they embarked on a detailed analysis which involved controlled statistical analysis of the running record of turnover by type of job against performance measures which allowed the organisation to determine if turnover was correlated with the specified performance measures even after accounting for the effects of other key business, workforce, and external market factors. This also allowed the bank to assess whether the changes in business results followed changes in turnover rates in different roles or if the relationships were the other way around. As a result, the bank was able to understand that turnover in customer-facing, front-line jobs was far more costly to the company than in back-office or even management roles. Whatever their level in the organisation hierarchy, those routinely interacting with customers were demonstrably more important to retaining and growing customers, as well as delivering branch-level profitability. As a consequence, the bank focused its efforts on the retention of front-line jobs even over managerial roles.

CASE STUDY

Segmenting the workforce in a state-owned bank to focus on mission-critical outcomes

A state-owned commercial bank in China, with a national network of more than 10,000 local branches, faced increasing competition from both domestic and global banks as well as heightened pressure from government economic reforms. In response, the bank planned to undertake a major transformation to increase market share, focused on sustaining its leading position in corporate banking, growing its consumer banking operations, developing fee-based service offerings and expanding its service offerings in select cities.

The human capital implications were significant. In support of this broader strategy, the bank would need to increase the number of employees in client-facing roles, while keeping overall workforce levels stable. This had to be accomplished in the face of a tight talent market where talent demand has outstripped supply. Moreover, the bank was under societal pressure to avoid workforce reductions.

A key decision initially would be whether to 'buy' needed talent from the external market or 'build' it from within. The organisation questioned whether it could rely on its existing workforce to adopt the latter strategy; *did they have enough people, who could be equipped with the critical skill sets, to deliver the business strategy?*

As a starting point, the bank realised that it needed to better understand the critical skill sets required for future business success. For this, the bank defined eight key job families aligned with the new business strategy and clarified mission-critical competencies for each of these. It mapped the current workforce distribution for each of the existing job families, at an overall level but also by region and by province. Thereafter, a competency inventory survey was administered to identify candidates who either already had desired skill sets or were on the right development path. It indicated that managerial and professional employees, given their backgrounds and training, lacked certain competencies critical to future business success. To deploy them effectively, the bank would thus need to focus on specific developmental interventions.

Another analysis assessed labour productivity in terms of net revenue per employee at the provincial-branch level to assist in making deployment decisions. The modelling revealed a number of branches that fell below the expected labour productivity standards. The combination of these analyses helped to identify where 'surplus' employees – those with relevant skills who could be reassigned to more mission-critical roles – were located within the organisation. Finally, the analysis determined the optimal allocation among three main segments of employees: client-facing employees, mid-office employees, and back-office supporting employees.

Based on these analyses, the bank was able to make informed decisions to better deploy its existing workforce. To support the reallocation and accelerate skill development, the bank also made significant changes to its HR management practices. For example, based on new competency models for eight key job families, the bank established a development and training system to help jobholders in key families prepare for higher-level roles. This system will also help cross-train employees whose jobs were identified as reduction targets to prepare for other entry- to mid-level roles.

By placing more emphasis on talent development and internal transfers, the bank is building an internal talent pipeline to meet its future workforce needs. It will accomplish this workforce restructuring without resorting to large-scale layoffs.

Leadership requirements

Many organisations are adopting the view that there are leaders at all levels who need to be developed and cultivated. Talent analytics can help these companies to carefully consider what types of capability and experience are required for different types of leader. As an example, a premier global hospitality organisation uses planned movement of managers from smaller to higher and from lower brand to higher brand properties or units as a key pillar in its approach to developing managerial talent. One measure to determine if the company is meeting its leadership requirements through this approach certainly would be to assess how the managers themselves responded to these kinds of opportunity. Did they have a favourable view? Did opportunities to move laterally help the company attract and retain its better managers? Of course, simple surveys, exit interviews, or focus groups could be used to inform the answers to this question. That is how many organisations proceed. But this organisation went further. It wanted to see if there was direct evidence of positive impact and know *how much* of an effect there was. The company undertook an internal labour market analysis to determine if lateral moves were helpful in retaining its managers. The answer was a resounding yes! Managers with more opportunities to move were significantly more likely to stay and grow with the company than those who remained in place longer.

Performance requirements

Assessing performance in organisations is always a challenge. For many roles, it is relatively straightforward to identify and measure individual performance. For some roles, it is decidedly not so easy. Sometimes individual performance may show up more in group outcomes, reflecting high interdependencies among employees. Depending on the context, how you measure performance and how much you differentiate between individuals in their assessments as well as in their pay may have very different effects on business outcomes.

In one example, a global media organisation with a number of different businesses sought individual performance data to help guide its rewards structure. Initially, company management followed the typical path to create a 'performance culture' among its employees and was concerned that laxity in its performance management system was standing in its way. A first step was simply to review the distribution of ratings to assess the extent of differentiation across its five-point ratings scale. Not surprisingly, it found ratings skewed to the higher end: 50 per cent of employees received one of the top two ratings. Armed with this knowledge, the company then deviated from the traditional path and modelled the relation between pay and ratings, accounting for multiple other factors (age, tenure, education, job family, location, etc.) that also could influence base and total compensation. By doing this, they were able to assess the incremental effect on individual pay of raising a performance rating and a subsequent return on higher individual performance. They found that the economic value of working hard to improve one's rating was relatively small. Overall, all else being equal, raising one's rating from the 'meets expectations' rating to an 'exceeds expectations' rating was worth about $1,000 per year, a rather small increase relative to average compensation levels. Most interestingly, however, the company found that the value of higher ratings tended to differ substantially across its businesses. One unit in particular differentiated higher- and lower-rated employees by pay far more than the others, especially at the lower end of the performance scale. Clearly, the company had much work to do to align the performance management system with the overriding concept of a performance culture. Analytics helped inform a major talent management issue with significant economic consequences – and proved a good return on the investment.

Understanding the employee value proposition

For companies, the employee value proposition (EVP), whether explicitly stated or not, expresses the terms of employment – what is expected of employees and what they can expect to derive from employment with the organisation. It is shaped by the talent strategy, which itself reflects the human capital requirements for accomplishing business goals.

Some organisations can easily articulate an EVP, but most have difficulty in measuring their employees' perception of EVP. In many cases, companies try to see it reflected in the perceptions of employees as captured in engagement surveys, but often these do not specify well what employees value in the employment relationship. A variety of analytical tools are available to avoid the pitfall of everything being reported as equally important.[3] Some organisations have turned towards more sophisticated ways of eliciting and handling perceptual data, such as conjoint analysis. This methodology forces choice among alternatives through a series of grouped comparisons and helps assess the degree of consistency across those choices.

Of course, what employees say they value and what, in fact, they act upon may be different. It is best then to know not only what employees 'say' in a survey or focus group, but what they actually 'do'.

For example, a company which asserted that its EVP was built on the foundation of its much-touted 'high-performance culture' used a combination of quantitative and qualitative analytics to assess perceptions and practices relative to what would be expected in a high-performance culture. Through this analysis, the company realised that what employees actually perceived was far removed from the purported EVP. For example, extremely low spans of control, reflecting strict governance and hands-on supervision, belied all the talk about the value of entrepreneurial initiative and risk taking. The company's very expensive management trainee programme, where MBA recruits from top schools were paid a premium, was found to be ineffective. The performance ratings and career progression of these 'high-potentials' were indistinguishable from those of their less-pedigreed counterparts, and they were about 25 per cent more likely to leave.

In a counterbalancing example, in the case of a large banking organisation, analysis revealed the dominance of what might be called a 'career culture' with opportunities for advancement, growth, and learning emerging as most salient to employees. These career factors, far more than pay, influenced employee retention. Drawing on this strength, the bank was determined to make that implicit culture more explicit in its EVP. The challenge of maintaining this EVP came to the fore when the bank acquired a competitor bank. Applying the same analytics, it found the acquired bank to have far more of a 'pay culture'. Understanding the stark contrast in the EVPs of the two entities, they were able to anticipate potential barriers to integration and work proactively to mitigate them.

Applying 'say–do' analytics to manage human capital costs in a call centre

A telecommunications company was experiencing high and rising turnover in its call centres. The level of turnover was estimated to be costing in excess of $150,000,000 annually, and it was placing huge demands on the company's human resources function. Having conducted numerous market studies to assess the competitiveness of its compensation programmes, management did not feel that pay played a significant role in voluntary turnover. HR leadership did, however, want to assess the degree to which the various elements of the employee value proposition – including pay but also benefits and career opportunities – were valued by employees. They also suspected that the company's recruiting and selection programmes needed refinement. Armed only with exit interview data, HR wanted to conduct additional employee surveys to better understand what was actually driving turnover. But could simply listening to what employees had to say be enough?

The call centre management decided to go one step beyond listening to employees, by combining research regarding employee *perceptions* ('say') with a robust analysis of employee *actions* ('do') (Figure 6.6) in order to get to the heart of the problem and develop the most effective solutions.

Capturing actionable insights into employee perceptions required more than exit interview data or a traditional employee survey; instead, the call centre conducted a conjoint analysis that asked employees to rank elements of their employment package and to indicate their willingness to make 'trade-offs' among them. This technique revealed that employees in the call centres valued competitive base pay and medical benefits more highly than any other aspects of their employment package.

Despite these findings, senior leaders were still not ready to increase investments in these areas without a deeper understanding. To gain this understanding, the HR team turned to its sophisticated modelling capabilities to analyse more than 20,000,000 company HRIS and payroll records. These statistical models examined the historical records to pinpoint the drivers of

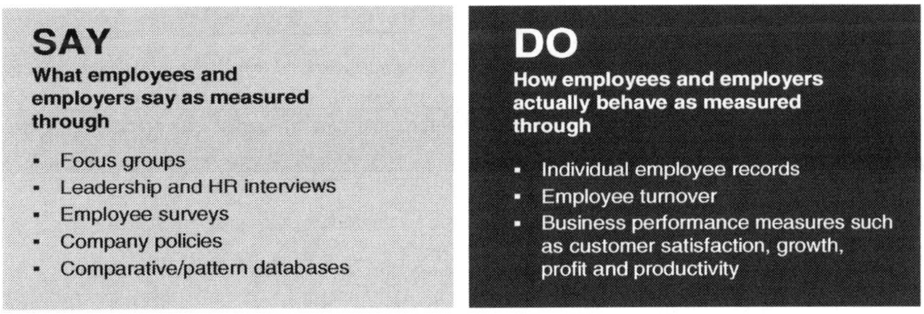

SAY	DO
What employees and employers say as measured through	**How employees and employers actually behave as measured through**
• Focus groups • Leadership and HR interviews • Employee surveys • Company policies • Comparative/pattern databases	• Individual employee records • Employee turnover • Business performance measures such as customer satisfaction, growth, profit and productivity

Figure 6.6 Measurement areas of 'say' and 'do'

voluntary turnover. The results of this analysis revealed that base pay was, in fact, a key driver of turnover. The analysis also enabled the company to quantify the effect: for every additional dollar of base pay per hour, the likelihood of the employee leaving voluntarily was reduced by more than 25 per cent, whereas changes in bonus pay and in promotions had no impact on the likelihood of leaving. Given the magnitude of the effect, increasing base pay was clearly a cost-effective way to staunch the flow of employees from the call centres.

Finally, the company also wanted a better grasp of local labour markets so it could sharpen its recruiting efforts. By carefully analysing various industry sectors within the company's geographical boundaries, they were able to identify those where the company was well positioned to compete for talent based on the number of workers available, their skill levels, and the relative competitiveness of pay. The hospitality sector, with its relatively large pool of talent and low hourly wages, for instance, emerged as a key market in which to target recruiting.

This multi-pronged approach enabled the company to pinpoint and quantify the most significant drivers of employee turnover. Initially reluctant to increase base pay in order to combat the problem, this analysis provided clear evidence that relatively small increases in pay would ultimately produce significant savings by dramatically lowering turnover. It also enabled the company to shift rewards investments away from those things that were either contributing to turnover or that failed to improve retention, such as bonus pay. Armed with rich and detailed information about where to find the right talent and how to attract and retain employees, the company was much better positioned to compete with other employers and to make the most of its human capital investments.

Monitoring results: Human capital dashboards

For companies that take advantage of a strong, fact-based talent strategy driven by analytics, the importance of ongoing measurement cannot be overstated.[15] Timely, efficiently updated, and accessible measurement of talent data is vital for renewing, revisiting, and adjusting strategy, and human capital dashboards are among the most effective tools that put information at the fingertips of decision-makers.

In general, there are three types of dashboard:

- Type I: Measure everything and benchmark

  - Headcounts, turnover, promotions, trend lines;
  - Data from the primary HRIS system;
  - Data quality issues.

- Type II: Simplification and expansion

  - More focus on selected metrics;
  - Vastly improved data quality;
  - Data from HRIS and supplemental HR databases (e.g. recruiting, payroll, engagement surveys).

- Type III: Integrate operational data

  - Data from non-HR sources (e.g. finance, marketing, quality control) and new metrics (revenue per employee, value added per employee, customer service levels).

The best dashboards are customised to display information of unique importance to an enterprise and its workforce. Dashboards also serve other functions, such as enabling easy data querying and issuing ready-to-distribute reports. Mainly, the dashboards help management understand two types of information essential to effective workforce management: one set of facts consists of accurate and timely descriptive information on outcomes, such as headcount, turnover rates, promotions, and pay changes. These are crucial for monitoring progress and providing leading indicators of an emerging problem. The second set of facts concerns the drivers or causes of critical outcomes, determined from statistical modelling. These are facts that explain important outcomes and also show the pathway to improving them. They are critical for making decisions about what to change and why and for tracking whether policy initiatives are, in fact, taking hold and changing realities. The monitoring function of human capital dashboards includes internal and external reporting, tracking progress toward strategic objectives, and responding to queries from business which is performed on an ongoing, frequently updated basis. The analytic function extends the dashboard's range to strategic planning, forecasting, proactive management, and problem-solving which is performed on an as-needed basis, with appropriate updates.

These observations and strategic examples underscore some basic requirements in utilising and optimising the value of analytic tools for talent management. Decisions about talent, as with other critical assets, must be based on the hard facts, the kind that can only emerge from the disciplined application of workforce analytics and measurement tools.[16]

Meaningful metrics must be customised to every organisation. However, below are some examples that organisations can use to link workforce management to business performance:

- Turnover/ retention by performance rating: retention of high performers and turnover of chronic underperformers;
- Merit and incentive distributions by performance rating;
- Gaps between external labour supply and projected demand by key jobs;
- Off-cycle versus year-end merit increases and promotions;
- Ratio of new hires to internal promotions ('buy' versus 'build');
- Value of promotions (to assess the calibration between promotions and compensation levels);
- Ratio of incumbent salary costs to new hire salary costs;
- Relationship between tenure and productivity (and wage growth);
- Headcount growth versus growth in salary costs;
- Relationship between employee engagement (survey scores) and critical outcomes (e.g. turnover, sales, customer retention);
- Spans of control by line of business;
- Impact of training (number of courses, type of training) on critical outcomes.

Figure 6.7 shows an example of a customised scorecard for a diversified services company.

BUILD OVER BUY		EMPHASISE GROWTH/PERFORMANCE		VALUE CAREERS	
METRIC	DIRECTION/ MAGNITUDE OF CHANGE	METRIC	DIRECTION/ MAGNITUDE OF CHANGE	METRIC	DIRECTION/ MAGNITUDE OF CHANGE
Ratio of hires to promotees in middle and upper levels	—	Skew of performance rating distribution for each segment and level	—	Return to transfer – sustained increase in pay and promotion likelihood associated with transfer	+
Difference in retention rates between top and average performers	+	Percent of workforce identified as high potential	+	Return to tenure – average pay increase associated with additional years of company experience	+
Percent new hires from agencies	—	Percent of employees with career development plans	+	Change in average base premium for new hires	—

Figure 6.7 Example of a customised scorecard for a diversified services company

---

CASE STUDY

Using dashboard data to refine talent strategy

In the competitive health care market, a major player had been focusing on external talent to meet its growing needs. It had been aggressively recruiting employees to address talent gaps and significant turnover, and to support its expanding business. But with almost one-third of its staff leaving every year and compensation costs spiralling, the leadership started questioning the fundamentals of the company's strategy.

The company had been relying on buying talent to fill positions, but leadership questioned whether building talent might prove to be a lower-cost, productive alternative for the enterprise. However, the human resources team lacked information on the talent profile and was unable to provide answers. The company realised that in order to implement the build strategy, it first needed clear information on its talent profile, such as talent availability and effective development practices.

On examination of its various databases, the company realised that it did have all the data available internally, but lacked a platform to bring this together in the form of key metrics which needed to be tracked. In order to ensure relevant metrics were available to make informed decisions, the company developed a customised web-enabled dashboard that focused on key metrics such as number of hires, promotions, transfers, terminations, spans of control, and promotion-based pay increases. The dashboard provided immediate and ongoing access to the company's network of HR personnel across the lines of business so that they could better focus on and manage talent development and other organisation-wide strategic HR priorities.

Armed with the right information, the HR team also undertook analytics to understand factors which led to employee advancement. Their analysis revealed that supervision could play a key role in development – broader spans of control increased turnover and led to fewer employees being promoted. Employees seemed to benefit from more on-the-job training provided by supervisors who had more time to invest in their development and understood the nature of their work. Other factors such as lateral movements also increased the likelihood of advancement and retention.

In only a few months, more than 100 HR personnel across the enterprise were granted access to the dashboard. The dashboard provided high-level scorecards for each business and allowed the team to drill deeper into the specific areas through detailed, customised data panels. As a result, the team was able to understand the talent profile, track progress of the build strategy, and proactively identify suitable strategies such as lateral movements and supervision spans to promote talent development. This enterprise is increasingly better positioned to leverage its human capital data to make better, more informed strategic decisions.

Workforce forecasting

Workforce forecasting is a critical foundation to workforce planning. It shows what the future holds for an organisation's workforce. It delivers a workforce forecast against business projections so that organisations can take actions in the short run to avoid costs and business risks in the long run.

Workforce forecasting provides basic projections of the future workforce profile and costs by:

- Projecting workforce size and cash compensation based on employee data;
- Comparing workforce projections to business forecasts;
- Modelling 'what-if' scenarios, showing the longer-term consequences of specific workforce changes in pay, hiring and turnover;

- Linking to labour market data;
- Highlighting potential talent gaps in the future workforce;
- Informing discussions on building a workforce to meet future business needs.

Properly done, workforce forecasting matches the talent demand stemming from the business requirements with the talent supply available. It also lays the foundation for defining people policies that can help to achieve the business goals.[17]

In the case of a financial services company in Asia, their plan was to grow 15 per cent per year so as to double the company in five years. However, they had not updated their HR practices. Somehow, it was assumed that 'HR will find the people'. The reality was that the company was promoting less than 10 per cent of its staff each year, plus it was losing nearly 20 per cent of people each year in the key markets of China and India. To compensate, the company was going out to the market to hire the managers they needed to fuel their growth, at a premium of 15 to 30 per cent over existing staff. The outcome is that costs had escalated, experience had dropped, and the likelihood of the company achieving its business targets in terms of both growth and profit were not good. By forecasting their needs five years out and in consequence adjusting their pay, promotion and employee engagement practices, the company is now more confident that their targets will be met.

CASE STUDY

Mitigating the business impact of an aging workforce in an energy company

A top energy company faced a problem common to its industry – an aging workforce. While the company had historically experienced low turnover, one-quarter of its workforce would be eligible to retire within the next five years. The prospect of so many exits – especially in critical jobs – raised serious business concerns. Future costs from these exits were estimated at up to $80,000,000 annually, not counting lost productivity and potential revenue losses for the business.

Given the historical stability of its workforce, the company had never developed a systematic method for projecting critical resource gaps or for assessing the adequacy of its workforce management practices to address those gaps. Instead, it had relied on one-off external hires to fill occasional vacancies. However, given the scale of the looming retirements, the leadership team understood that this approach would not be adequate to satisfy the company's long-term talent needs. So the challenge facing the team was to create a rigorous enterprise-wide workforce planning process that not only would identify but also would anticipate talent needs to support the business in the coming years.

Through structured interviews with key executives and statistical forecasting using the company's internal HR data, the company identified likely talent gaps in critical roles over the next decade. The main issues were around engineers and construction workers who would be needed five years ahead. The projected shortage limited the company's ability to meet future resource needs through an internal talent pipeline. Moreover, the company had no formal internal development programme, even though developing people generally is less costly than hiring from the outside.

For critical roles, such as engineers, an analysis of the external labour market indicated limited supply of senior talent. However, it also revealed a larger supply of early-career talent available in industries that the company had not traditionally tapped for candidates.

However, the company was not well positioned to tap this relatively early career talent as it had no formal internal development programmes. A detailed analysis of historical career movements within the company surfaced its specific shortcomings in this area (Figure 6.8). For one thing, the company was slow to move talent through career progressions – for example, engineers hired at the entry level spent an average of three and a half years at this level before taking on senior responsibilities and another six years before becoming supervisors.

Based on these analyses, the company decided to adopt a more rigorous approach to its workforce practices that would allow it to develop a more robust talent pipeline for critical jobs. This included:

- Accelerating career progressions for critical jobs;
- Investing more in the development of critical talent;
- Sourcing talent from a wider range of industries;
- Hiring and developing more entry-level and mid-career talent.

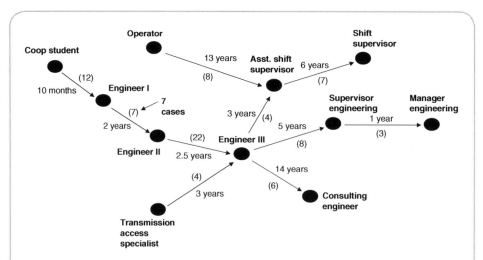

Figure 6.8 Estimated career progression time frame

Despite the impending loss of more than 57,000 person-years of experience from retirements alone – and a competitive marketplace for talent – the company is now prepared. Projected savings from better development and retention of human capital will amount to tens of millions of dollars, strengthening the company's business case for its current and future investments in workforce planning.

Reducing business risk through workforce planning

Organisations typically make a concerted effort to identify and mitigate risks that could hinder business success. But one risk is often overlooked: having the right workforce in place to execute the business strategy. As we have discussed throughout, a well-crafted business strategy has little value unless it can be implemented successfully by a qualified workforce.[18] Under any circumstances, it is counterproductive for an organisation to use its resources inefficiently. Considering that workforce investments account for a significant amount of company expenditures, maximising this investment is especially critical.

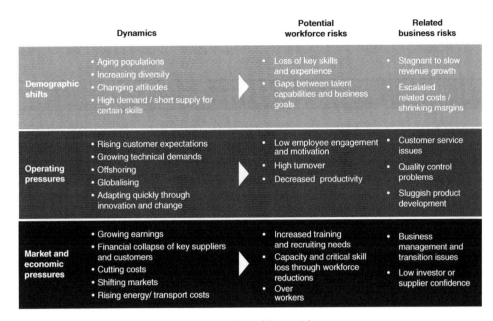

Dynamics	Potential workforce risks	Related business risks
Demographic shifts • Aging populations • Increasing diversity • Changing attitudes • High demand / short supply for certain skills	• Loss of key skills and experience • Gaps between talent capabilities and business goals	• Stagnant to slow revenue growth • Escalated related costs / shrinking margins
Operating pressures • Rising customer expectations • Growing technical demands • Offshoring • Globalising • Adapting quickly through innovation and change	• Low employee engagement and motivation • High turnover • Decreased productivity	• Customer service issues • Quality control problems • Sluggish product development
Market and economic pressures • Growing earnings • Financial collapse of key suppliers and customers • Cutting costs • Shifting markets • Rising energy/ transport costs	• Increased training and recruiting needs • Capacity and critical skill loss through workforce reductions • Over workers	• Business management and transition issues • Low investor or supplier confidence

Figure 6.9 Sources, causes, and effects of workforce risks

Workforce issues take on an even greater urgency as reliance on experienced, highly skilled employees, shifting demographics, and changes in the available talent pool are altering the traditional employer/employee relationship, whereby employees are less willing to stay in a single company for 'too many' years. Organisations that have not planned ahead face very real business risks. If they are not effective at meeting both current and future workforce needs, they could find themselves losing ground competitively and failing to meet business goals, as illustrated in Figure 6.9.

The most effective way to address these risks is through comprehensive workforce planning. The term 'workforce planning' is often used to describe operational tasks, such as work scheduling, headcount management, absenteeism management, and applicant tracking. While these actions are important to the efficient operation of a business, they only represent part of the picture.[19] Viewed from a broader, strategic perspective,

> **Three core questions regarding an organisation's workforce**
>
> **How many? (quantity)**
>
> • How many people are needed to operate – and grow – the business effectively?
> • How do these people requirements break down by business line, function, and level?
> • To what extent does the current workforce meet these

workforce planning is an integrated process that identifies and addresses the critical gaps between current workforce resources and future needs. It is a crucial part of an overall workforce strategy designed to drive business performance. A systematic approach to workforce planning forecasts workforce risks and finds the right balance of the quantity, quality, and location (as illustrated in the box) of critical talent – at the right cost – to drive business success over time.

The answers to these questions will be specific to each organisation. The process starts by focusing on both the talent demand and talent supply. The talent demand analysis documents the business requirements and articulates future workforce needs based on the business plan, including the capabilities and numbers of employees by location. The talent supply analysis on the other hand examines the current and projected internal and external supplies of talent.

The outcome is a gap analysis that identifies and prioritises workforce gaps – including when the organisation will be short on the necessary talent and where it might be able to find such talent. The next step is assessing which existing workforce policies and practices contribute most strongly to filling the gaps and identifying potential new workforce policies and practices to close the gaps. Design and implementation of new workforce policies and practices then follow.

requirements? How will the workforce be affected by future hiring, promotions, transfers, turnover, and retirement?

- How large are the workforce gaps and when will they occur?

What capabilities? (quality)

- What skills and capabilities are most at risk?
- Where are there critical gaps and how deep are they?
- What new skills and capabilities are needed to support changes in technology, products or services?
- What is the trajectory for internal candidates to fill these roles? Where can development be accelerated?
- How easily can external candidates be found? Are there alternative sources for high demand skills?

Where? (location)

- How do geographic choices affect product or service delivery and cost?
- What are the best future locations to find and locate talent? What will talent cost?

Attracting and developing health care talent in a competitive labour market

A health care network with six facilities in the USA faced increasing competition and felt the impact of industry-wide health care trends. In response, the organisation adopted a business strategy focused on expanding its service offerings in particular clinical areas and geographies. Success depended upon having enough key medical personnel – especially nurses, technicians, and therapists. In fact, certain clinical service lines were targeted to grow by as much as 55 per cent over three years. One option was to hire new talent. But were there enough candidates in the region with the needed skills and where specifically could they be found? Alternatively, the company could develop talent from within. But could it rely on its existing workforce management practices to retain and develop the right number of people with the right skills?

To address these questions, the organisation realised it needed to better understand the labour markets in which it operated – internally and externally. The external market analysis parsed census and other data to help pinpoint areas within the surrounding region that held the greatest supply of, and least competition for, medical talent. This included several pockets of appropriately skilled talent that had not been tapped by the organisation in the past.

However, analysis of the company's internal labour market – that is, who joined the organisation, who performed well, who moved up the ranks, who stayed and who left – revealed certain problems in relying strictly on external talent to fulfil growth needs. In the past, employees recruited from areas farther from the company's facilities had proven more difficult to retain. Furthermore, these external recruits tended to command greater pay premiums which, coupled with additional training costs, would impact the profitability of health care centres. It became apparent that the organisation would need to develop talent from within to ensure that it would have the supply it needed to meet its business demands.

The internal labour market analysis also revealed a number of barriers facing the company if it wanted to source the needed talent internally.

The most serious was the company's limited career development offerings, which resulted in few promotional opportunities and even fewer opportunities for employees to transition into new occupations.

Based on these analyses, the company developed workforce strategies to better tap its internal workforce. For example, having identified its critical talent needs and the best sources of talent to fill those needs, the company has selected a group of high-potential employees to go back to college at full salary in order to prepare for high-level clinical roles. Enhanced integration and mentoring programmes will give stronger support to new employees, while internal health career expos make all employees aware of career opportunities within the organisation. A new job-shadowing programme will similarly provide the opportunity to explore career alternatives.

The company also focused on enhancing its employment brand to convey to both current and prospective employees why the organisation is an attractive place to work and to be more consistent in delivering on that commitment. In addition, the company is now targeting non-traditional external sources of labour to fill key open positions. Following the implementation, the organisation saw the impact of its new workforce strategy, seeing a 15 per cent decrease in total separations and an 85 per cent decrease in first employment year separations.

The resulting workforce plan is a detailed roadmap for addressing an organisation's current and future workforce gaps. A well-crafted workforce plan identifies unique differences in both requirements and a company's employment proposition so that the organisation can more effectively attract and retain the right talent versus competing employers. A typical workforce plan contains:

- Workforce planning goals;
- Key challenges;
- Current workforce and future outlook;
- Gaps in critical and noncritical jobs;
- Company and/or business unit-level solutions;
- Action items;
- Accountability;
- Success measures and timing of workforce interventions.

Once the plan is ready, target your investments wisely. Focus on those workforce policies and practices that will most effectively help your company fill critical jobs versus other employers.

Future trends

One of the most impactful uses of analytics is the ability to quantitatively identify and model the workforce characteristics and workforce management practices that are the strongest drivers of business outcomes, such as productivity, profitability, growth, quality, and customer retention.[20] By uncovering facts about the human capital drivers of business success, management is able to address questions such as:

- *Does productivity rise with years of service?*
- *What is the impact of training on customer retention?*
- *Is incentive pay producing the desired effects?*
- *Does employee turnover affect profit?*
- *Are spans of control optimal?*
- *What is the impact of part-time employees on business performance?*
- *Is leadership development raising business performance?*
- *What is the return on investment (ROI) from specific HR interventions?*

These statistical models can also help anticipate the future, especially the returns (that is, improvements in business performance) that can be expected from a change in a human capital policy or practice. The insights gained from this approach significantly improve the ability of an organisation to settle quickly and objectively on the strategy and tactics best suited to achieving the desired business results.

Another fact-based platform for making many essential decisions about human capital is the analysis of the flow of people into, through, and out of an organisation, answering fundamental questions about a firm's workforce, such as who gets hired, who performs well, who advances and who stays. Such an analysis provides insights into the operation of an organisation's management system, reflecting actual (versus 'perceived') practices and their consequences. It focuses on causal links between critical workforce events and behaviours over time; thus, it reveals which attributes and management practices account for workforce outcomes, answering questions such as:

- *How is talent developed?*
- *What is actually getting rewarded?*
- *Is the organisation attracting, selecting, and retaining top performers?*
- *What is the value of internal job movement?*
- *How do employee attributes such as education or tenure impact performance for each job?*

As indicated earlier, dashboards, forecasting, etc. are also becoming more prevalent. And as technology improves further and as growth continues to be mainly curtailed by people issues, there will be more developments in this area.

Traditionally, HR has focused on functional metrics such as counts, rates, and tabulations to manage talent.[21] In other words, it has spent considerable time and effort measuring what is happening so as to answer questions such as: *'What is our turnover rate? How many promotions did we make? How many of those were women? What are our spans of control?'* As a result, it is able to produce descriptive reports, tracking progress toward goals and monitoring trends based on simple statistics. Interpreting trends is, in this scenario, an 'art'.

Advances in information technology and analytic methods are making it possible for organisations to manage investments in human capital in a way that can have a measurable impact on business performance. The need is great for HR to provide proven inferences about cause-and-effect relationships so as to know how to respond to events by answering questions like: *'Why do people quit? Do lateral moves make employees promotable? What experiences drive employee engagement?'* This type of analysis and metrics using statistical modelling techniques allows for strategy-making, forecasting, and problem-solving.

CASE STUDY

Workforce analytics at the industry level: aerospace industry

The business context

This fast-growing city in Asia had established its reputation as the leading hub for aerospace maintenance, repair, and overhaul (MRO) in Asia. In the decade leading up to 2006, the industry had grown at a blistering compounded annual rate of 12 per cent, and represented a quarter share of the Asian market. On the back of its stellar performance, the aerospace industry was looking to further accelerate its growth.

A key national investment in this direction was the setting up of a new Aerospace Park to support the aerospace industry including aerospace MRO, design and manufacturing of aircraft systems and components, business and general aviation activities, and an aviation campus for training. Overall, the Park was expected to contribute US$3 billion annually in value-added and consolidate the country's position as a leading player in the aerospace industry.

However, in addition to this physical infrastructure, another critical enabler for the industry was adequate and skilled workforce. Given the country's relatively small population and low growth rate, the industry raised concerns such as: *'Exactly how many new technicians and engineers will the industry need to recruit to meet its growth plans? How do we build a solid pipeline of qualified people to meet the industry's expansion? How do we compete with other attractive industries in this fast-growing market?'*

Applying workforce analytics

To address these questions, the industry realised it needed to collaborate and develop a robust understanding of the manpower demand and supply on a national level.

The assessment of industry demand saw the cooperation of thirty-five aerospace companies representing over 90 per cent of the industry workforce. The study revealed that the industry expected to need approximately 16,500 technicians and engineers by 2015, up from roughly 13,900 employees in these positions in 2009. However, the number of new industry recruits also had to take into account the fact that the industry faced talent losses to other industries as well. After factoring in this added recruitment, the industry estimated it required 4,195 new technicians and engineers by 2015 (Figure 6.10).

The study then looked to the national educational infrastructure to estimate the supply of qualified engineers and technicians. Prima facie, the number of graduates in various aerospace and related courses indicated that a sufficient pipeline of engineers was being educated. However, a survey of the students themselves revealed that a majority of them were considering other alternatives subsequent to graduation – indicating the industry needed to focus on enticing existing students from other options.

Another manpower challenge identified was fulfilling the supply of future technicians. The need for training and attracting technicians became even starker when the study revealed that 39 per cent of the special process technicians were foreign workers. To meet the supply of this critical role, the study identified opportunities for the industry to work with other industries, particularly those impacted by the financial crisis, to reskill local workers

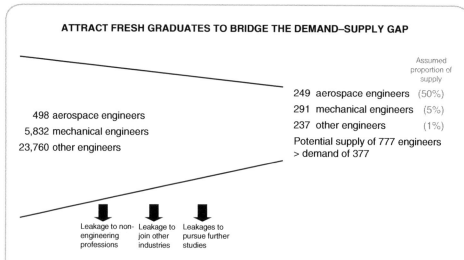

ATTRACT FRESH GRADUATES TO BRIDGE THE DEMAND–SUPPLY GAP

498 aerospace engineers
5,832 mechanical engineers
23,760 other engineers

Assumed proportion of supply

249 aerospace engineers   (50%)
291 mechanical engineers (5%)
237 other engineers   (1%)

Potential supply of 777 engineers > demand of 377

Leakage to non-engineering professions   Leakage to join other industries   Leakages to pursue further studies

Figure 6.10 Bridging the demand–supply gap

and absorb them. This analysis included a competency-based identification of roles with most similar skill sets, as well as a supply analysis – making it easier to identify those jobs that have an oversupply of labour as well as existing skill sets to enable faster retraining.

The detailed study also surfaced another issue the industry had previously not considered. It emerged that attracting new recruits was only half the battle as almost 1,700 employees were anticipated to leave the industry by 2015. Tackling industry attrition would significantly reduce recruitment pressures as well as costs associated with hiring, training, and reskilling. A pay comparison revealed that both aerospace engineers and technicians were better paid than counterparts in most other industries – in fact featuring in the top two to three industries for these roles. Since pay did not appear to be a key motivator for attrition, a cross-industry employee survey was undertaken to diagnose other reasons for attrition. Thereafter, individual companies were encouraged to develop initiatives to tackle top drivers of retention – such as career potential, promotions, learning, and development.

Results

Based on these analyses, the industry was able to clearly articulate its manpower demand in key roles and work with the educational system to ensure sufficiency of training. Further, the industry was able to identify and address a key issue – attracting future graduates to join the industry through promoting industry careers, providing exposure through internships, and reducing the long training period in collaboration with educational institutions and regulators. The industry also looked to tap alternate labour pools, such as retraining employees in other industries facing redundancies.

In addition to building a supply of fresh talent, the industry realised the importance of improving retention of its skilled workforce. Through various outreach platforms, individual companies were shown the impact of attrition as well as possible interventions to curb the same. Case studies of successful companies within and outside the industry were shared to spur retention initiatives.

With the host of initiatives in place, the industry seems well positioned to tap on the upcoming Aerospace Park and unlock its full potential.

Summary

Companies that seek to lead in their industries should be working to align their broad human capital strategy and supporting workforce management practices with business goals. Just as organisations have explicit, fact-based plans for their business, financial, and technology strategies, they can now craft such strategies and associated measures for managing the workforce.[22]

Designing a plan to help the organisation secure, motivate, and manage the workforce it needs to meet the long-term interests of its shareholders requires:

- Creating a focused picture of the current system by assembling reliable facts and data;
- Delineating the workforce implications of the organisation's business goals and establishing a set of criteria for what the organisation should look like;
- Viewing changes to workforce management practices as a potential source of new value as well as cost efficiencies;
- Substantiating the business case for change with data and tools that can accurately predict the outcomes of policy and programme changes;
- Executing the strategy so that people management practices enhance business strategy; and
- Building a set of metrics to measure progress.

Most CEOs and boards will soon expect human resources professionals to offer concrete recommendations for enhancing the value of human assets. The HR leaders in an organisation should be able to answer three types of question:

- *Is there a way to cut workforce costs without hurting business performance?*
- *Is there a way to keep spending at the same level and improve performance?*
- *Is there a way to increase spending modestly and gain significant improvements in performance?*

To answer these questions, HR leaders will need to leverage the unique portfolio of people, rewards, and other management practices in their organisation to influence the capabilities, behaviours, and attitudes of the workforce. Moving beyond the 'best intentions' approach to workforce planning, HR leaders can deliver new, fact-based plans for enhancing value through people.

Key questions for consideration

- *How well does the human capital strategy support the business objectives of the company and its segments?*
- *How aligned and integrated are the components of the human capital strategy, such as talent management and rewards?*
- *How is the talent strategy being measured and tracked by key stakeholders?*
- *What is the human capital scorecard used by the business to understand the people side of the business?*
- *How do you know that right HR measures are in place to make a positive impact on the business performance?*

FURTHER READING

Fitz-Enz, J. (2009) *The ROI of Human Capital: Measuring the Economic Value of Employee Performance.* New York, AMACOM.

Nalbantian, Guzzo, R. A., Kieffer, D., and Doherty, J. (2004) *Play to Your Strengths: Managing Your Internal Labour Markets for Lasting Competitive Advantage.* New York, McGraw-Hill.

Pfeffer, J., and Sutton, R. I. (2006) *Hard Facts, Dangerous Half-Truths, and Total Nonsense: Profiting from Evidence-Based Management.* Boston, MA, Harvard Business School Press.

REFERENCES

[1] Rousseau, D. M. (2006) 'Is There Such A Thing As "Evidence-based Management"?', *Academy of Management Review* 31(2): 256–269.

[2] Pfeffer, J., and Sutton, R. I. (2006) *Hard Facts, Dangerous Half-truths, and Total Nonsense: Profiting from Evidence-based Management.* Harvard Business Press.

³ Fitz-Enz, J. (2010) *The New HR Analytics: Predicting the Economic Value of your Company's Human Capital Investments*. New York, Amacom Books.

⁴ Becker, B. E., Huselid, M. A., and Ulrich, D. (2001) *The HR Scorecard: Linking People, Strategy, and Performance*. Boston, MA, Harvard Business School Press.

⁵ Becker, B., and Gerhart, B. (1996) 'The Impact of Human Resource Management on Organisational Performance: Progress and Prospects', *Academy of Management Journal* 39(4): 779–801.

⁶ Gong, Y., Law, K. S., Chang, S., and Xin, K. R. (2009) 'Human Resources Management and Firm Performance: The Differential Role of Managerial Affective and Continuance Commitment', *Journal of Applied Psychology* 94(1): 263.

⁷ Huselid, M. A., Becker, B. E., and Beatty, R. W. (2005) *The Workforce Scorecard: Managing Human Capital to Execute Strategy*. Harvard Business Press.

⁸ Huselid, M. A., Jackson, S. E., and Schuler, R. S. (1997) 'Technical and Strategic Human Resources Management Effectiveness as Determinants of Firm Performance', *Academy of Management Journal* 40(1): 171–188.

⁹ Thomas, H. R., and Horman, M. J. (2006) 'Fundamental Principles of Workforce Management', *Journal of Construction Engineering and Management* 132(1): 97–104.

¹⁰ Schuler, R. S., and Jackson, S. E. (1987) 'Linking Competitive Strategies with Human Resource Management Practices', *The Academy of Management Executive* 1(3): 207–219.

¹¹ Rousseau, D. M. (ed.) (2012) *The Oxford Handbook of Evidence-Based Management*. New York, Oxford University Press.

¹² Nalbantian, H. R., and Jeffay, J. (2011) New Tools for Talent Management: The Age of Analytics. In Berger, L. A., and Berger, D. R. *The Talent Management Handbook: Creating a Sustainable Competitive Advantage by Selecting, Developing, and Promoting the Best People*. New York, McGraw-Hill.

¹³ Nalbantian, H. R., Guzzo, R. A., Kieffer, D., and Doherty, J. (2004) *Play to Your Strengths: Managing Your Internal Labour Markets for Lasting Competitive Advantage*. New York, McGraw-Hill.

¹⁴ Cantrell, S., and Smith, D. (2010) *Workforce of One: Revolutionising Talent Management Through Customisation*. Harvard Business Press.

¹⁵ Neumark, D., and Cappelli, P. (1999) 'Do "High Performance" Work Practices Improve Establishment-level Outcomes?', *National Bureau of Economic Research, Inc.* NBER Working Papers 7374.

¹⁶ Davenport, T., Harris, J., and Shapiro, J. (2010) 'Competing on Talent Analytics', *Harvard Business Review* 88(10): 52–58.

¹⁷ Nolan, S. (2012). Talent. *Strategic HR Review* 11(4).

¹⁸ Kaplan, R. S., and Norton, D. P. (2000) *The Strategy-focused Organisation: How Balanced Scorecard Companies Thrive in the New Business Environment*. Harvard Business Press.

¹⁹ Cappelli, P. (1999) *The New Deal at Work: Managing the Market-driven Workforce*. Harvard Business Press.

²⁰ Guthridge, M., Komm, A. B., and Lawson, E. (2008) 'Making Talent A Strategic Priority', *McKinsey Quarterly* 1(1): 48–59.

²¹ Cascio, W. F. (2005) 'From Business Partner to Driving Business Success: The Next Step in The Evolution of HR Management', *Human Resource Management* 44(2): 159–163.

²² Crook, T. R., Todd, S. Y., Combs, J. G., Woehr, D. J., and Ketchen Jr, D. J. (2011) 'Does Human Capital Matter? A Meta-analysis of the Relationship Between Human Capital and Firm Performance', *Journal of Applied Psychology* 96(3): 443–456.

7   Change management

> If anything is certain, it is that change is certain. The world we are planning for today will not exist in this form tomorrow.
>
> Philip Crosby

Introduction

We have examined the elements of human capital strategy as components of a holistic system that supports the business strategy. Each component is critical in strategy execution and together create the human capital asset of the firm. Yet, each firm is hardly static. Movement in the marketplace, improvements in the processes, updates in technology, and the progression of people all require changes in the organisation. How a company is able to adapt and change is an important capability that is often correlated with long-term success.[1]

As firms develop new strategies and plans, the need for effective execution becomes critical. By addressing change management, companies have been able to more quickly adapt new strategies, new technologies, and processes to more rapidly achieve the benefits.

When businesses make changes based on new strategies, often there will be an impact on structures, operational processes, information technology, and expected behaviour. When these changes are determined, it is important to consider the aspects on human capital strategy components. Consider a company that develops a new strategy to automate factory operations across

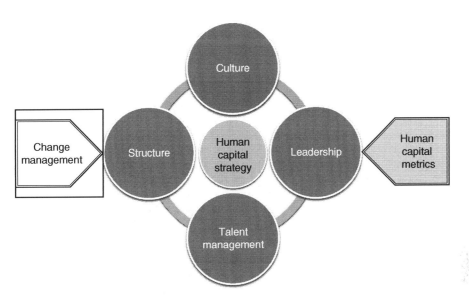

Figure 7.1 Change management

their manufacturing sites in Asia, Europe, and the Americas. With goals of improved efficiency, higher quality standards, and lower cost structures, management now has the task of introducing, managing, and sponsoring this change in the organisation. At the same time, they must find a way to keep operations going to meet current customer demands. It is often said that managing this type of change is similar to changing the tyres on a car while continuing to drive on the road. To introduce such a change, leaders will need to consider how to orchestrate such a change programme in a way that not only avoids risks, but also links to culture, leadership behaviour, structures, and talent management. As we will explore, each of these areas become critical in managing change.

In this chapter, we will cover the following key concepts related to managing organisational change:

- *What is the impact of change on individuals and organisations?*
- *What are the considerations for leaders of change?*
- *How should managers orchestrate a change programme?*
- *What are the ways to measure change?*

We will review these concepts of managing change and the impact on the dimensions of human capital strategy. Leaders who are able to successfully master the concepts associated with change management will be well prepared for the future challenges of strategy execution.[2]

The impact of change

The impact of change has been studied in the field of psychology for several decades in relation to individual motivation, cognition, and emotion. Organisational psychologists such as Hertzberg[3] pioneered the concepts related to collective work motivation in the famous 'Hawthorne studies'. Peter Drucker and others developed and refined management concepts to help leaders understand critical concepts for managing organisations and people.[4] These concepts have stood the test of time as a basis for management, yet the notion of managing through major changes remains a unique consideration and challenge for leaders. As the pace of change and globalisation started to accelerate in the 1980s, the concept of managing change surfaced as a critical issue for success. Leaders have recognised the importance of managing change and the disastrous results that may follow when change is not well managed.

Before looking at ways of managing change, we must first consider the impact of change and the process of change at both the personal and organisational level. After all, the organisation comprises a collection of individuals.

Personal change impact

At an individual level, we have some basic needs that are important to understand in the context of change. Psychologist Abraham Maslow first introduced the concept of a hierarchy of needs in his 1943 paper, 'A Theory of Human Motivation' and his subsequent book, *Motivation and Personality*. This hierarchy suggests that people are motivated to fulfil basic needs before moving on to other needs.

Maslow's hierarchy of needs is most often displayed as a pyramid (Figure 7.2). The lowest levels of the pyramid are made up of the most basic needs, while the more complex needs are located at the top of the pyramid. Needs at the bottom of the pyramid are basic physical requirements including the need for food, water, sleep, and warmth. Once these lower-level needs have been met, people can move on to the next level of needs, which are for safety and security, or certainty and control.

Needs related to esteem become most prominent in the workplace as our occupation and career often have measures for achievement. When new business strategies are introduced, potential changes to the organisation structure may create anxiety among the employees if there is a fear of loss in stature or respect. When our needs are not being met, or are being threatened, our

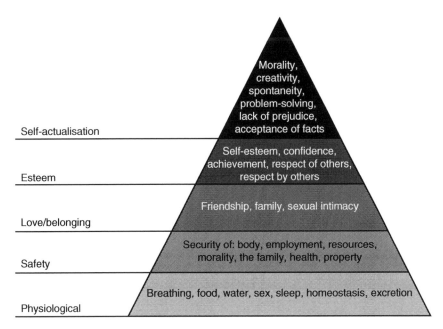

Figure 7.2 Hierarchy of needs
Source: adapted from Kübler-Ross, *On Death and Dying* (Macmillan, 1969)

behaviour will likely change. At the mere announcement of change, individuals may become concerned, anxious, or even angry.

Individual resistance to change is natural and generates from the fear of loss. This loss involves the letting go of something familiar and comfortable. Examples of types of loss can include:[5]

- **Loss of attachments** – friends, work groups, working relationships, mentor;
- **Loss of turf** – physical territory, field of responsibility, title, authority;
- **Loss of structure** – office, procedures, systems, reporting structure;
- **Loss of future** – plans, dreams, earning potential, career path;
- **Loss of meaning** – 'why things have to end', purpose of job;
- **Loss of control** – power, influence, freedom, autonomy.

Consider the example of a factory introducing new automation to help drive efficiencies. Imagine a factory supervisor, Chris, who has worked his way up after starting as a basic factory worker more than fifteen years ago. He is told that he will have a job and that they need his help to install the new automated line. He becomes quite anxious about this as he wonders if he will be able to measure up to expectations with the new complex computers, what would happen if upper management discovers that he is not so good with technology, how the people in the factory will view him if he does not know much about the technology, or if he will lose the respect of his loyal employees if he is seen to support this change. Each person may have their own reaction to the change based on their perception of the change's impact on their needs.

The reaction and potential resistance to change is magnified by uncertainty. When we are faced with uncertainty, we may imagine the worst of possible outcomes or may have trouble focusing due to unmet needs. It is precisely this anxiousness that also creates excitement while watching a favourite sporting event. We do not know the outcome and can get quite enthusiastic when cheering for our team to win! The uncertainty in this case generally creates nervous excitement and inability to focus on much else other than the game. In the workplace, we also create nervous excitement about changes which commonly results in distraction from normal activities due to this uncertainty.

This raises an important rule for managing change: people need certainty. If we cannot provide certainty of the outcome, we should provide certainty about the process. Consider a company that announced a plan to become more customer-centric. Leadership explained that by doing this the company would need to make a number of changes including the reassignment of sales territories for all of the sales representatives. While the leadership was delivering messages about the rationale for this change, the dynamics of the industry, the need for more representation, differentiation, and segmentation, the sales representatives had only one question on their minds: *'What is going to happen to my territory?'*. Uncertainty was high as there were no guidelines or assurances given by leadership as they had not yet developed the plan fully. In this case, the company was not prepared to address the fundamental need for certainty for the sales representatives. They did not know the outcome (*'What will be my territory?'*) and they did not know the process (*'How will this be determined and when?'*). By not addressing the need for some level of certainty, the sales representatives speculated, became distracted, or took action. The results were striking: over the next few months more than 30 per cent of the representatives left the organisation (created their own certainty), sales declined sharply (needs not addressed to create motivation), and rumours spread to the major customers who expressed concern about the company leadership. The change programme was eventually aborted, management changes were made, and the organisation worked to regain what it had lost due to poor management of change.

This example highlights the importance of introducing change in a way that helps provide certainty. Of course, we cannot always provide perfect clarity and need to balance the practice of open communications with providing a

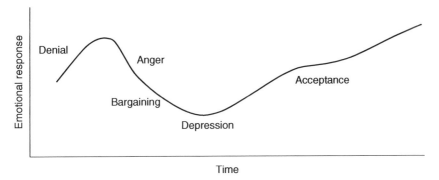

Figure 7.3 Stages of individual change
Source: adapted from Conner, *Managing at the Speed of Change: How Resilient Managers Succeed and Prosper where Others Failed* (Villard Books, 1993). Printed with permission of John Wiley & Sons, Inc.

degree of certainty. Of course, even when we are able to provide certainty, it does not mean that people will accept change.

The process of change

The process of change can be complex as there are many potential variables. Individual acceptance of change can be illustrated by the study of individuals who experience life-changing events. According to Elisabeth Kübler Ross, people go through five stages of grief when confronted with life-changing events (Figure 7.3).[6]

The first stage is *denial*. This is a conscious or unconscious refusal to accept facts, information, or the reality relating to the situation concerned. This is commonly viewed as a defence mechanism and is perfectly natural. Some people can become locked in this stage when dealing with a traumatic change that can be temporarily ignored.

The second stage is *anger*. This can show up in different ways depending on the person. People in this stage can be angry with themselves, or with others, especially those who may be close to them. This reaction to change can be confusing to others who may not understand the basis of the behaviour. In this case, it is important for others to keep detached and non-judgemental when experiencing the anger of someone who is dealing with a change.

After anger, the next stage is typically *bargaining*. At this point, people are attempting to negotiate in an effort to create an outcome they would be more comfortable in addressing. This is generally an attempt to gain some level of control over the situation. Depending on the circumstances, people can sometimes affect the outcome by bargaining and gain some sense of control.

Once the results of bargaining are realised, people will reach the stage of *depression*. Psychologists may refer to this as preparatory grieving. This is a sort of acceptance with strong emotional attachment. It is natural to feel sadness and regret, or fear, at this stage. At this stage people have started to accept the reality.

Acceptance is the final stage of the individual change process. At this stage, people may still have some emotional reaction when reflecting on the change, but have accepted the new reality and future. This stage varies based on the situation and it is generally found that there is increased emotional detachment and objectivity about the change.

Of course, not all changes in businesses are life-changing events. Our stages of change may be quite subtle when the change impact is not perceived as critical. Consider the organisation that announces the relocation of the office to the other side of the city. In this case, some people may view this as a positive change while others may view this as a very traumatic change. For those who see this relocation as a bad thing, they may enter denial with comments like: *'They will never be able to do this, we have been here too long ... it will never work!'* After management outlines the plans, people may become angry and may lash out at others: *'What are they thinking? Those people are crazy and I will give them a piece of my mind when I see them today!'* The anger may subside over time as people now consider this change of location and potential ideas. People may begin to bargain with comments like: *'I understand the plans for the new location, but a group of us should be allowed to continue to work in this location – this will provide the best alternative for everyone!'* After the attempts of bargaining show no results, people may enter a period of depression. During this period, they may project a negative outlook on a number of areas with statements such as: *'It doesn't matter if we get this done today, we will all be moving to a different place soon anyway.'* After a time, the acceptance of the new location will take place. Of course, this may not happen until after the actual move for some people. After the move we may hear people explaining: *'Yes, we moved our office to that side of the city a few months ago. It is a longer commute for me, but I am able to catch up on my reading on the train and enjoy the new office campus that is next to the shopping area.'*

Individual change results can vary dramatically and the psychology associated with human behaviour is well beyond our focus here. It is important however for managers to recognise the general stages of change acceptance when helping people through the process to acceptance. The time associated with the stages can vary by person depending on the degree of change impact and emotional attachment. It is also good for managers to recognise their own reactions to change as they are often both the recipients of change as well as the sponsors of change. As people have different reactions to change, then go through the process of change at different paces, the management of change at an organisational level can become quite complex.

The stages of organisation change

The firm comprises departments, teams, groups, networks, and individuals who may have different views on topics and on changes introduced in the enterprise. When considering change at an enterprise level, we must look at the aggregate view across various stakeholders. This aggregate view across the firm allows managers to consider phases or a natural progression of change acceptance. The organisational change process can be considered in four general stages (Figure 7.4), starting from awareness and ending with institutionalisation.[7]

Stage I: Awareness of change

Awareness is established successfully when individuals realise that change affecting them has now started to occur or is pending. Reaching awareness requires that initial communications about the change reach the desired audiences and convey the message clearly. This awareness, however, does not mean

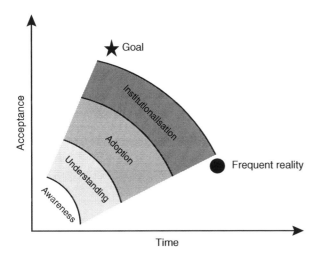

Figure 7.4 Stages of organisational change

people have a complete understanding of how the change will affect them. They may not have an accurate picture of the scope, nature, depth, implications, or even the basic intent of the change. For instance, people may perceive that a change is coming without knowing the specific ways they will need to alter their mindset and behaviours.

Regardless of the method, this first stage in the change process is intended to result in awareness that a change has taken place or may occur in the future. Since momentum and critical mass of commitment are essential to change success, careful attention should be given to how early contact (as well as later stages) will begin to promote the right energy movement toward realisation.

Initial efforts to contact people do not always produce awareness. It is important to separate contact efforts from people being aware of change. Managers should not assume that contact and awareness are synonymous; we can generally think about this stage as 'uninformed optimism' or '*Not sure what that is all about, but it sounds good.*' As Kotter's work in transformational change has shown, sponsors and change agents are often frustrated when, after many meetings and memos about an initiative, some people either are not prepared for the change or react with total surprise when it begins to affect them.[8]

Before people can progress further in acceptance, general awareness must be developed with a clear picture of the vision for the future and a general rationale for the change. Without a general awareness, confusion can result as people have different ideas about the change that has been introduced without explanation or basic information of the change implications.

Stage II: Understand the change

This is an important momentum and critical mass milestone as people shift from seeing the change as something 'out there' to seeing it as having personal relevance. While groups may pass to the understanding stage at different times, it is important to make the change relevant to their individual situation.

People often engage in individual activities designed to move themselves across this threshold in order to proceed from awareness to understanding. They ask questions, pose challenges, seek additional information, and make inferences in an effort to clarify their picture of the change. Sometimes leaders incorrectly interpret this behaviour as resistance to the change initiative. As we saw in the personal reaction to change, this may be a part of *bargaining* when people do not want the change. Although it is possible for people to use endless questions and challenges as part of their resistance strategy, true resistance to the specific change at hand (rather than to the notion of change in general) can be manifested only when people understand it well enough to be able to formulate an informed opinion.

In the understanding stage, people show some degree of comprehension of the nature and intent of the change and what it may mean for them. As they learn more about the initiative and the role(s) they are likely to play, people begin to see how the change will affect their work and how it will touch them personally. These insights enable them, for the first time, to judge the change. As Henry Knowles points out, this can take different forms when the change is planned versus when it is an unplanned change.[9]

Each person's judgement is influenced by their own cognitive and emotional filter systems – the unique set of lenses that they use to view the world. In addition, change of any significance usually has multiple aspects to it, and may produce both positive and negative reactions at the same time. For example, a person may have a negative view of a new company policy regarding relocation every four years, but sees positive benefit in the level of job security they will experience. People combine these positive and negative reactions to form an overall judgement of the change.

It is important to build an understanding of the system in a balanced way to avoid widespread negative perceptions of the change. Care should be taken when considering how to build understanding and the balance of information for each stakeholder group. While there will always be some concerns and negative perceptions at this early stage, managers of change should work to build some level of acceptance to create positive perception overall.

The later part of the understanding stage is critical in creating positive organisational momentum for the change. While people will decide whether to support or oppose the change on an individual basis, managers of change will take care to make sure that the aggregate view is positive. The forming of an opinion about change is not done in isolation – people typically weigh the costs and benefits of the change against the costs and benefits of other alternatives, including doing nothing. Ideally, the benefits of a change to an individual so clearly outweigh the benefits of any alternative course of action that it requires little thought to decide to move forward. However, this is not typically the case. In many organisational change situations, the benefits of moving forward are only marginally more positive than the benefits of the best alternative course of action. In some changes, the path forward has such significant costs associated with it that the individual reaches an overall positive perception only because all of the alternatives are worse – as *depression* may set in, as we saw in the personal reaction to change.

For instance, a leader may face a decision to lay off a large number of people from the business. He is likely to see this as a tremendously difficult and costly move. However, if he perceives that the alternative is the eventual failure of the organisation or the sale to a competitor that would be even more ruthless in the downsizing efforts, he may ultimately reach a positive perception about moving forward.

'Positive perception' is an important stage in the process of building commitment, but at this point the change is still rather theoretical. To reach true commitment, people must begin to try out the new way of operating in a hands-on manner.

Stage III: Adoption of change

There are many situations in which people will say that they view a change as positive. However, they will not actually take the first steps to alter their behaviour or mindset. There can be several reasons for this, including the lack of skill, insufficient time, missing tools, or improper setting. Commitment occurs when people see a change as more positive than negative and take action accordingly.

In the early part of the adoption stage, the organisation encourages individuals to take action to test a change. This is the first time people actually try out the change and acquire a sense of how it might affect their work routine. This stage is an important signpost that commitment building has begun, although greater support is possible.

The critical importance of this point is that no matter how positively people view a change prior to engaging with it, their actual experience with it will reveal a number of small or large surprises. Some of these may be positive, but others may involve unanticipated problems that have significant negative consequences. If problems become too costly, pessimism regarding the change will increase and may reach the 'checking-out' level. This occurs when early, uninformed optimism for a project transforms into informed pessimism, and the individual's original positive judgement shifts to negative.

Because of the inevitability of surprises, some degree of pessimism is unavoidable during change. Nevertheless, the confidence of those involved in a change increases as a result of resolving such problems. An environment that encourages the open discussion of concerns tends to solve problems, promote ownership, and build commitment to action. As these problems are resolved, a more realistic level of conviction toward the change builds. This conviction advances commitment to the adoption level.

Full adoption is reached after individuals have successfully navigated the initial trial period. The dynamics here are similar to that of the experimentation stage. Both stages serve as tests in which the individual and the organisation assess the cost and benefits of the change. Longer-term trials can reveal logistic, political, and economic problems with the new way of operating that can lead sponsors, agents, and/or targets to question the long-term viability of the new approach and potentially make a decision to terminate the change.

Although the level of time and resources necessary to reach adoption is great, a change project in this stage is still being evaluated and can possibly be stopped. If the change is successful after this lengthy test period, it is in a position to become the standard new way of operating. It is important to note that people will go through the change at different paces and timing. Managers should be prepared to allow their people to work their way through change at their own pace.

Stage IV: Institutionalisation of change

As the name suggests, institutionalisation reflects the point at which people no longer view the change as tentative. They consider it as standard operating procedure. Depending on the nature of the change in the institutionalisation process, the structure may be altered to accommodate new ways of operating, and rewards and recognition implemented to maintain new mindsets and behaviours. What was once a change requiring substantial sponsor support has now become part of the business operations that is monitored by managers.

The move from adoption to institutionalisation is a significant one, and a double-edged sword. The threshold that is crossed here is that of 'reversibility'. Once a change is institutionalised, it becomes the new status quo. Ending an institutionalised pattern that is ingrained into the fibre of an organisation is extremely difficult.

Although institutionalisation is sometimes all that is required to achieve the organisation's goals, it has some potential challenges if managers are only forcing a change for institutionalisation or compliance. If a change has been institutionalised but not internalised, those affected may be motivated to adhere to new procedures primarily to comply with organisational directives. Their compliance is achieved by using organisational rewards and punishments to motivate them to conform despite their own private beliefs about the change. If their perception of the change is generally negative, but they have chosen to go forward because the costs of not doing so are prohibitively high, they will likely only mimic acceptable behaviour. They learn to say and do the 'right' things, but their actions will not reflect their true perspective. Because their mindset (priorities and frames of reference) does not align with their behaviour, a great deal of managerial pressure will be required to ensure the ongoing presence of the desired behaviour.

The success of change does not always depend on the person's personal investment. Some projects require only that people 'do as they are told'. However, as the pace and complexity of change escalates, producing more turbulence in the workplace, many companies have modified their views about workers needing to understand or support organisational changes.

Forcing change implementation often results in a half-hearted effort without a full return on investment. Institutionalised change, as powerful as it is, only delivers compliance behaviour, not the commitment of mind and heart. This does not mean that institutionalisation is not the way to go sometimes because there are situations where leaders have to engage unpopular change. Beware of managers who might believe that they can achieve institutionalisation by force of compliance. While some can take this approach by exercising legitimate authority, long-term sustainability is at risk.

A pure form of institutionalisation occurs when people internalise the change. Internalisation represents the highest level of commitment people can demonstrate toward an organisational change. It reflects an internal motivation in which individual beliefs and desires are aligned with those of the organisation, and there is a high level of consistency between an individual's mindset and behaviour.

While company leadership can mandate the institutionalisation of a change, internalisation requires the active cooperation and careful change management for each individual. At this last stage, people 'own' the change and demonstrate a high level of personal responsibility for its success. They serve as advocates for the new way of operating, protect it from those who would undermine it, and expend energy to ensure its success. These actions are often well beyond what could be created by any mandate.

Enthusiasm, high-energy investment, and persistence characterise internalised commitment, and it tends to become infectious. Targets who have internalised a change often cannot be distinguished from sponsors and advocates in their devotion to the task and their ability to engage others in the change effort.

The time needed to move through the awareness, understanding, adoption, and institutionalisation phases will vary based on the group, the organisation, and the nature of the change project. If a change is mandated, it can become institutionalised very quickly (but, as mentioned earlier, at a high cost of monitoring compliance). In other cases, institutionalisation unfolds more gradually.

As people gain experience with the new way of operating, find ways to refine and improve it, and adjust to its long-range impact and requirements, the change gradually becomes a natural part of the organisation's culture or expected pattern of behaviour. Internalisation can begin very early in a change if the new way of operating is strongly aligned with individual beliefs and assumptions; it can also emerge along the way as individuals begin to see the advantages of the new approach.

Understanding the steps and sequence for building commitment is a powerful advantage for change practitioners when building momentum and critical mass for major change. The stages of organisational change provide a context and process that should be used when architecting a change programme across an organisation.

CASE STUDY

Post-merger change in a European information technology firm

Following its merger, the organisation immediately began integrating the operations of the two companies to achieve economies of scale, reduce the cost and complexity of information technology systems for business and improve the overall experience consumers have with technology. Performed on a country-by-country basis, this integration process involved physically blending the companies' resources, facilities, and people, and solidifying its image as a unified company.

The leadership quickly assembled a team to design, implement, and manage the key elements to facilitate the integration. The leaders were very aware of the change process that people would naturally go through and wanted to try to accelerate the change acceptance. Within a three-month period, the leadership had a goal to have all offices integrated and perhaps relocated. The focus on speed of integration required a robust change management effort. Key elements included the communications, active leadership involvement, comprehensive integration portal, office relocation event planning, project support for the local management teams, and access to a creative group to help communicate the critical issues and messages related to the integration.

The people quickly became aware of the change and there was quite an acute sensitivity to the new plans. To build a common understanding, leaders used standard messages in active two-way dialogue sessions with all the employees affected by this change. As a part of this change, many of the offices were combined around the world and/or relocated as part of this shift. Instead of 'unveiling plans', the leaders all worked to involve people to get input and ideas in rapid design sessions. As a result of this, people felt a degree of control and had a solid understanding of the impact of the change. The office and process changes were documented and reviewed with people to keep the momentum and minimise disruption. As the detailed plans were outlined, the employees all felt a sense of ownership and were ready to adopt the new plan. While not everyone was pleased with the results, nearly all employees felt that the process of change was handled well.

It was viewed by leadership as one of the most successful integration efforts in history and, most importantly, maintained its marketplace momentum during the move. With a strong change management effort that included detailed planning capabilities, integration tools, and creative on-the-ground assistance – all delivered in a very short time frame – 80 per cent of the workforce was operating at full capacity by 10 a.m. on the day of the transition. Within five hours, the entire company was operating as if a change had never occurred. The organisation achieved significant financial benefits from the well-executed integration and moves. It was a strong testimony to the power of proactively addressing the change programme elements.

Architecting change programmes

For managers facing the daunting challenge of leading a change programme, it is essential to understand how to organise or architect a change programme for success. As we have seen, moving the organisation through the stages of change requires diligence and planning that can be accomplished through architecting a change programme with care. When planning a new change programme, managers should consider three general levers (Figure 7.5):

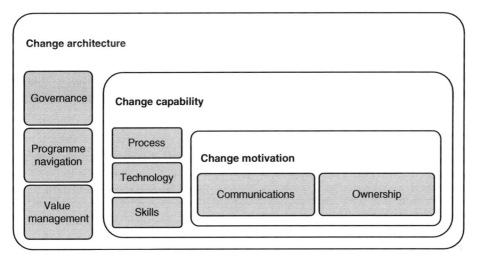

Figure 7.5 Levers in managing change
Source: copyright © 2006 Accenture. Reproduced with permission. Changetracking® is a registered trademark of Accenture

1. **Architecture** – the context for change in the organisation and management of the programme to achieve value;
2. **Capability** – the supply of tools, information, processes, and skill development to enable change;
3. **Motivation** – the understanding for the need to change, sense of pain with the status quo, and participation in creating the new future.

These three levers are necessary in both large and small change programmes as imperatives for any manager charged with leading a new change programme.

Change architecture

Three components of architecture include governance, programme navigation, and value management. It is the architecture of a change programme that quickly determines success or failure. If the overall programme is not set for success, the details on managing change are rather negligible. The change architecture ensures the alignment of the change programme with the business plans and the proper support from business leaders across the company. If the governance, ability to navigate, or orientation to value are not in line with the top-level leadership, the change effort will soon develop 'cracks' in the foundation that will create larger problems as the change effort continues.

In smaller change projects, little attention may be paid to the overall architecture; this lever becomes important when a project crosses organisational boundaries, involves multiple leaders, or is longer than several weeks in duration. Consider a change effort to remodel the interior of one bank branch to update the look for an improved customer experience. The project is sponsored by the bank manager and only included one branch. The project will take a few weeks and will affect the employees and customers of the branch. After reviewing the plans with the regional manager, the project is launched with one of the assistant branch managers overseeing the effort. In this case, the governance is straightforward as any critical decision-making will go to the branch manager if needed. The programme navigation consists of various project components (flooring, wall treatments, layout, furnishings, electrical, etc.) in a coordinated schedule that provides minimal disruption to operations. Depending on the preference of management, there may be limited attention to value management for a project such as this. However, the branch may do pre- and post-project customer satisfaction measures along with employee surveys to gauge the effects of the change on these key groups.

Imagine a much larger effort with the bank that involved the implementation of a new product line that had an impact on every branch, the financial systems, the core banking systems, employee training, and customer communication. In this case, many bank leaders need to be involved and sponsoring the effort, clear decision-making is required, as the pilot is implemented, careful programme navigation and adjustment is required based on the results by region. The multiple impact areas across each of the functional areas requires careful monitoring and programme coordination while a change team addresses the employee questions and feedback on the new product line. All the while, close attention must be paid to the business case or value realisation plan to make sure that this new set of products will meet the objectives for the bank. This type of change will require significant attention to the 'change architecture' as it is critical to getting this new product line implemented appropriately across the enterprise.

While it may seem easy to consider that change programmes are small and do not require the full 'change architecture' effort, it is important for managers to consider all aspects of the change architecture for each change effort as some may apply, even on small projects.

Governance

The initial area to consider in 'change architecture' is how the programme is set up to be led. In general, governance pertains to the structure of the programme, accountability for results, and roles required for execution of the programme. Challenges can arise when it is not clear who has the responsibility to direct, implement, and manage the change in the organisation when there are project team roles, line management roles, and perhaps even functional roles in a matrix structure.

An effective change structure and governance effort provides a framework to enhance decision-making, promote the achievement of strategic objectives, build business commitment to the changes, and enable effective leadership of change. It helps to ensure that issues are identified and resolved in a timely and effective manner, so that changes are achieved and sustained as intended. Key elements to address include:

- *Who is accountable for the ultimate success of the programme?*
- *How will the change programme resources be organised most effectively?*
- *What decisions will be made by the programme team versus the line management team?*
- *How will authority levels be defined across organisational boundaries and by level?*
- *Do the key sponsors have the commitment and clear roles to drive change?*
- *How does the programme structure map to the ultimate?*
- *Do programme leaders have control over the needed resources which will be required to deliver the change?*
- *What are the management processes for escalation of issues and risks?*
- *How will strategic direction and intent be cascaded in the organisation?*
- *How will the accountabilities and responsibilities be aligned across the change programme and embedded into the performance management processes?*

In complex change programmes, clarity of the governance and structure can be a critical factor in making the change programme work. Setting up the governance is an important initial activity because it often becomes difficult to change after the programme is launched in the organisation. Programme governance is not a one-time set-up activity, it needs to be reinforced throughout the change lifecycle and regularly communicated. Once the governance areas are addressed, proper attention should also be given to how the change programme will operate, or how management will navigate through the change.

Programme navigation

It should be noted here that we are defining a project as a collection of related activities that are done in a coordinated way. We are defining programme as a collection of projects. Change programmes are larger in scope than projects and often involve several individual projects needed to accomplish the programme goals. We use the word navigation for the simple reason that when entering a new change programme, we do not always know what we will encounter along the way. It becomes important to navigate through the effort just as the crew of a ship would navigate through a storm. Without strong programme navigation, many change efforts or ambitious goals would not be achieved.

For example, when Airbus launched a major change initiative in the early 1990s to design and build the A380 aircraft, this was set up as a large effort with many projects contained within it. The project was conceived to create the new aircraft and several project teams were focused on component areas (fuselage and cabin, wing and pylon, empennage and aft fuselage, transport, etc.).[10] This large and complex effort faced a number of challenges along the way and needed strong programme navigation not only to keep all the project efforts coordinated, but also to address the unforeseen issues and risks along the multi-year journey. Airbus had a goal to create a large competitive aircraft as a result of Boeing's success with the 747 design at a time of increasing need for long-haul, large aircraft for global travel. From those early days of concept in 1991 to the first commercial flight in October 2007 (Singapore Air from Singapore to Sydney, Australia), Airbus successfully navigated a complex global programme that now has the company busy in delivering the 253 orders for the A380 aircraft around the world (71 delivered of the 253 orders as of February 2012). While most of us will not be asked to lead a programme as large and complex as the A380, we can learn some important lessons from large-scale programme management and navigation.

In a simple view of running a programme, projects are identified and individual project managers report to the programme manager on progress, process, and expenditure of resources. The programme manager looks for relationships among the individual projects and at what they are producing to understand how they are or are not helping accomplish the goals. While this may seem rather straightforward, there are a number of areas to consider in navigation. A structured and comprehensive programme navigation approach is important for the delivery of outcomes as expected. Most leaders will include the following components (required from start to end, independent of the phase of the programme): planning and standards, stakeholder management, risk and issue management, financial management, communications and reporting, quality management, resource administration, release and integration planning, and scope and schedule management.

It is important to not only address these critical areas of programme and project management, but to also include a dedicated attention to managing the change process within the organisation. Areas to include within the programme navigation include:

- **Change identification** – this would include the capabilities, behaviours, culture, organisation, process, and system changes and how they will affect the stakeholder groups or individuals.
- **Change impact** – this will address the size and type of impact each change will have on specific stakeholder groups. This can be gauged based on various parameters such as volume, degree, or complexity for each of the groups in the organisation (departments, locations, functions, employee groups) that are impacted by the change.
- **Change management interventions** – to move stakeholder groups through the change commitment curve, we must define the appropriate change interventions to manage each impact and drive the change.
- **Change monitoring** – provide insight to programme leadership regarding key change challenges and how the change project activities will move stakeholder (that is, targets) along the change commitment curve. Establish initial awareness for the change(s) for each stakeholder group with project leadership.

Programme navigation is an ongoing and active function in any change programme. While each effort will have unique aspects, it is important to adopt not only good project management disciplines, but also active programme navigation. Without proper navigation it is difficult to steer the programme in the right direction when unexpected activities and events take place. Several questions should be addressed on an ongoing basis in programme navigation:

- *What are the risks associated with the programme and how are they being mitigated?*
- *Is the programme on track with financial, human, and other resources?*
- *How are the sponsor and stakeholder expectations being managed?*
- *What are the current issues in the programme and how are they being resolved?*
- *What interdependencies exist between projects and how are these being addressed?*
- *How might external factors influence the planned programme journey?*

- *How might other internal programmes influence the planned programme journey?*
- *What are the ways that the programme is ensuring quality of the solutions?*
- *How will we know when the programme is on track to achieve the timeline and benefits?*
- *What mechanisms will be in place to keep the programme organised along the way?*
- *How will internal programme communication and people management be addressed?*
- *Does the team have a set of guiding principles to help ensure alignment?*

The area of programme navigation can be complex and significant in scale with large programmes. Regardless of programme size, it is important for change managers to step out of the details of change and consider the direction, progress, and condition of the programme at regular intervals along the journey of making change.

Value management

With any planned change, a strong business case or rational is often used as a justification for the effort. This is not only important for the sponsors of the programme who want to make sure to meet the objectives, but also important for those involved in the change as a way to help ensure alignment to priorities, needed adjustments, and plans. It is also critical to communicate the value of the programme to help people understand the rationale for change.

When navigating a change project with many adjustments and decisions along the way, it is important to stay anchored to the ultimate goal or value. A value plan will:

- Establish milestones in line with project milestones to drive the business case and business objectives.
- Define a plan for what the sponsoring organisation is going to do to achieve the expected results defined in the business case.
- Define accountability and create ownership within the sponsoring organisation for delivering the expected results.

Achieving the financial, operational, and performance benefits (the value) is important for any project. There are few reasons why an organisation would embark on a project not delivering value. The ability to deliver the value depends on clearly articulating the required actions and accountabilities. The value plan captures this information by defining what each stakeholder needs to do, why they are involved, and the value they are driving. The goal is to create ownership and accountability within the sponsoring organisation. Several questions should be addressed with a value plan:

- *How will the change programme contribute to the organisation strategy?*
- *What are the articulated business benefits of the programme?*
- *Have the business benefits been factored into business plans and budgets?*
- *What are the goals of the change programme – both short- and long-term?*
- *How will the success of this programme be measured – and when?*
- *Which aspects of the programme are most critical to achieving the goals?*
- *Are the sponsor goals for the programme viable? Have the goals been validated by others?*
- *Do the key stakeholders buy-in to the goals for the change programme?*
- *Do the sponsors have an understanding of the challenge associated with the change?*

If the project is a part of a larger programme, similar work efforts may occur in value management tasks within the programme and project management methods. It is important that the value plan ties in to these efforts, but is also managed at the project level.

CASE STUDY

Change architecture in a Middle Eastern oil exploration organisation

The company was making plans to build a new refinery with a capacity of 450,000 oil barrels per day in the next five years. At the same time, the organisation leadership introduced a number of strategic initiatives to drive improvement in operations, including projects in safety, reliability, supply chain, and business process reengineering. Given the range and scale of the initiatives, leadership was concerned that the business would struggle to assimilate the scope and depth of change required.

The organisation decided to add change management architecture to the overall programme. While change management was not necessarily part of similar programmes in the past due to cultural considerations, the leadership was committed to minimise business disruption and improve organisational performance. The team took the initiative to address some of the key aspects of the change programme:

- integrating initiatives into a coherent journey that can be easily understood, communicated, and assimilated by the whole organisation;
- designing and implementing a systematic approach to prioritise, align, measure and drive a successful transformation of performance;
- developing and implementing the overall transformation governance model with a clear accountability framework;
- defining and implementing a new programme methodology to ensure successful management of change;
- refining the strategic management system and organisation architecture;
- designing and implementing a structured communication process;
- putting in place a corporate transformation office and governance structure to manage and support the transformation;
- improving organisational commitment to the transformation programme;
- providing senior management with a clear assessment of strategic programme progress, interdependencies, and risks;
- an integrated standardised approach to programme management;
- fostering project management, change management, and communication skills.

As a result of the strong change implementation, the organisation successfully architected the programme in a way that allowed management and each of the programme leaders to execute in a way that achieved their strategic goals and business outcomes.

Change capability

Most new change programmes get squarely centred on the capability for change. In other words, determining 'what' is going to change with new processes, technologies, structures, policies, and other areas of the business. In many change programmes, most of the project effort is centred on developing the capabilities needed to make the change. While there can be many facets of change programmes, these can generally be considered in three primary groups: processes, technology, and skills/talent.

Processes

The business processes can be a key anchor for aligning the other components of the change. Many change efforts will consider the entire end-to-end perspective such as 'procurement to payment' or 'order-to-cash'. By taking a more holistic view of the processes, instead of just looking at accounts payable for example, the change team can look for synergies and ways of improving without the risk of suboptimising.

Most change programmes involve some type of process or procedure change. When changing processes there are several considerations that managers generally consider:

- *Has the organisation established clear ownership for processes and authority for making changes?*
- *What process expertise exists in the organisation that should be leveraged for the change programme (Six Sigma, LEAN capability, etc.)?*
- *How will process changes impact the roles and responsibilities of the people performing each part of the process?*
- *What will be done to understand the links between IT application workflow and the process changes?*
- *When should the process follow the IT application design and when should changes be made?*
- *How will the new processes be documented and communicated to others?*
- *What measures will be put in place to ensure process compliance and effectiveness?*
- *How will performance of the process be supported (job aids, help aids, training, experts, etc.)?*
- *What mechanisms will be in place to ensure consistency across locations and regions?*

In many change programmes the processes can serve as the base template for changes. The organisation structure to support the new processes can be anchored to the process template. Of course, the IT systems must also be anchored to the process. In this way, the process, technology, and people components of the change become interlocked, yet separate components of providing the capabilities for change.

Technology

Information technology has become an integral part of every organisation as we keep records, process data, track transactions, and report performance. The advancement of information systems and new technology in all aspects of business has had both a disruptive impact with the intrusive nature of such systems as well as a competitive advantage for those organisations that harness the power of information. Much of the attention on change management comes from the many failed and challenged IT programmes of the last few decades as organisations have learned painful lessons on assimilating new technology.

Often the information system changes create large change efforts in an organisation. When implementing a large integrated system such as SAP or Oracle, the technology system will drive changes across many processes and organisation areas. Often, organisations will adopt the default processes embedded into the system logic to minimise the cost of customising standard software. New trends in cloud computing using applications that reside in the Internet such as Salesforce.com, allow easy access to information, but limit any customisation. Regardless of approach to balancing the technology and process, it is critical that the process design fits with the functionality of the information technology programmes.

Whether the change programme involves a large complex IT system or a customised local application, it is important to consider a number of areas related to managing IT change:

- *How will the IT system integrate with other existing IT systems?*
- *What is the impact for data records (part numbers, customer IDs, etc.)?*
- *What special skills are required to maintain and support the new system?*
- *How will users of the system get help when they need it?*
- *Has the organisation established clear responsibilities for the ownership of the system, data, reports, and interfaces?*
- *What will be done to test the system with the users to ensure quality and buy-in?*
- *How will the conversion be managed and stakeholders affected?*
- *What measures will be taken to ensure security, risk, and backup?*
- *What cross-border data requirements and privacy issues may emerge?*

- *How will the ongoing compliance and utilisation of the system be managed?*

While most managers will rely on IT experts and perhaps external consultants for help when implementing new technologies, it is important for leaders to consider the change readiness and the business impact for such changes. New IT tools and applications can be a powerful asset in the organisation, but can also lead to massive disruption. In 1999 Hershey Foods installed a large SAP system in an accelerated thirty-month time frame (initially estimated to take four years). The system went live during the busiest order season and created massive challenges with order management, inventory tracking, and supply chain. This contributed to a 19 per cent drop in revenue during the third quarter of 1999. It took close to a year to recover from this unfortunate IT change programme.[11]

The integration of the new technology changes with the processes and the organisation becomes the critical linkage for providing new capability to the enterprise. The implementation of a new system may also require a different set of skills and talent in the organisation based on the type of technology, nature of user interfaces, and knowledge required to perform roles.

CASE STUDY

Technology change at a national health care provider in Asia

The organisation was implementing new processes and technologies in a large-scale change effort that would impact 6,200 employees. People who need to assimilate to these changes, applying these new processes and systems in performing their respective roles and responsibilities, were a vital component of the overall success.

The change management approach ensured that all levels of the organisation (e.g. C-level executives, department/functional leaders to individuals) are addressed in preparing for the changes associated with the deployment of the new business capability across the hospitals. The comprehensive and structured approach involved the following streams of work:

- Assess the impact of change to each stakeholder group, their attitudes towards the changes and define specific interventions (e.g. through communications and involvement process) to help individuals feel 'ready' for the changes.

- Understand the unique needs of each stakeholder group, define specific messages, timing and channels for communications; also define specific activities to involve them, encouraging ownership/commitment and help each group progressively move up the change commitment curve.

- Refine roles and responsibilities and map individuals to the new roles. Prepare the workforce to execute new processes by training individuals on role-specific procedures within which system-specific training is embedded.

- Manage organisation risks proactively to ensure minimal disruption to the business throughout the project.

- Develop communication efforts to allow users to fully understand and 'buy into' the new standardised best practice processes to deliver patient centric service to customers.

- Create a sense of ownership through the 'change network' across many areas of the organisation.

- Train people to build the right skills and knowledge to operate their day-to-day responsibilities on the new systems productively from day 1 of 'go-live'. Changes were sustained post-implementation.

The effort was a tremendous first step towards building an ongoing change management capability in the organisation. The goals of building the credibility, momentum, and capability for future change management were achieved.

Skills/Talent

The third critical component of change capability is the people. Change capability is not only about the processes and technology needed to perform in a new way, but also about the talent needed to execute. If we have the processes and technology in place, but lack the skills to perform them well, we will likely have challenges in meeting the desired outcomes. It is therefore necessary that a manager of a change programme address the 'people' capability needed for executing the change.

Here we address the capability (skills, competencies, talents, etc.) of the people only. We will describe the willingness (motivation, desire, interest, etc.)

in the 'change motivation' section of our model. However, it is important to note that the people capability building closely links with the ability for people to move through the change acceptance curve. For example, moving from awareness to understanding can be partially addressed by sharing the impact on roles and responsibilities. Likewise, the training people receive on the new ways of working can go a long way in helping to move from understanding to adoption.

Three areas to address in the people capability include roles/responsibility alignment, skill acquisition, and performance support. As covered in the other 'change capability' areas, it is important to ensure the alignment of roles or responsibilities of people with the defined processes. It is often helpful for changes teams to break down the processes into activities and then map those activities to roles that perform them. This can entail a lot of detailed cross-linking of activities between the organisation structures and processes, but is often critical to ensure alignment between people and processes. Creating a clear set of responsibilities for each role and job can be a critical step in the change programme.

When introducing new changes, the people in the organisation may need to learn new skills related to the processes, policies, or technology. An effort to design and implement training for people is typically a project within the change programme that starts with understanding the behaviours, skills, capabilities, and knowledge required to effectively perform new or improved ways of working. Typically the design and development of training sessions, materials, and experiences becomes both a way of developing skills, and also a method to provide more information about the coming changes. Conducting the training in the organisation can be disruptive and should be carefully orchestrated and timed to ensure receptivity as well as the application of acquired skills. This is ideally timed to help people move further in under-standing and on to adoption of the change. Following the training, evalua-tions of the effectiveness should be completed to make sure that the design is effective in achieving the desired skill acquisition. Many organisations will want to make sure that the training for the change is not a one-time event and work to embed the training into an ongoing curriculum for future joiners or refresher training in the future.

The third area to address with the people capability is the ongoing per-formance support. After the change is implemented, questions will likely arise and new situations be encountered. In other cases, people may forget or need a bit of assistance on occasion. Performance support can help ensure the adoption of change and assist people with institutionalisation of the new ways of working. It is good to consider how the people will be supported on an ongoing basis to minimise future disruptions or quality issues. Often, key users or process experts are identified in each department as 'go-to' people for help. This can be an additional responsibility that they hold to provide a level of expertise to the group or local department. Other performance support efforts can include reference guides, online help aids, quick reference cards, or even real-time, online Q&A forums. It can be important to track the nature of the questions and inquiries to help identify continuous improvement opportunities.

Preparing the people capability for change includes the roles, training, and performance support which provide the ability to perform in the new way of working. The people capability coupled with the process capability and technology capability creates a holistic approach to managing most changes. Of course, these items are focused on the change itself, not necessarily the context and motivation for change. Considerations related to the people capability for a manager addressing a change programme might include:

- *How are organisational roles aligned to processes and technology designs?*
- *Have clear levels of authority and accountability been determined in line with the responsibilities and roles?*
- *What is the skill gap in the organisation when comparing new competency requirement to the current levels?*
- *What training approaches are most effective, given the audience and demographic requirements?*
- *How will the effectiveness of the training be evaluated and the competency levels assessed?*
- *How will the ongoing performance support be provided to each of the areas impacted by the change?*

When planning a new change effort of any type it is easy to become centred on the change itself rather than taking a balanced approach of looking at both the supply and demand for change. In other words, if a change involves putting a new procedure in place for employees, the change project will typically drive the documentation, training, and specifications for the new procedure. These all deal with the supply side of change – what we are going to introduce to the organisation. It is important to balance the change we are supplying with the demand for change – or change motivation.

Change motivation

If we provide the capability but not the motivation, we are helping people with their question of *'Can I make this change?'* yet not addressing the question of *'Will I change?'* There is a critical difference between the 'can' and the 'will' for change. People may have the ability to make the change, but lack the motivation to really make it work. This relates quite directly with the organisational change curve and the general stages of acceptance covered earlier in this chapter. While there are many facets to motivation and the psychology of change, we will address communications and ownership in multiple dimensions.[12]

Communications

Communications play a critical part in every change programme regardless of size and can be one of the more complex areas of the change programme to manage. Often the communication can be put into a general plan, but will need to be constantly adjusted and adapted to the changing needs of the stakeholders and in response to the feedback from the messages. Key elements of a communication programme include stakeholder management, message planning, and feedback.

Good communication starts with understanding the audience or, in this case, the people we will call stakeholders of the change. We need to identify the people who will be affected by the change and classify them by group to then understand types of needs. Often people may fall into more than one stakeholder group when lines are drawn by geography, function, and process. A stakeholder analysis will help surface the needs of each group as well as potential issues associated with the upcoming change.

Stakeholder management (consisting of engagement with and communication to stakeholders) will move target groups to the appropriate level of commitment by informing, educating, and motivating. Stakeholder interventions, not just traditional communications, are critical to winning stakeholders' 'hearts and minds' as often noted by Kotter.[8] The identification of stakeholders is required to understand which of the stakeholders will be critical to the success of the change effort and understands their needs. By executing stakeholder management correctly, there will be a raised acceptance and awareness, it will accelerate the speed of change and it improves stakeholders' ability to embrace the change. A set of activities might include the following:

- Identify key individual stakeholders and stakeholder groups.
- Understand stakeholder goals and expectations throughout the project.
- Identify the degree of impact the project will have on stakeholder groups.
- Analyse the overall sponsors' and stakeholders' commitment and willingness to change based on whether the change is supportive or disruptive.
- Define the required movement along the change commitment curve for each stakeholder and stakeholder group, in the context of before and after the change project.
- Ensure that stakeholders are positioned to maintain the desired level of commitment as the capability is being embedded and deployed in the organisation.

Planning of messages is another critical aspect of communication during change. Here the change project team members will determine the key messages, consider communication vehicles, and the timing of the communication efforts. Often, these can include events, meetings, videos, workshops, posters, social media posts, email notes, websites, and other media to get messages out to the stakeholders at the right times. While an overall comprehensive plan can be developed for major milestones in the programme plan, adjustments and special messages are regularly needed to address the ongoing needs and concerns of the stakeholder groups. A set of activities for the communication team might include:

- Develop an 'Engagement strategy and communications plan' that identifies the timing, messages, vehicles, and events used to address and engage the stakeholder groups regarding the change.
- Continuously review needs to help move stakeholders through to their targeted level of change commitment.
- Ensure that the 'Communications and engagement plan' is synchronised with the overall project's release schedule.
- Develop and deliver effective messaging, templates, and branding for the change programme.
- Evaluate whether the communications activities and messages are effective in achieving the desired movement of stakeholders along the change commitment curve, and adjust the 'Communications and engagement plan' accordingly.

Often the communication teams will create a set of guiding principles to help guide the team and management on appropriate actions. Since many of the line managers will execute the communications directly it is important for them to receive some level of instruction or training on addressing the sensitivity associated with communicating changes.

Sample of communication guiding principles

- Honest, informative, consistent and timely
- Customised to audience needs
- Utilising all existing channels
- Measurable, with feedback mechanism
- Positive and fact-based messages
- Emphasis on face-to-face communication, high involvement of stakeholders
- Reporting both good and bad news
- Avoiding under- and over-communication

Feedback from the communication efforts is an essential element in the communications area. Ample care should be taken to seek feedback both formally as well as informally from audiences for each major communication. In addition, regular pulse checks or samplings from stakeholders can greatly help make sure that the communication is having the desired impact and reaching the target audiences.

Through stakeholder management, message planning/execution, and communication feedback, the motivation for change can be affected. Key considerations for a manager involved in a change effort might include:

- *How does the communication effort generate awareness and understanding of project initiatives, timelines, scope, and value?*
- *Will the plan address all key stakeholders and build commitment to change at all levels in the organisation?*
- *How will the organisation and the leaders promote open and honest, two-way communication and provide opportunities for raising questions and concerns?*
- *What processes exist for aligning stakeholder expectations and minimising the 'rumour mill' which can disrupt plans?*
- *What will be done to create dissatisfaction with the status quo?*
- *How will the plan help explain and sell the benefits and implications of the programme to affected audiences?*
- *Does the plan acknowledge and celebrate milestones and progress of the project implementation activities?*

- *What will be done to maintain visibility and momentum throughout the project within the team and in the organisation?*

Communication is not only a key lever in introducing and driving change, but also a key aspect for creating the motivation for change.[13] The efforts for communicating are often not fully estimated when considering the plans for a change programme, yet communication remains as a critical interface between the plans for change and the audience or targets of the change. Along with the communication efforts, care must also be taken to address the ownership for change.

Ownership

To make a sustainable change, clear ownership is required. Ownership refers to the way that people can participate in the change – be a part of the change planning and overall efforts so that they feel a part of the programme. This can fit closely with the communication plans, but is often best considered separately as it relates more to the informal networks, sponsors, and advocates for change. Creating ownership can be difficult and time-consuming, but important for creating the buy-in needed for longer-term success.

Creating a change 'network' with defined roles is a way of clearly setting out the responsibilities and expectations for people during times of change. Change sponsors are typically leaders who initiate or have responsibility to bring about successful change. Change agents are typically associated with the project effort and take a role in addressing assigned stakeholder groups. Change advocates are generally defined as people in the organisation who are not part of the formal project efforts, but may be identified as influencers who can assist within their area or department in supporting the change. When we begin to identify these roles, the people in these roles, and this group as a network we can begin not only to understand the degree of commitment or ownership in the organisation, but also to receive important feedback from others.

In large programmes it is important to provide education on core change management principles and topics so that the change network organisation will understand the basics on managing change. By doing so, the 'change network' is better prepared for what lies ahead, can manage expectation, increase the speed of acceptances and improve communication effectiveness. By preparing and coaching leaders to engage with stakeholders, change leadership support is built and alignment towards a common goal is formed in a clear, simple and action-oriented manner.[14] Leaders and stakeholders will be inspired to commit to the change, resulting in acceptance, increased speed to adoption, financial benefits of change.

In addition to the education, the ownership team must start by working closely with senior leaders and sponsors to help them understand how to demonstrate commitment and ownership. It is also important to ensure alignment on messages between organisational leaders. As noted by Herold, even slight differences in messages between leaders of different groups can create confusion in the organisation as these messages are passed along to others.[15] If the change involves a reshaping of the organisation culture, this leadership alignment and ownership becomes even more critical to ensure consistency.

In addition to sponsorship, it can be powerful to have a strong network of change advocates in the organisation. A good advocate will be a person who has influence in the organisation at their own level, in other words – not the boss. Advocates can be identified as people who are well connected to others in their peer group, command a degree of respect, and generally have a pulse on the group they are in. They can help in achieving a level of trust associated with the change and leveraging their own networks.[16] Seeking help from advocates by giving them advanced notice of communications, getting their feedback and buy-in, and asking for their support can be a powerful way of bringing about change. It is one thing to have the boss explain a new change; it is quite another for this to be followed up by a peer who understands and helps support the new direction.

The concept of ownership can help in creating a change network and then using the sponsors, agents, and advocates of change to bring about the desired behaviours from both the outside-in as well as the inside-out.[17] When the ownership and communication efforts are working together, they powerfully create the demand and interest for change that eases in the acceptance and ultimate commitment for the new ways of working. For a manager involved in a change programme, there are several considerations:

- *How will we determine the degree of sponsor support for the change?*
- *What are the measures of success for the behaviour changes we are seeking?*
- *How do the defined desired behaviours link to the business objectives of the change programme?*
- *Do we have the right change agents and advocates identified in the organisation?*
- *How will we move target groups to the appropriate level of commitment by informing, educating, and motivating?*

- *What are the best ways to create a sense of ownership for this change in our organisation?*
- *What stakeholder interventions, not just traditional communications, are critical to winning stakeholders' 'hearts and minds'?*
- *When do we make examples and stories of the change success to share and build momentum?*
- *How do we prepare the leadership to lead during the change process?*

Adequate management attention to ownership and communication will help develop the motivation or demand for change as people move through the stages of change acceptance. As mentioned, it is important to keep the balance between the demand (change motivation) and the supply (change capability) of change. A key element in balancing is having change-capable leadership where change sponsorship needs are understood from board-level to mid-level leadership. It is ideal when all levels of management are engaged and able to act as active role models in leading the change agenda.

We have explored a comprehensive change architecture that addresses how the change programme is assembled and planned as well as how to address the demand and supply of change. In addition to architecting a programme for change, we must also determine how to measure the change and change progress.

Measuring change

As we explored in the change architecture, one of the aspects critical for success in a change programme is the measurement of value realisation. Recently more effort has also been given to measuring the progress of change more directly. Here most change experts specifically look at the key variables in achieving change acceptance and understanding change impact for the business.[18] Change measurement activities are initiated at the early stages of a project to provide baseline measurements and repeated on major milestones or at four- to six-month intervals.

One such global tool has emerged from an organisation called ChangeTrack Research.[19] Their change navigation system, ChangeTracking®, is a patented analytical system that has defined the most successful change pathways. ChangeTracking® combines the power of several surveys into one integrated measurement system to review benefits realisation, change readiness, risk analysis, communications, climate, and culture.

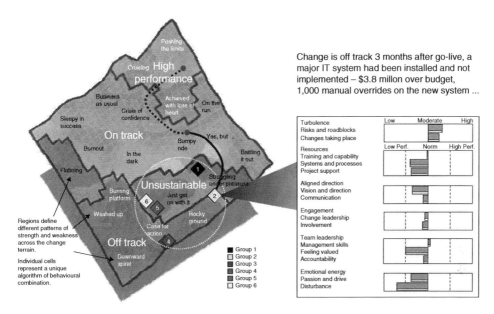

Figure 7.6 Sample output from ChangeTracking® tool

The results of the change surveys are shown on a 3D change map as shown in Figure 7.6. The four zones on the map show the level of performance and capability from 'off track' to 'high performance'. Since change progress is not linear, this map shows where different stakeholder groups are by using more than 20 regions to reflect strengths, challenges, and weaknesses the groups face in the change journey. For each group, detailed measures are available to help pinpoint problems and determine clear actions to help manage the change.

In addition to using tools for measuring the progress and results of change, the emergence of social network analysis in conjunction with change programmes has also added new ways of understanding change networks and connections. Research has shown that trust plays a large role in the social networks and this can be a critical aspect of managing change.[20] Social network analysis can be used to assess a situation pre- and post-change. For example, social networking can be used for tracking best practice transfer as one means of driving operational efficiency.[21]

Additional analytic capabilities in organisations will continue to drive the use of data and feedback to help us improve the effectiveness of change management programmes in the future. As we reviewed in Chapter 6, the use of analytics to gain insight on various elements of human capital and human behaviour patterns is increasing. The future of change management will likely be shaped by the increasing insight gained from measurement at all vantage points in and outside an organisation.

CASE STUDY

Human resource function change at a national oil company in Asia

This national oil and gas company embarked on a journey to be a world-class organisation and was constrained by human resources functions (HRF) that are unable to meet the demands that come with aggressive business growth. There were challenges in terms of inaccurate and incomplete talent data to make informed decisions on leadership succession planning and capability development, and fragmented human resource systems leading to lack of visibility at the management level. The company decided to establish a Human Resource Shared Services Centre and to implement a global integrated system as a common regional human resource service platform in thirty-four companies globally.

After having completed an assessment, the team worked to define the desired end state that includes greater line ownership and accountability, empowerment of the business units and operating unit business partners to drive business activities, and initiatives to deliver its strategic and financial goals. Change management was one of the four key work streams of the project and key activities implemented were:

- Stakeholder engagement
- Communications
- Change network
- Change readiness assessment
- Training and performance support
- Go-live readiness

Change management was a key enabler in ensuring the business and end users are committed to adopt the new system, operating structure, processes, and new ways of working introduced via the project. Key values delivered included the following:

- Stakeholders across the organisation and businesses were effectively engaged via various and frequent engagement modes.
- 24,000 end users were informed in proactive and timely manners throughout the project to support them through the transition.

- A network of 950 business change agents was established to support the business transition to the new end state.
- Effectiveness of change activities was monitored and tracked with interventions identified to enhance effectiveness of change effort.
- System and process knowledge was effectively transferred to the business via the 'train the trainer' approach.
- E-learning courses were developed to support the learning of 24,000 end users in using the new application.

The change effort was a large success in addressing the complexity of this organisation and helping to drive the new technology and ways of working across not only the HR team, but also the line business organisation.

Sustaining change

In this chapter we have reviewed challenges and approaches to managing change. While there are many aspects to addressing a comprehensive change programme, the true success of the change programme may not be evident for several months or years after the change. The ability to sustain the change over time is a critical consideration for leaders of change. To address sustainability, we consider the key elements of human capital introduced in this book (Figure 7.7).

Leadership is critical not only in sponsoring change, but also in sustaining the efforts of change. Leadership development programmes should include topics related to managing change to prepare leaders at all levels for the challenges that come with change leadership. The alignment of leaders is needed not only during times of change, but also for optimum effectiveness in creating teamwork and consistent leadership direction. As we saw in Chapter 3, there are many ways to develop leaders and care should be given to the development and identification of future leaders during times of change. Change programmes are a great opportunity to involve future leaders and high-potential talents in creating the future of their organisation.

Culture can be a factor in a large change programme and the team should determine how the change can be embedded into the culture for future success. If the change programme requires new sets of behaviours that are not consistent with the current culture, the programme will not be successful unless the

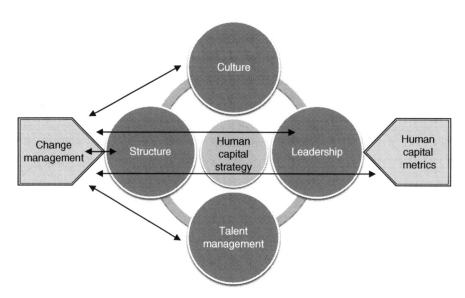

Figure 7.7 Change management interdependencies in human capital components

culture of the organisation is addressed. As we reviewed in Chapter 2, culture change is not easy and should be managed carefully and proactively in the organisation. Of course, changing the culture is itself a large change programme that requires the planning and change architecture we have reviewed.

Organisation structure also plays a role in helping to sustain a change programme. As we described, change programmes often impact the roles and responsibilities of people affected by the change. In addition to micro-level organisation changes (job and position changes), macro-level changes may also be required with reporting lines, structural orientation, and interfaces. As we reviewed in Chapter 4, the organisation design must be consistent with the future direction, and this includes the changes introduced in an organisation change programme. The structure must facilitate and support the introduced changes and can help encourage the sustainability of the change programme.

Talent management plays an integral part of change management sustainability. The use of performance management and rewards during and after a change programme is a powerful mechanism for reinforcing behaviours and sending clear messages. In the area of talent development, learning skills for managing change can help build future capability for addressing change and improve the adaptability of the organisation. As discussed in Chapter 5, talent management is an ongoing system of obtaining, developing, and growing the human capital of the organisation. To sustain the change, the needed behaviour changes should be reinforced with talent management systems.

Human capital analytics and measurement can bring about insight to the change process as described earlier in this chapter. Measurement is important for the sustainability of change, and the additional management attention on measures and indicators for success will help ensure not only compliance but interest in improving the current state; after all, most organisations continue to be in a constant state of change.

Summary

Managing change is a key element in the success of executing a successful human capital strategy as it provides the tools and approaches needed for addressing each of the components. To be effective at managing change, managers must understand the human change process and the needs for certainty and control, balanced with the movement of change efforts. The change commitment curve and stages of commitment provide a way for change managers to measure the progress and goals for moving stakeholders through levels of commitment.

Architecting a change programme can be a complex undertaking that involves the right architecture (governance, programme navigation, value management), the supply of change capability (process, technology, skills), and the motivation for change (communications, ownership). During the process of change, appropriate measures can help provide feedback and insight on the direction and progress of the overall programme. The sustainability of the change programme is anchored to the human capital components to drive consistency with the business strategy on a long-term basis.

Key questions for consideration

- *What change programmes have you seen work well to bring about effective change?*
- *What are some of the challenges you have seen with introducing change?*
- *How will you determine the change impact on people in the organisation over time?*
- *What are ways you can leverage the elements of human capital in your change programme?*
- *Do you have the resources needed to bring about the change?*
- *How will you sustain the change over time?*

FURTHER READING

Bridges, W. (1991) *Managing Transitions: Making the Most of Change*. Reading, Mass, Addison-Wesley.

Conner, D. (1993) *Managing at the Speed of Change: How Resilient Managers Succeed and Prosper where Others Fail*. New York, Villard Books.

Kotter, J. P. (2007) Leading Change: Why Transformation Efforts Fail. *Harvard Business Review* 85(1): 96–103.

Schein, E. H. (2009) *The Corporate Culture Survival Guide*. San Francisco, CA, Jossey-Bass.

REFERENCES

[1] Kotter, J. P., and Heskett, J. L. (1992) *Corporate Culture and Performance*. New York, Free Press.

[2] Hughes, M. (2011) 'Do 70 Per Cent of All Organizational Change Initiatives Really Fail?', *Journal of Change Management* 11(4): 451–464.

[3] Herzberg, F. (1959) *The Motivation to Work*. New York, Wiley.

[4] Drucker, P. F. (1954) *The Practice of Management*. New York, Harper & Row.

[5] Bridges, W. (1991) *Managing Transitions: Making the Most of Change*. Reading, Mass, Addison-Wesley.

[6] Kübler-Ross, E. (1969) *On Death and Dying*. New York, Macmillan.

[7] Conner, D. (1993) *Managing at the Speed of Change: How Resilient Managers Succeed and Prosper where Others Fail*. New York, Villard Books.

[8] Kotter, J. P. (2007) 'Leading Change: Why Transformation Efforts Fail', *Harvard Business Review* 85(1): 96–103.

[9] Knowles, H. P., and Saxberg, B. O. (1988) 'Organizational Leadership of Planned and Unplanned Change: A Systems Approach to Organizational Viability', *Futures* 203: 252–265.

[10] Airbus (2012) [Online] Available from: www.airbus.com [Accessed: June 2012].

[11] Koch, C. (2002) Chain: Hershey's Bittersweet Lesson. *CIO* [Online] 15 November. Available from: www.cio.com [Accessed: June 2012].

[12] Lepine, J. A., Erez, A., and Johnson, D. E. (2002) 'The Nature and Dimensionality of Organizational Citizenship Behavior: A Critical Review and Meta-analysis', *Journal of Applied Psychology* 87(1): 52–65.

[13] Locke, E. A., and Latham, G. P. (2002) 'Building a Practically Useful Theory of Goal Setting and Task Motivation: A 35-Year Odyssey', *American Psychologist* 57(9): 705–717.

[14] Kerr, S. (1975) 'On the Folly of Rewarding A, While Hoping for B', *Academy of Management Journal* 18(4): 769–783.

[15] Herold D. M., Fedor, D. M., Caldwell, S., and Liu, Y. (2008) 'The Effects of Transformational and Change Leadership on Employees' Commitment to a Change: A Multilevel Study', *Journal of Applied Psychology* 93(2): 346–357.

[16] Dirks, K. T., and Ferrin, D. L. (2002) 'Trust in Leadership: Meta-analytic Findings and Implications for Research and Practice', *Journal of Applied Psychology* 87(4): 611–628.

[17] Anderson, D., and Ackerman-Anderson, L. S. (2001) *Beyond Change Management Advanced Strategies for Today's Transformational Leaders*. San Francisco, Jossey-Bass/Pfeiffer.

[18] Ford, J. D., and Ford, L. W. (2009) 'Decoding Resistance to Change', *Harvard Business Review* 87(4): 99–103.

[19] Changetrack Research (2012) *How Change Tracking Works* [Online] Available from: www.changetracking.com [Accessed: June 2012].

[20] Ferrin, D. L., Dirks, K. T., and Shah, P. P. (2006) 'Direct and Indirect Effects of Third-party Relationships on Interpersonal Trust', *Journal of Applied Psychology* 91(4): 870–873.

[21] Cross, R. L., and Thomas, R. J. (2008) *Driving Results through Social Networks: How Top Organizations Leverage Networks for Performance and Growth.* San Francisco, Jossey-Bass.

8 Conclusion

> We tend to look at people from the perspective of management
> instead of looking at management from the perspective of people.
>
> Lale Kesebi

Introduction

As we continue to evolve the idea of strategy as a core concept in management theory, we must find ways to more clearly incorporate human capital as a part of strategy. As we have argued throughout this book, human capital strategy and each of the elements are a core part of strategy implementation and essential to leadership processes in strategic change.

The dynamics of global business strategy include the external context, enterprise goals, and resources and capabilities. Strategic analysis is often centred on the external context as firms correctly review the competitive situation, global market shifts, and technology advances as globalisation evolves. More attention should be directed towards the internal resources and firm-level dynamic capabilities that create sustainable competitive advantage.

As we conclude this review of human capital strategy, we will demonstrate how firms can incorporate human capital strategy into their business strategy efforts and integrate the elements of human capital into strategy implementation.

Figure 8.1 Conclusion

Incorporating human capital in global business strategy

As discussed throughout this book, the elements of human capital are linked to business strategy as they can either 'enable' or 'disable' the strategic logic and organisational intent. It is important to consider these together as an integrated human capital strategy. Framing a strategy as a set of goals and policies is often much simpler than implementing that strategy in practice. Therefore, strategists must be aware of the elements of organisational structure and human capital as an integral part of the strategy process and in questioning critically the suitability of the strategy. The ability to exploit human capital must be considered an important dynamic capability of the firm.

As depicted in Figure 8.2, a holistic view of strategy includes implementation as a key aspect of strategy process. Just as we would not ignore a strategic resource or asset of the firm when formulating strategy, nor should we frame strategy without examining implementation considerations. The human capital strategy of a firm is clearly one of the key aspects of successful implementation.

When we examine the process of strategy, it is often hard to clearly define a clear and deliberate process. Some strategies are intended and deliberate, while

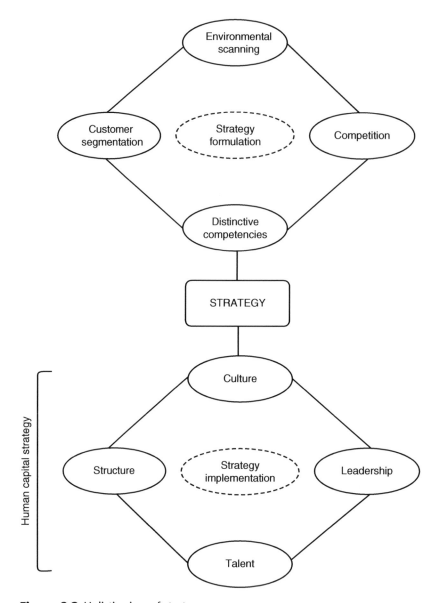

Figure 8.2 Holistic view of strategy
Source: adapted from McGee, Thomas and Wilson, *Strategy Analysis and Practice* (McGraw Hill, 2010)

others emerge from the situational context. A somewhat typical strategy process is shown in Figure 8.3. Important and valuable managerial processes are typically associated with the effective development of the stages in this process.

While organisations may develop more formal processes for developing strategy, many of the core activities remain consistent. Regardless of specific

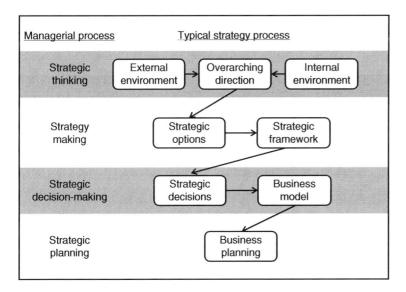

Figure 8.3 Strategy process
Source: adapted from McGee, Thomas and Wilson, *Strategy Analysis and Practice* (McGraw-Hil, 2010)

strategy process, the consideration of human capital comes into play in many areas. For example:

- **External environment** – with globalisation and the international competition for talent, it may be necessary to review management capabilities and talent across competitors and the geographic landscape when reviewing the external environment. Here managers should consider if the organisation has the talent to grow globally to meet the strategy.
- **Internal environment review** – while this process may normally be focused toward internal performance measurements, there should also be an organisational review that assesses the organisation from a human capital perspective. Developing a clear understanding of the strengths and challenges associated with the culture, leadership, talent (bench strength), and structure can create potential insight for the effective implementation of the strategy. For example, many firms develop strong growth plans in Asia yet sometimes fail to consider the availability of key talent to drive the growth agenda.
- **Overarching direction** – once an overarching strategic direction is set, a simple gap assessment might be a good way to quickly identify potential risks associated with strategy implementation. If a significant shift in direction is proposed, management attention will need to address the organisational capacity for change in a timely fashion. Thus, recognising strategic

capabilities or noticing their absence can provide greater insight into the potential of the set of alternative strategy options.

- **Strategy options** – therefore, when considering options for business strategies, strategists must judge whether the organisational elements and human capital capabilities will enable certain options to be implemented effectively. They may also question the strategic skills and capabilities of the senior managers.
- **Strategic framework** – once an overall framework for the strategy is developed, it is important to map how this will fit with the key elements of human capital. Having the leadership, culture, talent, and structures aligned is critical to success.
- **Strategic decisions** – in every strategy implementation process, alternative strategic choices are evaluated and important decisions on how the strategy will be executed are made. Human capital considerations are a key part of this process.
- **Business model** – human capital, in conjunction with the continuing refinement and adaptation of the human capital strategy, is a key component in addressing the feasibility of successfully modifying the business model.

In any organisation, the strategic planning process is a continuous process reacting and adapting to ongoing change. Therefore, the strategic plan should provide a comprehensive framework in which the organisation and management of human capital is an essential element in the process of strategic execution and strategic change.

Integrating the elements of human capital for strategic change

In previous chapters we have discussed each of the human capital elements to highlight their importance. These elements should not be examined in isolation, but as an integrated set of variables that drive the performance of the organisation. This is especially critical when planning for strategic change.

Strategic change is seemingly a constant phenomenon in many industry groups and at the forefront in the discussions of senior executives today.[1] In particular, the effects of global competition, advancing technologies, and geopolitical dynamics create additional requirements that drive strategic change in organisations. Research on approaches for navigating change, as discussed in Chapter 7, has generated a number of ideas, frameworks, and concepts.[2] Many of these frameworks address organisational values, culture, structure, leadership communication, operating environment, talent, and performance measures. In other words, the fundamentals of human capital strategy are seen as 'core' to managing strategic change.

Change is called strategic (versus operational) when its impact on the organisation is significant relative to the structures, processes, and core businesses of the organisation. Strategic changes are generally viewed as somewhat novel to the organisation, which may create new precedents for subsequent decisions made in the organisation. The pace of strategic change may be driven by internal or external factors and is often difficult to manage at a rapid pace due to its comprehensive nature. Some argue that strategic change is a continuous incremental process, while others argue that it is more of a discontinuous and radical shift, but this may depend upon the competitive environment.

With incremental change, often the change process is taken in small steps so that each change component continuously builds on the previous phase of activity. Thus, strategy implementation efforts fit with existing practice or add in some way to what is already in place. Advocates of this incremental strategic change approach argue that there are three key principles for success, namely, continuous improvement, continuous learning, and constant adaptation.[3] These must all be built into the nature and plan for human capital of the organisation.

Others suggest that strategic change is more radical and can be disruptive to the organisational status quo. Harvard Professor Clayton Christensen highlighted the phenomenon of disruptive innovation in his 1997 book, *The Innovator's Dilemma*.[4] Christensen argues that some firms fail to stay atop their industries when they are confronted with market shifts or major technological change. This could be driven by the discontinuity of competition, bureaucracy, poor planning, short-term investments, or even the firm's current success in generating profits. The argument is that organisations are generally quite effective in creating stable practices and processes that then act as strong barriers to change. These stabilisers can be found in the formal and informal systems, standard operating procedures, structures, and organisational culture. This phenomenon of resistance to change can, of course, be found at an individual level, as discussed in Chapter 7. However, radical change can be required when unforeseen innovations disrupt the status quo of an industry or market sector such as we have seen in the mobile phone market. The launch of the iPhone by Apple with advanced touch-screen technology created a disruption in the current practices by Nokia, RIM, and Samsung. This disruption quickly changed the industry. Those who were able to rapidly adapt to the change were able to keep or increase their market share. For others, the change was too disruptive to current practices. The idea of strategic change as a disruptive or radical process advocates a strong orientation towards identifying human capital strategies that promote organisational flexibility and capability to anticipate and react quickly to change.

As we have argued throughout this book, strategic change implementation requires deliberate attention to the core elements of human capital. These elements of leadership, culture, structure, and talent management are inter-related in many aspects. They cannot be treated in isolation and must be considered together as a group of factors that will shape the direction and success of a strategic change.

If we consider the case of General Electric (GE) and the strong orientation to strategy execution driven by Jack Welch and his successor, Jeffrey Immelt, we can see the integrated nature of the corporate human capital efforts. This is observed by noting the key elements: GE values as a part of the leadership model, the leadership growth traits, the importance of the vision and goal-setting processes, the GE operating system, and the influence of the corporate culture. In essence, GE has a strong 'corporate glue' that binds the organisation together around the world. The common suite of organisational leadership and training programmes that helps drive constant change and improvement is an anchoring element in the corporation's ability to execute strategy. The strong corporate culture is certainly linked to the leadership programmes, the direction of the CEO, and the operating model. All the elements of human capital are addressed in executing strategy. GE has aligned the strategy, structure, leadership, culture, and talent to drive strategic change. The dedication to management training at the GE Crotenville centre has provided a common platform for developing future leaders and a forum for eyeing the talent pipeline. While the organisation had many challenges with the results of GE Capital in recent years, the strong nature of building leaders has helped it weather the storm of re-evaluating the portfolio of businesses and ventures. GE still holds as a great example of strategy implementation with a strong human capital orientation in a global multi-business organisational setting.

The power of human capital for competitive advantage

While more research is needed to review the impact of human capital on business strategy and planning, the evidence of the important link is found in many business situations today. Several successful businesses have incorporated human capital strategy as a core part of their planning. Deliberate attention to human capital strategy is growing in business circles and we see this in some of the leading organisations today.

The Tata Group in India is now quite global in its reach and has a strong foundation rooted in values that make up the core of its culture and orientation to business. The values and purpose guide much of the group's business strategy decisions and shape the nature and direction of the firm.[5] There have been many cases and articles on the success of the Tata Group, and its attention to the human capital of the firm is clear. This focus on structure, talent management, leadership, and culture has certainly had an impact on business performance.

Management attention to people and values at Google has contributed greatly to its ongoing success. Unlike other technology start-ups, Google has been able to keep a unique culture and way of working through a deliberate orientation to human capital.[6] The idea of leveraging and over-investing in human capital as a strategic asset while creating generative chaos and precision output has been a lasting advantage for this technology player.

Other examples of success stories with human capital strategy include GE, Accenture, Nissan, and many others that have been covered throughout this book. We hope that the number of examples continues to grow as strategists embed human capital components as an integrated part of global business strategy.

Conclusions and conjectures

In this book we offer a simple conceptual model of human capital elements that link to global business strategy. We have argued that human capital is an integral part of strategy execution and strategic change, and have discussed how each of the elements of human capital can have a direct impact on the performance of business, yet should be viewed in a holistic way.

We are at a critical point in the evolution of practices related to human capital strategy and suggest that we will continue to see shifts in the thinking in both the literature as well as in practice. As globalisation continues to change business results and economic prosperity, human capital will undoubtedly continue to surface as a key factor. Consequently, we expect to see more attention on human capital as a part of national agendas, board-level strategy reviews, and strategy implementation planning.

In recent years we have seen national human capital agendas and talent efforts emerge in developing nations as countries such as India with significant technical skills leverage this for economic prosperity. In the 1980s we witnessed the strong rise of the Japanese and German economies due in large part to the human capital in quality management and technical skills.[7] The skills and human capabilities of a nation will continue to play a key role in attracting business enterprise and retaining national organisational interest. While regulatory and fiscal policies will also play a role in the economic value of human capital for a nation, those countries with a strong focus on building future talent will certainly be better positioned for long-term economic growth.

At a firm level, boards and top-level leaders will continue to see human capital as a critical element of success. The Conference Board CEO Challenge 2013 survey identifies human capital as the number one issue that top teams are grappling with around the world.[8] As the aging workforce demographics continue to create gaps in some locations, the need for talent in emerging markets creates needs that were not previously identified. Having the human capital is a critical element, but then retaining it and growing it can equally be a challenge, especially in emerging markets across Asia.[9] Organisations are starting to more deliberately consider human capital as a core part of the strategy implementation process as corporate directors are now asking the tough questions related to the ability to execute.

We expect that more public and private sector organisations will proactively develop a human capital strategy that supports the corporate and business strategy. Creating a plan for the development of the organisation, key talents, future leadership, and even the organisational culture requires discipline and focus on the people aspects of business in the context of the corporate strategy. As firms advance in their consideration of human capital as a dynamic capability, we will see an increase of activity in this aspect of strategic planning.

As leaders increasingly concentrate their attention on the strategic aspects of human capital, additional focus will be brought to the human resources function. In many firms, the HR function is burdened with administrative, compliance, and process-oriented tasks while also being under pressure for cost reduction. This pressure on HR professionals to be more strategic while being operationally efficient without the luxury of automation or other investment will ultimately come to a turning point in the coming years. Firms will either reinvest in the HR function to build a more strategic capability and steward-ship for the human capital, or they will empower other more strategic leaders or groups in the organisation with the charter of human capital strategy.

Human capital in organisations is often intertwined with knowledge capital as firms work to capture, share, and leverage institutional knowledge for com-petitive advantage. Knowledge management holds a promise to help leverage human capital through the use of knowledge architectures to enable the trans-fer of knowledge and know-how when and where needed.[10] The Internet is quickly breaking barriers to knowledge and firms with a strong human capital strategy will determine how to leverage knowledge management as an integral part of addressing the challenge.

With the attention of business leaders on the human capital in their organ-isation, we expect to see new research and theories to help address the many challenges associated with the people side of business. Perhaps surprisingly, much of the organisational and management research does not emerge from nor tie back to the human capital theory originally developed by Gary Becker in 1964. His book, *Human Capital*, provided a potential basis for human cap-ital and even attempted the distinction of various types of human capital linked to economic outcomes.[11] We expect to see more research in the area of human capital from a strategic advantage viewpoint to help organisations determine how to address this important resource. Potential research areas might include enhancing our understanding of the human capital strategy process as it relates to strategy implementation planning; the measurement of human capital as a dynamic capability of the firm; the sustainable competitive advantage offered by differentiated human capital strategies; and strategic group impact on human capital strategies. We see this more strategic aspect of organisational studies as a rich area for future research.[12]

Human capital strategy is a natural part of strategy implementation and a critical part of executing the strategy of the firm. A good strategy is achieved through an understanding of not only how to create strong competitive advan-tage, but also how to execute that position and the competitive vision over time. This execution of strategy requires a strong focus on human capital at a time when human capital is a key issue for business leaders.

As we proposed at the beginning of this book, the topic of human capital strategy is a needed, yet often overlooked, part of the strategy process. We hope that our approach, which highlights the importance of human capital as part of a global business strategy process, brings new light to leaders and researchers on how to think about human capital strategies and opens up new questions for further research and inquiry.

REFERENCES

[1] Wilson, D. C. (1992) *A Strategy of Change*. London, Routledge.

[2] Hambrick, D. C., Nadler, D. A., and Tushman, M. L. (1998) *Navigating Change*. Boston: Harvard Business School Press.

[3] Rajagopalan, N., and Spreitzer, G. M. (1997) 'Toward a Theory of Strategic Change: A Multi-lens Perspective and Integrative Framework', *Academy of Management Review* 22(1): 48–79.

[4] Christensen, C. M. (1997) *The Innovator's Dilemma: when new technologies cause great firms to fail*. Harvard Business Press.

[5] TATA Group (2012) [Online] Available from: www.tata.com [Accessed: June 2012].

[6] O'Callahan, T. (2011) *What's the Google Approach to Human Capital?* Interview with Laszlo Bok, Head of People Operations for Google. Yale Insights, Publication of the Yale School of Management.

[7] Streeck, W. (1991) On the Institutional Conditions of Diversified Quality Production, in Matzner, E., and Streeck, W. (eds.), *Beyond Keynesianism: The Socio-Economics of Production and Full Employment*. Aldershot, UK and Brookfield, US, Elgar: 21–61.

[8] The Conference Board (2013) CEO Challenge 2013 Survey Results. [Online] Available from: www.ceochallenge.org.

[9] Doh, J., Smith, R. R., Stumpf, S. A., and Tymon Jr, W. G. (2011). 'Pride and Professionals: Retaining Talent in Emerging Economies', *Journal of Business Strategy* 32(5): 35–42.

[10] Evers, H., Gerke, S., and Menkhoff, T. (2011) Knowledge Hubs and Knowledge Clusters in Menkhoff, T., Evers, H.-D., Wah, C. Y., and Pang, E. F. (eds) *Beyond the Knowledge Trap*. Singapore, World Scientific.

[11] Becker, G. (1964) *Human Capital*. New York, National Bureau of Economic Research.

[12] Sherer, P. (2011) Looking into the Future: Bringing Organizations Deeper into Human Capital Theory, in Burton-Jones, A., and Spender, J. (eds.), *The Oxford Handbook of Human Capital*. Oxford University Press.

INDEX